OXFORD ENGLISH MONOGRAPHS

General Editors

Shakespeare and the Constant Romans

GEOFFREY MILES

CLARENDON PRESS · OXFORD
1996

This book has been printed digitally and produced in a standard design in order to ensure its continuing availability

OXFORD
UNIVERSITY PRESS

Great Clarendon Street, Oxford OX2 6DP

Oxford University Press is a department of the University of Oxford. It furthers the University's objective of excellence in research, scholarship, and education by publishing worldwide in

Oxford New York

Athens Auckland Bangkok Bogotá Buenos Aires Cape Town Chennai Dar es Salaam Delhi Florence Hong Kong Istanbul Karachi Kolkata Kuala Lumpur Madrid Melbourne Mexico City Mumbai Nairobi Paris São Paulo Shanghai Singapore Taipei Tokyo Toronto Warsaw

with associated companies in Berlin Ibadan

Oxford is a registered trade mark of Oxford University Press in the UK and in certain other countries

Published in the United States by Oxford University Press Inc., New York

Reprinted 2001

ISBN 0-19-811771-X

The jacket illustration shows the figure of Constancy from an eighteenth-century edition of the Cesare Ripa's Iconologia, *taken from a modern reprint:* Baroque and Roccocco Pictorial Imagery : The 1758-60 Hertel Edition of Ripa's 'Iconologia',*ed. Edward A. Master (New York: Dover, 1971).*

To my mother

and

to the memory of my father

Preface

The material in this book was first presented as an Oxford D.Phil. thesis in 1987, and I have been engaged in the process of turning it into a book for so long as to give the phrase *Constant Romans* a whole new meaning. Despite the lapse of time, I believe its argument has not been superseded. Recent criticism, in dealing with Stoic constancy in the Roman plays, has tended either to repeat the conclusions of the first studies from the 1970s, or else to deny the relevance of Stoicism altogether. What I have tried to provide is a closer analysis of 'constancy' that acknowledges the complexity of its meanings and the tangled roots from which it springs.

This is not of course the last word on the topic. One fruitful area for future investigation would be constancy in the sense of 'fidelity', and its relationship to Stoic constancy (steadfastness and consistency). I have largely ignored this topic, since to do it justice would involve exploring traditions of love, friendship, and gender roles, which would have vastly expanded the book. However, the potential conflicts between 'constancy-to-oneself' and 'constancy-to-others' are visible in all the plays, not only in the love tragedy of Antony and Cleopatra, but also in Brutus' betrayal of his friend Caesar and Coriolanus' treason to his nation and family in the name of an ideal of steadfastness. I hope in the future to look more closely at the questions begged by Polonius' complacent conclusion,

> . . . to thine own self be true,
> And it must follow, as the night the day,
> Thou canst not then be false to any man.
>
> (*Ham.* 1. 3. 78–80)

Some other aspects of the book's scope and structure may need explanation. In spite of the arguments and example of Robert Miola in *Shakespeare's Rome*, I have stuck to the traditional definition of 'the Roman plays' as *Julius Caesar*, *Antony and Cleopatra*, and *Coriolanus*. As I argue in Chapter 6 below, the three Plutarchan plays can be read as a triptych on the theme of constancy. *Titus Andronicus* and *Cymbeline*, with their fictional plots and fairy-tale vagueness of chronology, seem to belong to a different species, using Rome as an archetype of civilization and empire rather than as a subject whose history and ethos are of interest in their own right.

I deal with *Coriolanus* before *Antony and Cleopatra*. This does not signal any challenge to the conventional dating of the two plays (*Antony c.*1606, *Coriolanus c.*1608), merely that it was convenient to my argument to treat Coriolanus' testing of the limits of constancy before Antony's experiment with the benefits of inconstancy. I do think it likely, though, that the two plays were conceived, if not written, very close together.

In dealing with the views of Stoic writers I have consistently used masculine forms such as 'the wise man' and 'his constancy'. I realize that this may offend some readers, but such forms are an inextricable part of the Stoic tradition, and to substitute gender-neutral language would be positively to misrepresent a tradition in which the idea of virtue is intimately bound up with that of 'manliness' (*andreia*, *virtus*).

My greatest debt is to my two D.Phil. supervisors, John Wilders (at Oxford) and Alistair Fox (at Otago). Dr Miriam Griffin read and commented helpfully on early drafts of the chapters on Cicero and Plutarch. I am grateful to the English Department at Victoria University of Wellington for the respite from administrative work which enabled the book to be completed, and to my colleagues, especially Kim Walker, Heidi Van de Veire, David Norton, and Paul Millar, for advice and support of manifold kinds, Janet Hughes generously helped with the preparation and checking of the index. Deborah, Jennifer, David, Celia, Barry, Marian, and Marjan my manager have kept me provided with 'Diverting and Diversions' and with encouragements to be constant; my thanks for both.

Contents

Bibliographical Note

All references to Shakespeare are to the Oxford Shakespeare: *William Shakespeare: The Complete Works*, ed. Stanley Wells and Gary Taylor (Oxford, 1986), large-format edition (the line-numbering of the compact edition is occasionally different).

References to Latin and Greek texts (unless otherwise noted), and unattributed translations, are taken from the Loeb Classical Library editions. The principal texts in English are as follows:

Cicero

Those fyve questions, which Marke Tullye Cicero, disputed in his Manor of Tusculanum [*Tusculan Disputations*], tr. John Dolman (London, 1561); STC 5317.

Marcus Tullius Ciceroes thre bookes of duties, to Marcus his sonne [*De officiis*], tr. Nicholas Grimalde (2nd edn., with parallel Latin text, London, 1558); STC 5281.8.

References are to book and section (i.e. the marginal numbers, rather than the chapter divisions in the text) in Loeb, followed by page number in Dolman or Grimalde. Translations of other works are taken from the Loeb editions.

Seneca

The Workes of Lucius Annaeus Seneca, Newly Inlarged and Corrected, tr. Thomas Lodge (2nd edn., with corrections, London, 1620); STC 22214.

References are to Loeb chapter and section, followed by page number in Lodge.

Some translations from the plays are taken from *Seneca His Tenne Tragedies Translated into English*, ed. Thomas Newton [1581], introd. T. S. Eliot (London, 1927).

Plutarch

The Lives of the Noble Grecians and Romanes, Compared Together by that Grave Learned Philosopher and Historiographer, Plutarke of

Chaeronea, tr. Sir Thomas North (2nd edn., London, 1595); STC 20067. References are to page number in North, followed by Loeb chapter and section number.

References to Jacques Amyot's translation are to *Les Vies des hommes illustres, Grecs & Romains, comparees l'une avec l'autre par Plutarque de Chaeronee* (2nd edn., Paris, 1565).

Neostoic writers

Sir William Cornwallis, *Essayes of Sir William Cornwallis, the Younger*, ed. Don Cameron Allen (Baltimore, 1946).

Guillaume Du Vair, *The Moral Philosophie of the Stoicks* [*La philosophie morale des stoiques*], tr. Thomas James, ed. Rudolf Kirk (New Brunswick, NJ, 1951).

Guillaume Du Vair, *The True Way to Vertue and Happiness: Intreating specially of Constancie in publike Calamities, and private Afflictions* [*De la constance*], tr. [Andrew Court] (London, 1623); STC 7373.2. [Repr. with new title-page of *A Buckler against Adversitie: Or A Treatise of Constancie* (London, 1622).]

Joseph Hall, *Heaven on Earth, and Characters of Vertues and Vices*, ed. Rudolf Kirk (New Brunswick, NJ, 1948).

Justus Lipsius, *Two Bookes of Constancie* [*De constantia*], tr. Sir John Stradling, ed. Rudolf Kirk (New Brunswick, NJ, 1939).

Montaigne

Essays, tr. John Florio, Everyman's Library (3 vols., London, 1910; repr. with introd. by L. C. Harmer, 1965). References are to essay and page number (since the Everyman volumes correspond to the three books of the *Essays*, I omit volume numbers).

References to the French text are to *Les Essais de Michel de Montaigne: Édition conforme au texte de l'exemplaire de Bordeaux*, ed. Pierre Villey, rev. V.-L. Saulnier *et al.* (Paris, 1965), cited as *EMM*.

In quoting from old-spelling texts I have silently expanded contractions and normalized *i/j*, *u/v*, and long *s*.

Abbreviations

Clem. Seneca, *De clementia*
CompD *Comparative Drama*

Const.	Seneca, *De constantia sapientis*
ELR	*English Literary Renaissance*
EMM	*Les Essais de Michel de Montaigne* (see above)
Ep.	Seneca, *Letters* (*Ad Lucilium epistulae morales*)
F	First Folio (1623)
Fin.	Cicero, *De finibus*
Ira	Seneca, *De ira*
JEGP	*Journal of English and Germanic Philology*
JHI	*Journal of the History of Ideas*
MLQ	*Modern Language Quarterly*
MLR	*Modern Language Review*
N&Q	*Notes and Queries*
OCD	*Oxford Classical Dictionary*
Off.	Cicero, *De officiis*
PBA	*Proceedings of the British Academy*
PMLA	*Publications of the Modern Language Association of America*
PQ	*Philological Quarterly*
Prov.	Seneca, *De providentia*
RenD	*Renaissance Drama*
RES	*Review of English Studies*
RORD	*Research Opportunities in Renaissance Drama*
RQ	*Renaissance Quarterly*
SEL	*Studies in English Literature, 1500–1900*
ShakS	*Shakespeare Studies*
ShS	*Shakespeare Survey*
SQ	*Shakespeare Quarterly*
Tranq.	Seneca, *De tranquillitate animi*
Tusc.	Cicero, *Tusculan Disputations*

The standard abbreviations are used for the works of Shakespeare.

1
Constant Romans

When Brutus in *Julius Caesar* tells his fellow conspirators to

> bear it as our Roman actors do,
> With untired spirits and formal constancy
>
> (2. 1. 225–6)

he is calling on what was for Shakespeare and his contemporaries perhaps the quintessential Roman virtue. For Shakespeare's audience the word 'constancy' would have had a penumbra of Roman associations, evoking Roman courage, resolution, integrity, consistency, temperance, endurance of suffering, heroic death and suicide 'after the high Roman fashion' (*Ant.* 4. 16. 89). More educated spectators would have recognized it as a Stoic term, raising echoes of classical discussions by Cicero and Seneca or, more immediately, of contemporary debates provoked by the works of Continental 'Neostoics' like Justus Lipsius or Montaigne. It is of course rash to say what a Renaissance audience would have thought, but such spectators of *Julius Caesar* (and later of *Antony and Cleopatra* and *Coriolanus*) would at least have been in a position to recognize that 'constancy' was not merely Roman local colour but a necessary question of the play; that Shakespeare was gesturing towards a genuine debate, both contemporary and long-standing; and that the teasing ambivalence of his treatment reflected the ambivalence of traditional attitudes to this very problematic virtue. For the modern reader, on the other hand, 'constancy' means little; and even those modern critics who have focused on the constancy of Shakespeare's Romans have tended to over-simplify the complexities of the word's meaning and of the tradition Shakespeare is drawing on.

Critical attention to constancy in the Roman plays is part of a general interest over the last three decades in Shakespeare and the classical world. One sign of this interest is the tendency to read the Roman plays as plays about Rome. This approach, perhaps initiated by T. J. B. Spencer's 1957 article 'Shakespeare and the Elizabethan Romans',[1] informs most recent book-length studies: J. L. Simmons's *Shakespeare's Pagan World*, Paul A. Cantor's *Shakespeare's Rome: Republic and Empire*, Michael Platt's *Rome and Romans According to Shakespeare*, Robert S. Miola's *Shakespeare's Rome*, Vivian Thomas's *Shakespeare's Roman Worlds*.[2] All regard Rome not merely as a setting but as a subject of the plays; all emphasize the plays' concern with Rome as an alien society, with the nature of 'Romanness' or *romanitas*, and with the 'mutually defining, paradoxical relationship' (Simmons) between Rome and the Romans, who see themselves as 'citizens' rather than 'men' (Platt).[3]

[1] *ShS* 10 (1957), 27–38. Later articles by G. K. Hunter, 'A Roman Thought: Renaissance Attitudes to History Exemplified in Shakespeare and Jonson', in B. S. Lee (ed.), *An English Miscellany Presented to W. S. Mackie* (Cape Town, 1977), 93–118, and Paul Dean, 'Tudor Humanism and the Roman Past: A Background to Shakespeare', *RQ* 41 (1988), 84–111, extend and modify Spencer's study of English Renaissance views of Rome. Gary Miles (no relation) provides a classicist's perspective in 'How Roman Are Shakespeare's "Romans"?', *SQ* 40 (1989), 257–83. Two useful works now seriously in need of updating are John W. Velz's bibliography *Shakespeare and the Classical Tradition: A Critical Guide to Commentary* (Minneapolis, 1968), and his 'The Ancient World in Shakespeare: Authenticity or Anachronism? A Retrospect', *ShS* 31 (1978), 1–12.

[2] Simmons: Brighton, 1974. Cantor: Ithaca, NY, 1976. Platt: London, 1976; 2nd edn., Lanham, Md., 1983. Miola: Cambridge, 1983. Thomas: London, 1989. The last of these is disappointingly thin, but the others have all been valuable. My greatest debt is to Simmons, despite reservations about his Augustinian framework; his reading of the plays' central conflict, between Rome's purely secular world and the impossible desire for transcendent perfection which it instils in its heroes, has helped to shape my own sense of the tensions between 'Ciceronian' and 'Senecan' constancy. Judah A. Stampfer, *The Tragic Engagement: A Study of Shakespeare's Classical Tragedies* (New York, 1968) deals with *Troilus* and *Timon* as well as the Roman plays. Charles Wells's recent *The Wide Arch: Roman Values in Shakespeare* (London, 1993) surveys a wide range of 'Roman values' (*amicitia*, *fides*, *pietas*, *mos maiorum*, etc.) in Shakespeare's six 'Roman' texts and throughout the whole of his work; the treatment is inevitably breathless and superficial, though Wells does assemble some useful material and draw attention to the neglected Roman dimension of topics like friendship and service.

Other studies, of course, take less Rome-centred approaches: Maurice Charney's *Shakespeare's Roman Plays* (Cambridge, Mass., 1961) focuses on imagery; John Wilders' *The Lost Garden* (London, 1978) and Alexander Leggatt's *Shakespeare's Political Drama* (London, 1988) are two excellent studies of the 'English and Roman history plays' which do not sharply distinguish between the two groups.

[3] Simmons, *Pagan World*, 7; Platt, *Rome and Romans*, 87–8. Three articles which take up this contrast between 'Romans' and 'men' are J. L. Simmons, 'Shakespeare and the Antique Romans', and David L. Kranz, 'Shakespeare's New Idea of Rome', both in P. A. Ramsey (ed.), *Rome and the Renaissance: The City and the Myth* (Binghamton, NY, 1982), 77–92 and 371–80, and Kranz's '"Too Great a Mind": The *Mentis Integritas* of Shakespeare's Roman Heroes',

A related trend, not limited to the Roman plays, is the exploration of classical influences on Shakespeare, especially the influence of classical concepts of virtue and heroism.[4] A key figure in such explorations has been Seneca. Much of the discussion has revolved around the influence of Seneca's tragedies on the development of Elizabethan tragedy, and hence has focused on themes and conventions only marginally related to Senecan Stoicism; but some critics, like T. S. Eliot in his two classic 1927 essays, focused directly on the nature of Stoic heroism.[5] The case for the influence of Senecan drama is now widely accepted,[6] but the relevance of Stoicism to that tradition is still debated. Opposing positions are represented in two books published almost simultaneously in 1984–5. Gordon Braden sees Senecan Stoicism as having a profound though paradoxical influence: the legacy of Seneca's tragedies was 'a style of autarkic selfhood', expressed in anger and desire for power, which is 'not altogether paradoxically mirrored in the dispassionate philosophy' of Stoicism.[7] Gilles Monsarrat, defining Stoicism much more narrowly, argues that the loose and baggy definitions of earlier critics have caused its influence to be greatly overrated, and underlines his claim that 'there is . . . little to be said about

Classical and Modern Literature, 4 (1984), 143–65. In the last decade the critical focus has tended to shift from *romanitas* back towards a concern with the plays' Renaissance context, or with more universal issues of power and gender. However, some of the best recent work keeps a balance between Roman and Renaissance concerns: for instance, Gail Kern Paster's chapter on 'Shakespeare's Idea of Rome' in *The Idea of the City in the Age of Shakespeare* (Athens, Ga., 1985), 58–90, or Wayne A. Rebhorn's comparison of Roman and Elizabethan forms of aristocratic 'emulation' in 'The Crisis of the Aristocracy in *Julius Caesar*', *RQ* 43 (1990), 75–111.

[4] For instance, Eugene Waith, *The Herculean Hero in Marlowe, Chapman, Shakespeare, and Dryden* (London, 1962); Reuben A. Brower, *Hero and Saint: Shakespeare and the Greco-Roman Heroic Tradition* (Oxford, 1971).

[5] 'Seneca in Elizabethan Translation' and 'Shakespeare and the Stoicism of Seneca', both first pub. 1927, repr. in *Selected Essays* (3rd edn., London, 1951), 65–105 and 126–40. The latter essay has been criticized by Gilles D. Monsarrat, *Light from the Porch: Stoicism and English Renaissance Literature* (Paris, 1984), who calls its influence 'pernicious' (130), and by G. F. Hartford, 'T. S. Eliot on the Stoicism of Seneca', *English Studies in Africa*, 33 (1990), 1–14. Hartford makes some damaging criticisms of the essay's obscurities and perversities (such as the odd choice of Othello as a typical Stoic figure), but I still believe, like Gordon Braden, *Renaissance Tragedy and the Senecan Tradition: Anger's Privilege* (New Haven, 1985), 69, that Eliot seized on an essential truth about the self-dramatizing quality of Stoicism.

[6] See Robert S. Miola, *Shakespeare and Classical Tragedy: The Influence of Seneca* (Oxford, 1992), ch. 1.

[7] Braden, *Renaissance Tragedy*, 2.

Stoicism in Shakespeare' by allotting him twelve pages out of 300-odd.[8]

The importance of Stoic constancy in *Julius Caesar* was first argued (independently) in 1966 by John Anson and Phyllis Rackin, followed in the early 1970s by R. J. Kaufmann and Clifford J. Ronan, Ruth M. Levitsky, and Marvin L. Vawter.[9] Many subsequent critics have accepted and acknowledged their arguments; Marvin Spevack, for instance, in his 1988 edition, calls constancy 'the major dramatic, psychological, social, and political ideal' of the play.[10] Some have extended the concept to other Roman plays: Miola treats constancy, along with honour and *pietas*, as one of the 'three Roman ideals whose thematic implications Shakespeare explores through the Roman plays'; and Charles and Michelle Martindale, in a discussion of 'Shakespeare's Stoicism', deal with the constancy of Coriolanus, Antony, and Cleopatra.[11]

There is disagreement, however, about how Shakespeare presents

[8] Monsarrat, *Light from the Porch*, 137; 135–47 deal with Shakespeare. Monsarrat's scholarship is encyclopaedic, and his disentangling of Stoic from non-Stoic elements often extremely useful, but his criticism tends to be unsubtle. In identifying Stoic influence only in what squares precisely with the doctrines of classical Stoicism, he disqualifies much that Elizabethan writers and audiences would surely have labelled as 'Stoic' or 'stoical'. His most questionable assumption is reflected in the chapter title 'In Quest of Stage Stoics': Monsarrat looks for characters who perfectly fulfil the ideal of Stoic virtue, and unsurprisingly finds few. Only Horatio is accepted out of Shakespeare's characters, and even the senators in Massinger's *Roman Actor* who enact on stage the rhetorical trope of the Stoic smiling on the rack are dismissed as 'rather doubtful Stoics' (229) for their earlier political trimming. By the same reasoning it could be argued that Renaissance drama is not influenced by Christianity, since it contains few saints. Stoicism is much more commonly and usefully present as an ideal than as an achievement. (For Monsarrat's comments on *Julius Caesar* see Ch. 7 below.)

[9] Anson: '*Julius Caesar*: The Politics of the Hardened Heart', *ShakS* 2 (1966), 11–33. Rackin: 'The Pride of Shakespeare's Brutus', *Library Chronicle (Univ. of Pennsylvania)*, 32 (1966), 18–33. Kaufmann/Ronan: 'Shakespeare's *Julius Caesar*: An Apollonian and Comparative Reading', *CompD* 4 (1970), 18–51. Levitsky: '"The Elements Were So Mix'd ..."', *PMLA* 88 (1973), 240–45. Vawter: '"Division 'tween Our Souls": Shakespeare's Stoic Brutus', *ShakS* 7 (1974), 173–95, and, on related themes, '*Julius Caesar*: Rupture in the Bond', *JEGP* 72 (1973), 311–28, and '"After Their Fashion": Cicero and Brutus in *Julius Caesar*', *ShakS* 9 (1976), 205–19.

[10] *Julius Caesar*, New Cambridge Shakespeare (Cambridge, 1988), 11–12, 17–18, 23–7 (24).

[11] Miola, *Shakespeare's Rome*, 17 (see also 98–100, 119, 200–3); Martindale and Martindale, *Shakespeare and the Uses of Antiquity* (London, 1990), 165–89 (179–81 on *Coriolanus*, 181–9 on *Antony*). See also Wells, *Wide Arch*, 60–79, 100–7, 109. The *mentis integritas* discussed by Kranz ('"Too Great a Mind"') is a concept closely related to constancy.

constancy. The earlier discussions tend to be hostile to Stoicism, at times virulently so: Anson's Caesar is petrified into a marble statue by Stoic pride, Vawter's Brutus by killing Caesar 'unleashes his demented mind upon the already sickened world'.[12] They see Shakespeare as writing within a dominant 'anti-Stoic tradition', stretching from Cicero through Augustine to Erasmus and Montaigne, which condemns Stoicism for pride, arrogance, inhumanity, and impossible aspirations. The Martindales, on the other hand, deny that Shakespeare is 'ideologically hostile to Stoicism', and insist that constancy, however 'repellent' we post-Romantics may find it, appealed profoundly to Renaissance minds.[13] There is also debate over the depth and seriousness of Shakespeare's engagement with Stoicism: views range from Vawter's picture of a scholarly Shakespeare familiar with such difficult texts as Cicero's *De finibus*, through the Martindales' view that he merely made use of ancient commonplaces in a spirit of 'creative opportunism', to Monsarrat's flat denial of any influence.

On both these debates I would take a middle position. I believe that there is no evidence that Shakespeare had a scholarly knowledge of Greco-Roman philosophy, but that he was aware of, and deeply engaged with, current debates about Stoic 'constancy'. And I see his attitude as neither unequivocally hostile nor admiring, but ambivalent. Such ambivalence, moreover, runs deeply through the entire Western tradition of responses to Stoicism, and is especially strong in such key figures as Cicero, Erasmus, and Montaigne, whom Anson and Vawter define simply as 'anti-Stoic'.[14]

More important, however, I believe that previous discussions of constancy have underestimated the ambiguity and complexity of the concept. In particular, by focusing on Senecan Stoicism, they have overlooked an equally significant but rather different concept of constancy in Cicero. It is, I shall argue, to a large extent out of the tensions between these two kinds of constancy, and within each of them, that Shakespeare constructs the moral and political conflicts of the Roman plays.

[12] Vawter, 'Division', 182. Levitsky's more sympathetic reading is flawed by misreadings (the misquotation in the title is symptomatic). The most balanced and convincing of these essays (despite at times impenetrable thickets of jargon) is that of Kaufmann and Ronan, to whom my reading of the play is indebted.

[13] Martindale and Martindale, *Shakespeare and the Uses of Antiquity*, 167, 169.

[14] On Erasmus, see Anson, 'Politics of the Hardened Heart', 13–14; on Cicero and Montaigne, see Vawter, 'Division', 174–6 and 182–3.

The problems of 'constancy' as a moral term are inherent in the ambiguity of the word. It derives from the Latin noun *constantia*, and thence from the verb *constare* (to stand firm). Its basic sense is thus 'not moving, remaining fixed', and hence 'not changing, remaining the same'. The *OED* distinguishes three senses of the word as a moral term, which may be labelled constancy (steadfastness), constancy (consistency), and constancy (fidelity). The last of these (*OED* 2: 'Steadfastness of attachment to a person or cause; faithfulness, fidelity') is unquestionably important in Shakespeare, but, as I have already noted, lies largely outside the scope of this present study.[15] My concern is with the Stoic tradition of constancy, which is essentially a compound of the first two senses: steadfastness and consistency.

Constancy (steadfastness) is 'The state or quality of being unmoved in mind; steadfastness, firmness, endurance, fortitude' (*OED* 1).[16] In this sense, constancy is a form of courage or endurance. It means remaining unmoved under pressure, internal or external; the constant man maintains his fixed resolves, unshaken either by his own emotions or by outward pressure to change or submit.

Constancy (consistency) is 'The quality of being invariable . . . ; uniformity, unchangingness, regularity' (*OED* 3). In this sense, 'constancy' is the opposite of 'mutability', and virtually synonymous with 'consistency'.[17] Though *OED* refers this sense only to abstract or inanimate subjects (except in the limited sense of 'persistence, perseverance', 3b), it can easily be applied to a mental state or, metaphorically, a person: so Julius Caesar claims, 'I am constant as the Northern Star' (*JC* 3. 1. 60). The constant man in this sense is self-consistent, always the same, uniform and unvarying in his beliefs, principles, feelings, and way of life.

In theory these two senses can be distinguished; in practice they are so linked that the one usually implies the other. When Caesar calls himself 'constant as the Northern Star', he means primarily that he is self-consistent, but also that he will not give way to

[15] For an interesting discussion of constancy (fidelity) see Marilyn French, *Shakespeare's Division of Experience* (New York, 1981), esp. chs. 5 and 8—though her assertion that 'constancy had come by Shakespeare's time to refer exclusively to the sexual dimension of life' (124) is of course quite misleading.

[16] 'Steadfastness' has the same root meaning as *constantia*: 'standing firm, remaining in place'.

[17] The two words are etymologically linked: Latin *constare* and *consistere* largely overlap in meaning, and both derive ultimately from *stare* (to stand).

political pressure. When Brutus urges 'formal constancy', does he mean steadfastness in the face of danger, or consistency in playing a part, or both? The ambiguity of the word is neatly (if unintentionally) captured by a note in M. A. Screech's fine recent translation of Montaigne: '*constantia* (inner consistency and steadfast constancy) were the ideals of Stoic philosophy.'[18] The grammatical hiccup suggests a perfectly justified uncertainty as to whether *constantia* is in fact one thing or two.

The idea of constancy in English literature is at least as old as *The Battle of Maldon*, but the words 'constant' and 'constance' (later 'constancy') entered English from French in the fourteenth century. In Chaucer's 'Clerk's Tale' we find them used as a leitmotif in all three senses: fidelity, steadfastness, consistency.[19] In the Renaissance 'constancy' came to be more explicitly associated with the moral ideals of classical Stoicism, and especially in the later sixteenth and early seventeenth century, when it was taken up as a keyword of the Neostoic movement, it came to sum up Stoic and Roman virtue.[20] In translations of classical works, such as North's Plutarch (1579) and Lodge's Seneca (1614), 'constancy' and 'constant' are used to translate a wide range of Greek or Latin words and phrases denoting an equally wide range of virtues: manliness, strength, courage, patient endurance, peace of mind, magnanimity.[21]

How does constancy come to be seen in this way as central to Stoicism and Roman virtue? To answer this question we must go

[18] Michel de Montaigne, *The Complete Essays*, tr. and ed. M. A. Screech (Harmondsworth, 1993), 373.

[19] Griselda's constancy is essentially fidelity, but she is also steadfast, and the sense 'consistency' is implied in lines 1047–8 ('And she ay sad and constant as a wal, | Continuynge evere hire innocence overal'; compare 708–11, though the word 'constant' is not there used). Her constancy is contrasted with both the fickle inconstancy of the populace (995–1001) and Walter's irrational obstinacy (701–5). (*The Riverside Chaucer*, gen. ed. Larry D. Benson (Oxford, 1988).)

[20] Kaufmann and Ronan note the Elizabethan tendency 'to make a four-way identification between stoic, constant, heroic, and Roman behaviour' ('*Julius Caesar*', 28); see 27–9 and notes.

[21] Some examples from Lodge's translation of Seneca's *De constantia sapientis*: 'a more constant course' = *virilem viam* (1. 1, p. 658); 'one only man remained quiet and constant' = *uni homini pax fuit* (6. 2, p. 662); 'a willing and constant heart' = *aequo placidoque animo* (8. 3, p. 665); 'vertue, [of] constancy and patience' = *virtute ... dura tolerandi* (10. 4, p. 667); 'constancy and greatness of his mind' = *magnanimitatem* (11. 1, p. 667). North's use of the words is analysed in Ch. 6.

back ultimately—as so often—to Plato. One of the basic Platonic assumptions is (in Karl Popper's formulation) '*that change is evil, and that rest is divine*'.[22] This assumption rests upon Plato's distinction between the realm of Being, the unchanging world of the Forms and the gods or God, and the mortal realm of Becoming, governed by movement and change, growth and decay. The distinction corresponds to that between the human soul and body: 'The soul is most like that which is divine, immortal, intelligible, uniform, indissoluble, and ever self-consistent and invariable, while the body is most like that which is human, mortal, multiform, unintelligible, dissoluble, and never self-consistent.'[23] This Platonic dichotomy—on the one side God, the soul, constancy, perfection; on the other the mundane world, the body, mutability, imperfection—is one of the most influential in Western thought. From it follows logically the ethical assumption that to become more perfect, more like the gods, human beings must become more constant, unchanging, and self-consistent. On the level of practical ethics this means, as the *Republic* makes clear, that each person should 'persist unswervingly in the pursuit of [his] single natural bent', playing a single social role with unvarying consistency.[24]

The Stoics take over from Plato, along with much else, the axiom that rest is better than change. They approach the idea of constancy, however, by way of a rather different set of assumptions.[25] One of the most fundamental Stoic ideas is *homologia*:

[22] Quoted in Jonas Barish, *The Antitheatrical Prejudice* (Berkeley, 1981), 18 (italics in original). This paragraph is indebted to Barish's ch. 1, esp. 17–18; see also John Passmore, *The Perfectibility of Man* (London, 1970), 39–41.

[23] Plato, *Phaedo* 80b, in *The Last Days of Socrates*, tr. Hugh Tredennick (Harmondsworth, 1954).

[24] Barish, *Antitheatrical Prejudice*, 18; cf. 22–3.

[25] This outline of Stoicism is based principally on A. A. Long, *Hellenistic Philosophy: Stoics, Epicureans, Sceptics* (2nd edn., London, 1986), 107–209 (the most lucid summary), and R. D. Hicks, *Stoic and Epicurean* ([London, 1910]; repr. New York, 1962), which brings out most clearly the central importance of the idea of consistency. I have also drawn on the works of Seneca and Cicero discussed in the following chapters, especially Cicero, *De finibus* 3 and 4, and *Academica* 1. 35–9, and on the texts collected in Jason L. Saunders (ed.), *Greek and Roman Philosophy after Aristotle* (New York, 1966), sect. 2, and A. A. Long and D. N. Sedley, *The Hellenistic Philosophers* (2 vols., Cambridge, 1987). Other secondary works consulted include E. Vernon Arnold, *Roman Stoicism* (Cambridge, 1911); Edwyn Bevan, *Stoics and Sceptics* (Oxford, 1913); J. M. Rist, *Stoic Philosophy* (Cambridge, 1969); *Oxford Classical Dictionary* (cited as *OCD*), 2nd edn. (Oxford, 1970), s.v. 'Stoa (1)'; F. H. Sandbach, *The Stoics* (London, 1975); Monsarrat, *Light from the Porch*, 9–19 (a good account with particularly full references to the classical sources).

harmony, regularity, consistency. Zeno of Citium (335–263 BC), the founder of Stoicism, defined the aim of the philosopher as to live *homologoumenôs*, harmoniously or consistently. The definition was later expanded, by Zeno himself or one of his successors, into *homologoumenôs têi physei*, consistently with nature.[26] Implied in this formula is the Stoic view of the universe as a perfectly harmonious, ordered, unified whole, animated and guided by a power which can be called, more or less synonymously, Reason (*logos*) or Nature or God.[27] Our human reason is a reflection of the cosmic Reason ('right reason') which governs the universe. The philosopher is the person whose reason is perfectly in tune with right reason and who willingly submits to it, becoming a harmonious part of the grand design. Such a harmony or consistency inevitably involves internal harmony and self-consistency. In the words of R. D. Hicks, the Stoic end is 'a life consistent and harmonious, the smooth flow of existence unchecked by eddies and cross-currents'.[28]

> To Zeno . . . the first mark of reason was self-consistency. A rational life must follow a single harmonious plan, whereas the paths of folly are many and various, but always stamped with inconsistency and self-contradiction.[29]

This seems to be implied in Zeno's original, cryptic formula: since reason is inherently consistent and unreason inconsistent, to live consistently (*homologoumenôs*) necessarily implies consistency with right reason and nature, and hence a life of wisdom and virtue.[30] The Stoics' assumptions thus lead them back to the Platonic ideal of being always the same.

[26] The relevant texts are quoted in Long and Sedley, *Hellenistic Philosophers*, 63A–C (translation i. 394–5, Greek texts ii. 389–90); for commentary see ibid. i. 398–401; Arnold, *Roman Stoicism*, 282; J. M. Rist, 'Zeno and Stoic Consistency', *Phronesis*, 22 (1977), 161–74. Braden, in a stimulating discussion (*Renaissance Tragedy*, 19–20 and n. 22), suggests that Zeno's formula was expanded to remove the 'antinomian' implication that self-consistency is all that matters, and each individual can define virtue for himself. The formula is often translated, following the Latin *secundum naturam*, as 'according to nature', which obscures its relation to constancy.

[27] Long, *Hellenistic Philosophy*, 146–9. Long and Sedley, *Hellenistic Philosophers*, i. 383, note that '*Homologia* . . . was ideally suited to capture the essence of Stoic virtue, since its linguistic form (*homo-logia*) is interpretable as "harmony of (or with) reason".'

[28] Hicks, *Stoic and Epicurean*, 77.

[29] Ibid. 10.

[30] This assumption is made explicit by Seneca in *Ep.* 20. 5 (p. 202).

To see how this concept of consistency develops into the rather different concept normally thought of as 'Stoic constancy', we must look in more detail at the Stoic ethical system and the theory of knowledge on which it rests.[31]

The Stoics, like Plato, draw a sharp distinction between true knowledge and mere belief or 'opinion', and identify knowledge with virtue: a person who knows what is good will necessarily act rightly. Virtue depends on making correct judgements. Hence the Stoics normally speak not of 'good' and 'bad' men, but of 'wise' and 'foolish' ones. The Stoic moral ideal is the 'wise man' or 'sage' (*sapiens* in Latin), whose reason is completely in tune with right reason. The wise man makes consistently correct judgements, and is incapable of error; hence he is morally perfect.

The basis of the wise man's wisdom is the knowledge that nothing is 'good' except what is morally good (that is, life in harmony with nature), and nothing 'bad' except what is morally evil. All other things which in everyday language are called 'good' (health, wealth, power, and so on) or 'bad' (sickness, poverty, disgrace, and so on) are in fact 'indifferent'—morally neutral, neither to be desired nor feared by the wise man. It is true that some of these indifferent matters can be classed as 'preferred' and others as 'rejected': all other things being equal, in most circumstances the wise man will prefer to be healthy than sick, prosperous than poor, and so on, and will attempt to arrange his life accordingly. Ordinary day-to-day virtue—the performing of 'appropriate acts', in Stoic terminology—consists in the correct selection and pursuit of such 'preferable' objects. But the wise man will not allow himself to *care* about his success or failure in such aims. He remains indifferent to everything which is outside his own mind and hence outside his control, and cares only about the one thing which is within his control: his own moral state. Even life and death are not good or bad in themselves. In most circumstances to remain alive will be preferable, but the wise man will face death, or even commit suicide if this seems an appropriate act, with undisturbed equanimity.

Virtue is thus identified with knowledge of what is good, and vice with wrong moral opinions. In the words of Epictetus, 'What

[31] For a more detailed account of Stoic epistemology see Long, *Hellenistic Philosophy*, 123–31.

disturbs men's minds is not events but their judgements on events.'[32] The false opinion that something indifferent is good or bad (for instance, that money is desirable, or that death is fearful) will produce an emotional reaction of desire or fear towards that thing. For the Stoics, thus, the mind is not the traditional battleground between two forces labelled 'reason' and 'passion'; it is a single, rational faculty, but it may either act in accordance with right reason, or be swayed by false opinions into undesirable emotional states. When these states become ingrained they are called 'passions', which are diseases of the mind and cause a kind of insanity. Such passions must be not merely controlled but completely eradicated. The wise man, whose reason is in complete harmony with right reason, lives in a state of complete freedom from passion, *apatheia*.

This is not, as later anti-Stoics assumed and as the English associations of 'apathy' would suggest, a state of total emotionlessness. The wise man has no passions, but he has feelings—moderate and rational feelings such as happiness and benevolence. Cicero translated the Greek term for these feelings, *eupathai* (good emotional states), as *constantiae* (consistent states).[33] This suggests the essential distinction: 'The Stoics distinguished good men from others by reference to the consistency of their *logos* [reason].'[34] Whereas most people act sometimes rationally and sometimes irrationally, the wise man is consistently governed by right reason. His state of mind is characterized above all by stability, regularity, harmony, constancy (consistency).

Stoic ethical doctrine, in its original form, is not as inhuman as later anti-Stoics painted it. Stoic teachers often formulated it, however, in 'paradoxes', which put the concept of the wise man in its most extreme form: that only the wise man is rich (because he has virtue, the only possession which matters), that only the wise man is a king (because he has absolute sovereignty over himself), that the wise man will be happy even while being tortured on the rack (because no physical suffering can disturb the happiness that comes from virtue). Such paradoxes provocatively express the Stoic sense of an absolute disjunction between external events and internal states of mind. Once you have attained Stoic wisdom,

[32] *Manual* (*Enchiridion*) 5, in Saunders, *Greek and Roman Philosophy*, 134.
[33] Long, *Hellenistic Philosophy*, 206–7; Cicero, *Tusc.* 4. 14.
[34] Long, *Hellenistic Philosophy*, 177.

nothing that happens to you, however 'bad' (or for that matter however 'good'), can disturb your absolute tranquillity and equanimity. You cannot be deterred from virtue by any threats, since you know that pain and death are not to be feared. The idea of the wise man's consistency of *logos*, his maintenance of the same beliefs and feelings, thus turns into a celebration of the defensive strength of the mind, unshaken by adversity. Constancy (consistency) merges into constancy (steadfastness).

This side of Stoic ethics was emphasized by the Roman Stoics. More moralists than philosophers, they largely ignored physics, metaphysics, logic, and the technicalities of ethics, to concentrate on practical moral advice and exhortation. The result was in some ways to soften, in others to increase, the austerity of the ancient Stoa. On the one hand, following Greek philosophers of the 'Middle Stoa' like Panaetius (180–109 BC) and Posidonius (135–51 BC), the Roman Stoics tended to focus more on everyday 'appropriate acts', less on the ideal sage.[35] On the other hand, they laid an even heavier stress on suffering, adversity, and endurance. This is not surprising when we consider that the leading Roman Stoic writers were also active in politics, and wrote for readers who were likewise of the governing class. Cicero, politician and orator, finally murdered on the orders of Antony and Octavian; Seneca, Nero's adviser, finally compelled by him to suicide; the Emperor Marcus Aurelius—all had reason to look to philosophy primarily for guidance on the steadfast bearing of danger and death.

It is this Roman form of Stoicism, 'first and last a practical moral doctrine',[36] which has had most influence on later centuries. In the words of Herschel Baker, 'Stoicism has always exerted its profoundest influence as an attitude rather than a philosophic system'[37]—an attitude of patient endurance, absence of passion, indifference to externals. It is this attitude which (as Long points out) is summed up in the popular use not only of the words 'stoic' and 'stoical' but also of the word 'philosophical'.[38] Shakespeare's characters, indeed, use 'philosophy' in this way. When Romeo rejects the Friar's proffer of 'Adversity's sweet milk, philosophy'

[35] Long, *Hellenistic Philosophy*, 211–16 (on Panaetius), 233–4. [36] Ibid. 233.
[37] Herschel Baker, *The Dignity of Man* (Cambridge, Mass., 1947), 71.
[38] Long, *Hellenistic Philosophy*, 107.

with the cry 'Hang up philosophy' (*Rom.* 3. 3. 55–7), or when Leonato dismisses philosophers who cannot endure the toothache patiently, 'However they have writ the style of gods, | And made a pish at chance and sufferance' (*Ado* 5. 1. 35–8), it is primarily Stoic philosophy that is in question.

The most important writers in transmitting Stoicism to later generations (though neither was purely a Stoic in the strictest sense) are Cicero and Seneca. Both make *homologia* or constancy central to their ethics, but the one stresses consistency, the other steadfastness.

Cicero's *De officiis* ('On Duties' or 'Moral Obligations') is the classic account of Roman virtue, setting out a rational public-spirited code woven from Stoic thought and Roman traditions. Perhaps its most influential passage is the discussion in Book 1 of 'decorum'. Interpreting *homologia* in terms of the literary and dramatic concept of decorum (appropriateness or propriety), Cicero here outlines an idea of virtue as the consistent playing of a part appropriate to human nature, one's personal character, and one's social role.

Seneca, in his moral epistles and essays such as *De constantia sapientis*, celebrates a more heroic ideal of the constancy of the wise man. For Seneca *constantia* means strength and stability of mind, unmoved by passion, unshaken by disaster, always the same whatever the external circumstances (*unus idemque inter diversa*). His *sapiens* combines the imperviousness of a rock with the serene detachment of a god. His is the ideal most commonly identified by posterity as 'Stoic constancy', repeatedly attacked by Christians as arrogant and inhuman, and revived in the Renaissance as the cornerstone of Neostoicism.

The contrast I have here drawn is oversimplified—it is not hard to find passages in Cicero exalting 'Senecan' constancy, and passages in Seneca on 'Ciceronian' decorum[39]—but it reflects genuine and obvious differences in tone and emphasis between the two

[39] For example, Cicero's *Tusculan Disputations* contain most of the 'Senecan' ideas on passion, suffering, and death (though treated with an un-Senecan touch of reserve and scepticism); Seneca's *De tranquillitate animi* (based on a work by Panaetius) sets out a more moderate, everyday, 'Ciceronian' view of Stoic virtue than that described in *De constantia sapientis*, and his Epistle 120 summarizes the Ciceronian-Panaetian concept of decorum.

writers. And the differences reflect very different directions in which the basic principle of being always the same can be taken. Ciceronian decorum is a moderate, social virtue, that of a good citizen who fulfils with consistency and temperance his proper role in society. Senecan constancy is the virtue of a heroic individual who stands alone like 'a Colossus' (*JC* 1. 2. 137) or 'a great sea-mark' (*Cor.* 5. 3. 74), is primarily concerned with his own self-sufficiency and self-perfection, and aspires to the nature of a god. There is obviously a potential conflict between the two.

There is also a potential internal conflict within both ideals, between reality and role-playing. The metaphor of life as a play is a traditional Stoic one, classically stated by Epictetus:

> Remember that you are an actor in a play, and the Playwright chooses the manner of it . . . your business is to act the character that is given you and act it well; the choice of the cast is Another's.[40]

Cicero's decorum is explicitly described in theatrical metaphors, and many critics have seen something histrionic in Senecan Stoicism—most notoriously Eliot, who labelled Seneca's ethics 'a matter of postures', well adapted to 'the natural public temper of Rome'.[41] Both Seneca's and Cicero's concepts of virtuous action depend upon being performed on a public stage for the approval of others. The good man must not only be virtuous but must be seen to be virtuous: *esse est percipi.* This external, self-dramatizing strain in Roman Stoicism contrasts oddly with the 'inwardness' of Stoic ethics, its theoretical stress on morality as 'an affair of the inner life'.[42] There is a particular irony in the fact that to conceive virtue as a public performance means that the performers' success must be publicly judged by others—and so places them at the mercy of that mere 'opinion' which, in Stoic epistemology and ethics, is the root of all evil.

Shakespeare's treatment of constancy in the Roman plays is shaped by these potential conflicts. This is not to suggest that Shakespeare had a detailed knowledge of or interest in Stoic philosophy; he had probably never heard of Zeno, or *homologia*, or appropriate acts. He had, however, almost certainly read *De*

[40] *Manual* 17, in Saunders, *Greek and Roman Philosophy*, 137.

[41] Eliot, 'Seneca in Elizabethan Translation', 72 (the passage is quoted in full in Ch. 3 below).

[42] Hicks, *Stoic and Epicurean*, 152.

officiis at school (as T. W. Baldwin demonstrated);[43] and even if he had not read Seneca's moral essays and epistles, or even his tragedies, he could not have avoided hearing his aphorisms quoted. Moreover, in the 1590s and early 1600s Stoic virtue and constancy were topical issues. Works by the European Neostoics, who made constancy the central virtue of a revived and Christianized Stoicism, were being translated into English: Justus Lipsius' *De constantia* in 1595, Guillaume du Vair's *Philosophie morale des stoiques* in 1598.[44] Shakespeare may have known these books; he certainly read Florio's translation of Montaigne's *Essays* (possibly before its publication in 1603), and would there have encountered both the Neostoic concept of constancy and a critique of it. Montaigne circles endlessly round the themes of constancy and inconstancy, while moving from a Neostoic position to a rejection of the Stoic ideal as impossible, self-contradictory, and even undesirable; his fascination with the topic, and a number of his specific ideas, parallel and perhaps influenced Shakespeare's.

Constancy was thus familiar to Shakespeare both as a classical and a topical issue. As the defining virtue of the Romans, it is central to his reconstruction of the ethos of ancient Rome. But he must also have been aware that this ancient virtue was being revived by contemporary writers as a cure for present-day problems, and it seems likely that the prominence of the theme in the Roman plays is in part a response to that current debate.

[43] T. W. Baldwin, *William Shakspere's Small Latine & Lesse Greeke* (Urbana, Ill., 1944), ii. 581–610. The possible influence of *De officiis* on Shakespeare has been little noted, and treatments of decorum in his work have focused on its linguistic and literary rather than its ethical aspects. T. McAlindon, *Shakespeare and Decorum* (London, 1973), concentrates on decorum as a linguistic principle and its relationship with cosmic order; he touches only briefly (11–12) on its connection with 'constancy', and barely mentions what I see as the central concept of role-playing; and, dealing only with *Antony* (ch. 6), he does not note its special importance for Shakespeare's Romans. Simmons's discussion of the *De officiis* passage in *Coriolanus* (*Shakespeare's Pagan World*, 38–42, 53–6) first drew my attention to its importance; but he also concentrates on the linguistic sense of decorum, with reference to the appropriateness or 'propriety' of public opinions and honours to their subjects, and does not relate it to Stoic constancy. Some discussions of decorum in *Antony* are noted in Ch. 9 below.

[44] 'Neostoicism' is variously spelt and variously defined (some classicists use the term, confusingly, for 'Late', i.e. Roman, Stoicism). Monsarrat (*Light from the Porch*, 77–80) argues that the term should be dropped, as carrying the misleading implication of a formal school with a unified body of doctrine; his cautions are valid, but I nevertheless retain the word as a useful shorthand for distinguishing Renaissance 'Stoicism' from classical.

This is not to say that his treatment of constancy is simply polemical. It is one of the strange features of the tradition I am tracing that so many of its central figures, from Cicero to Montaigne, can be described both as proponents and opponents of the Stoic ideal. Shakespeare is no exception, and his treatment of constancy seems to be, in Yeats's phrase, a quarrel with himself more than a quarrel with others. Clearly he is drawn to the ideal of constancy. Mutability is one of his preoccupations throughout his career; his favourite classic text was clearly Ovid's *Metamorphoses*, with its sinister-delightful representation of a world in perpetual motion.[45] The *Sonnets*, his most apparently personal work, are haunted by 'the conceit of this inconstant stay' (15)—the inevitability of time and death, the fickleness of human emotions, the impermanence of human achievements—and the desire for something that will remain, whether a love that 'alters not' (116) or poetry that outlives marble and gilded monuments (55). Sins of inconstancy—fickleness, treachery, ingratitude—are handled with particular horror throughout both the sonnets and the plays. Shakespeare is clearly sympathetic to the ideal voiced in perhaps his first play, *The Two Gentlemen of Verona*, by the inconstant Proteus: 'O heaven, were man | But constant, he were perfect' (5. 4. 109–10).

At the same time he is also conscious of the folly of this desire to be 'perfect'—an aspiration which drives a series of tragicomic figures from the academicians of *Love's Labour's Lost*, through the would-be angelic Angelo, to the Olympian Caesar and Coriolanus imitating the graces of the gods. Shakespeare is aware of the criticisms traditionally levelled at the Stoics, from Cicero and St Augustine onwards, for arrogantly and foolishly attempting to rise above the human condition, and setting up the inhuman and unattainable ideal of a 'wise man' who is rigid, emotionless, and fixated on death rather than life. These traditional criticisms are proverbially summed up in the hoary pun which Tranio inflicts on his master in *The Taming of the Shrew*: 'Let's be no stoics nor no stocks, I pray' (1. 1. 31).[46] They also, as earlier critics have noted,

[45] The lifelong influence of Ovid (especially the *Metamorphoses*) on Shakespeare is demonstrated in Jonathan Bate's *Shakespeare and Ovid* (Oxford, 1993).

[46] Braden, *Renaissance Tragedy*, 240, has a useful note on the 'stoic/stock' pun. (Tranio's speech, incidentally, can be seen as the germ of *Love's Labour's Lost*.)

inform Shakespeare's treatment of Stoic constancy in the Roman plays.

The originality of Shakespeare's treatment lies in his awareness of the complexity of 'constancy', the different senses of the word and the potential conflicts between them. To be 'constant' can mean to aspire to the immovable and godlike virtue of the Senecan *sapiens*, or to play with unwavering consistency and decorum the social role in which one is cast. Constancy as aspiring individualism and constancy as social role-playing can easily come into conflict, as Coriolanus finds. In Shakespeare's Rome, moreover, a society governed by opinion, decorum tends to become divorced from the self-knowledge on which Cicero insisted, while even Senecan constancy can become a matter of acting a part.

These problems are encapsulated in Brutus' lines quoted at the beginning of this chapter: 'bear it as our Roman actors do, | With untired spirits and formal constancy.' '[U]ntired spirits' suggests the inner strength of the Senecan Stoic hero, enduring and immovable; 'formal constancy', picking up the image of 'Roman actors', suggests Ciceronian decorum, the consistent acting of an appropriate part. More subtly, the contrast may suggest a problem which is inherent in both the Senecan and Ciceronian ideals: is constancy a spiritual reality or a matter of outward appearances? Or—as is suggested by the perverse attribution of 'constancy' to actors and the submerged theatrical pun in 'untired'—is it impossible to separate the two? The tension between the two halves of this densely packed line encapsulates the tension which runs through the entire Stoic tradition, and through the three Roman plays.

2

Cicero and the Roman Actors

More than any other writer, Marcus Tullius Cicero defined for posterity the concept of 'Roman virtue'.[1] His philosophical works blended an eclectic but Stoic-flavoured version of Greek ethical thought with traditional Roman values to produce a distinctively Roman Stoicism: moderate, public-spirited, placing all its emphasis on the social virtues, and inculcating courage, temperance, honour, and duty in the service of Rome. Cicero made no claim to originality, but his works survived when their Greek sources were lost, and, backed by his eloquence and the immense prestige of his name, became accepted as epitomes of the best kind of classical virtue. In particular their influence on the Renaissance was incalculable: 'Insofar as Tudor England had any sense of Roman values it was owing largely to Cicero.'[2] Most popular of all was Cicero's last work, his treatise on civic virtue, *De officiis*. It has been called 'arguabl[y] . . . the most influential secular prose work ever written', and in the sixteenth century it was second only to the Bible as a source of moral wisdom.[3]

If there is one classical text, outside Ovid and Plutarch, that Shakespeare must have read, it is *De officiis*. T. W. Baldwin has shown that it was the standard text for moral instruction in the upper forms of Elizabethan grammar schools; if Shakespeare attended Stratford grammar school (and Baldwin's massive

[1] On Cicero texts and references, see Bibliographical Note.

[2] Geoffrey Bullough (ed.), *Narrative and Dramatic Sources of Shakespeare*, v (London, 1964), 6–7.

[3] A. E. Douglas, 'Cicero the Philosopher,' in T. A. Dorey (ed.), *Cicero* (London, 1964), 135–70 (149). For the comparison of *De officiis* and the Bible, see Roger Ascham, quoted in Baldwin, *Small Latine*, ii. 585–6, and Grimalde's 'Epistell to the reader', sig. 2[v]: 'so rightlye pointing out the pathway to all vertue: as none can bee righter, onely Scripture excepted'. On the influence of Cicero and *De officiis* in Renaissance England, see also John Higginbotham, introd. to *Cicero on Moral Obligation: A New Translation of Cicero's 'De Officiis'* (London, 1967), 23–30; Long, *Hellenistic Philosophy*, 211; Ralph Graham Palmer, *Seneca's 'De Remediis Fortuitorum' and the Elizabethans* (Chicago, 1953), esp. 17–18; Baldwin, *Small Latine*, ii. 581–610 (on Cicero in 16th-cent. education).

accumulation of evidence makes this overwhelmingly likely), he would have studied it in Latin, and probably also in Nicholas Grimalde's 1553 translation (the version quoted in this chapter).[4] His early reading of *De officiis* must have done much to shape his idea of Rome, as a society whose life was public and political, morally serious, and self-conscious in its exercise of the Roman virtues.

Most important for Shakespeare, in my view, was the section of *De officiis* (1. 93–151) dealing with the quality of *decorum*: a moderate and temperate version of Stoic constancy defined as the consistent playing of an appropriate role, a playing of the part of oneself. Shakespeare's conception of his noble Romans as actors, I shall argue, derives ultimately from these passages. He is fascinated by the questions raised by Ciceronian decorum, and its ambiguous relationship with other, more heroic forms of Stoic constancy.

Before coming to this central question, however, it is necessary to define Cicero's own ambiguous relationship with Stoicism, especially in his treatment of the problems of knowledge, opinion, and honour.

Stoic and sceptic

It is one of the paradoxes of Cicero's philosophical position that it is possible to call him both a Stoic and a founder of the 'anti-Stoic' tradition.[5] He studied in youth with all three of the main philosophical schools of his day: Stoic, Epicurean, and Academic.

[4] Baldwin, *Small Latine*, ii. 601–10, demonstrates Shakespeare's knowledge of *De officiis* in a roundabout way by arguing that Hamlet's 'To be or not to be' soliloquy and the Duke's speech on death in *Measure for Measure* draw upon passages in *Tusc.* 1 in the original Latin (see also Marion H. Addington, 'Shakespeare and Cicero', *N&Q* 165 (1933), 116–18); if Shakespeare studied the *Tusculans*, he 'had pretty certainly' studied *De officiis* previously (ii. 601). On Grimalde's translation, ibid. ii. 585.

[5] On Cicero's philosophy I am indebted, apart from the general works on Stoicism cited in Ch. 1, to Douglas, 'Cicero the Philosopher'; Torsten Petersson, *Cicero: A Biography* ([London, 1920]; repr. New York, 1963), ch. 16; H. A. K. Hunt, *The Humanism of Cicero* (Melbourne, 1954); G. B. Kerferd, 'Cicero and Stoic Ethics', and R. G. Tanner, 'Cicero on Conscience and Morality', in John R. C. Martyn (ed.), *Cicero and Virgil* (Amsterdam, 1972), 60–74 and 87–112; Paul MacKendrick, *The Philosophical Books of Cicero* (London, 1989); M. T. Griffin and E. M. Atkins, introd. to Cicero, *On Duties* (Cambridge, 1991).

He was most attracted to the scepticism of the New Academy, which taught that certain knowledge is impossible, and the only attitude proper to a philosopher is suspension of judgement.[6] Nevertheless, it is possible to arrive at an approximation of the truth by a rational calculation of possibilities. Being an Academic, Cicero insists, does not prevent him from holding opinions as probable, only from claiming them as dogmatic certainties.[7]

Cicero the sceptic thus maintains an eclectic position, willing to take probable doctrines from any school.[8] He contrasts his own open-mindedness with the rigidity of more dogmatic philosophers, such as (by implication) the Stoics,

> which bynde them selves to anye certayne opinion, as men wholye gyven to the same, so that sumtimes they are constrayned, to get theym opinion of constancie [*constantiae causa*], to maynteyne such thynges, as otherwyse they woulde not allowe. But I who in al thinges folowe probabilitie, and can go no farther then likelyhode, am readye both to wryte agaynst others without any stubbernes, and also to be writen agaynst, without anye anger. (*Tusc.* 2. 5, sigs. I3^{v}–4^{r})

By *constantia* Cicero primarily means '(philosophical) consistency'; yet John Dolman's translation may not be entirely inaccurate in implying the moral sense of the word. The Stoics, Cicero implies, are fixed in their intellectual positions, and as unwilling to be moved by argument as by adversity.

Cicero's eclecticism is clearly reflected in his treatment of Stoicism. The essentially Stoic framework of his most famous works, the *Tusculan Disputations* and *De officiis*, and the almost undi-

[6] On the Academics, see Douglas, 'Cicero the Philosopher', 142–4; Long, *Hellenistic Philosophy*, 88–106; Bevan, *Stoics and Sceptics*, lecture 4. The New Academy nominally descended from Plato's Academy, but emphasized the scepticism inherent in Socratic dialogue, while abandoning Plato's positive dogmas. It must be distinguished from the confusingly named 'Old Academy' founded by Cicero's contemporary Antiochus of Ascalon, an eclectic school which claimed to return to the original teachings of Plato (Long, *Hellenistic Philosophy*, 222–9). The relations between the various Hellenistic schools are greatly clarified by a diagram in Griffin and Atkins, *On Duties*, p. xxxiv.

[7] *Fin.* 5. 76. Cicero follows the 'probabilism' of Carneades and his own teacher Philo of Larissa, rather than the more thoroughgoing scepticism of Arcesilaus, the founder of the New Academy. His Academic scepticism must also be distinguished from the absolute scepticism of the Pyrrhonians (see Ch. 5 below), who reject 'probability' and claim that all beliefs are arbitrary. Cicero discusses these epistemological questions in detail in the *Academica*.

[8] *Tusc.* 5. 83; compare 5. 32–3, where Cicero jokingly refuses to be bound by consistency (*constantia*) with what he has said elsewhere.

luted Stoicism of passages such as the account of emotions in *Tusculans* 4, justify the custom of referring to him casually as a 'Stoic'.[9] On the other hand, he is sharply critical of some Stoic doctrines. In *De finibus* ('On the chief good and evil'), Books 3–5, and in *Tusculans* 5, he conducts a running debate with the Stoics over their claims that virtue alone is 'good', and that the virtuous man can be happy even in extreme pain and deprivation. Such hyperbolical claims—very similar, as we shall see, to claims made by Seneca for *constantia sapientis*—Cicero treats as arrogant, unrealistic, and absurd. Nevertheless, in both works he finally comes round to a very hesitant support for the absolutism of the Stoic position, as in his superbly hedged conclusion in *Tusculans* 5: 'Thus you have that, whyche I thynke to be moost stoutelye spoken, of a blessed and happy life. And (as the case standeth) unlesse you can bryng any proofe, that also, which is as trulye spoken, as it may be' (5. 82, sig. C[C]8^{r}). Cicero's eclectic posture enables him, while accepting much Stoic doctrine, to maintain a thoroughly ambiguous mixture of scepticism and wistful half-belief towards its more extreme claims.[10]

Academics and Stoics, despite their differences, agree on the moral importance of problems of knowledge. The Academics stress the difficulty or impossibility of perceiving truth and the dangerous ease of error. The Stoics, on the other hand, believe it is possible to distinguish truth from falsehood on the basis of a certain quality of 'clearness' possessed only by true sense-impressions; consequently, error must arise from negligence or wilful blindness. In Stoic thought, as we have seen, the choice of false opinion over true knowledge is the root of all evil. The two epistemologies are almost diametrically opposed; nevertheless, their common concern with the dangers of false opinion means that throughout this study we will find Stoicism and scepticism strangely intertwined, and in the Renaissance almost identified with each other.

Cicero, influenced by both schools, is doubly conscious of the problem. As he advises in *De officiis*, we must be careful

[9] As Douglas refers to the 'moderate popular Stoicism' of the *Tusculans* ('Cicero the Philosopher', 147–8), and Long to the 'humane Stoicism' of *De officiis* (*Hellenistic Philosophy*, 321). Monsarrat, on the other hand, complains that the 'humanistic casuistry' of *De officiis* 'often blurs and softens the specific features of Stoicism' (*Light from the Porch*, 10).

[10] Vawter, 'Division', in attempting to portray Cicero as a pure anti-Stoic, ignores the important final turn of the argument in *Fin.* 5.

that we take not thinges, we knowe not, as though we knewe them, & rashlie assent to them. Which fault whoso will eschew (and all ought to be willing) must employ to the considering of maters both leasure, & diligence. (*Off.* 1. 18, sig. A8^{v})

Cicero's most eloquent treatment of the dangers of taking things we know not as though we knew them is in *Tusculans* 3, where he argues Stoically that our moral failings arise from our inability to see nature clearly. We are born with only a few sparks of divine knowledge in us,

which with noughtye fashions & erronious opinions we doe lyghtelye quenche, in such wise, that not so much as any glymse of the lyghte of nature can appeare ... As soone as we are borne & brought foorth into this light we are forthwith continuallye trayned in al noughtinesse and perverse opinions, so that it maye well be sayd, that even with the milke of oure nurses, we do sucke errour.

First our parents, then our teachers, then the poets we read teach us their prejudices and false beliefs. Finally the most powerful teacher of all, public opinion, 'the commen voice of the multitude', completes our flight from the light of nature into 'erronious opinions' by instilling into us the most dangerous and plausible fallacy: 'that nothing is more necessary, more to be desired, or coveted then honour, empire & the praise of the common people'. Most men, including the best [*optimus quisque*], take this ideal of honour for true virtue, but they

are foulye deluded and mocked. For they do not obtayne any perfect picture of vertue, but the shaded image of glorye. For, true glorye is a sounde and perfect thynge, and no coloured shadowe. And that is the incorrupted and universall prayse, of al good men, proceeding of the right report of the excellencie of vertue.... Which inasmuch as commonly it foloweth al good deedes, is not to be refused nor despysed of such, as are good men. But it which will needes be an imitatour of the same (the commen brute [i.e. bruit, fame] of the people I meane) is often time rashe, unadvised, and most commonly a commender of vice, and naughtines, and under the shape of honestie, stayneth the forme and beauty of unfayned glorye. With the ignoraunce of the whyche mens mindes beynge blynded, and coveting alwayes to do some fact, wherby they myghte be renowmed [*cum quaedam ... praeclara cuperent*], knoweinge not neverthelesse, how or whych waye they might perfourme the same, have fallen into great inconvenience. For some have rased theyr owne cities and some have slayne them selves. (*Tusc.* 3. 2–4, sigs. N1^{v}–3^{r})

Cicero's treatment of false opinion as a morally corrupting force which blinds us to the light of nature is Stoic; his sense of the inevitability of such corruption, in a world of illusion and confusion where we drink in error with our nurses' milk, is profoundly sceptical.

Cicero returns repeatedly to the problems raised in this passage concerning public opinion and honour. In Platonic and Stoic thought, the opinion of the crowd is necessarily irrational, blind, and fickle; to rely on it is to be foolish and inconstant, for you cannot be 'always the same' and unmoved if continually swayed by shifting popular opinions. The desire for 'honour', therefore, if that is defined as the good opinion of the crowd, must be corrupting. But Cicero's attitude to honour is more complex; it is, as he admits in *De officiis*, 'a very slypper place' (1. 65, sig. D5[r]). In one context he can declare that popular favour is worthless and praise Democritus as 'constante' and 'grave' for rejecting it: 'a wise man . . . will despise all honoure, though it be profered unto him' (*Tusc.* 5. 104, sig. D[D]8[v]). In another, he can demand respect for the opinions of all men, not only of the best: 'For it is not onelye a signe of an arrogante bodye, but also of one altogyther lawlesse, to be rechles, what every man thinketh of him' (*Off.* 1. 99, sig. F4[r]).

Cicero's most extended treatment of honour, in *Tusculans* 2, is complicated by the ambiguity of the key word *honestum*, which is Cicero's term for 'the Good' or 'moral virtue', but also means 'honourable' or 'honoured'. In fact part of Cicero's purpose seems to be to identify Stoic virtue with the desire for honour. He argues that contempt for pain can only be taught by the Stoics, 'whyche thinke that whiche is honest, to be the chiefest good . . . In theyr presence trulye, thou durste not syghe, nor yet to bragge of such trifles.' Endurance of pain is not unnatural; on the contrary, there is nothing more in harmony with nature

> then honesty, then prayse, then dignitie, then worship. By these divers names, I meane but one thinge. But I use them to shewe the thing more evidently by many names. But my meaninge is this, that that thing, is farre above al other most convenient for eche man, whiche is to be desyred for it selfe: as a thing eyther issuynge out of vertue, or els beyng it selfe placed amonges some one of the vertues, and of his owne nature praise worthy. Which trulie, I would rather terme the singuler and onelye, then the chiefest or greatest good. (*Tusc.* 2. 45–6, sig. L7[r])

The profusion of explanatory synonyms in fact confuses rather than clarifies, since all of them—*honestas*, *laus*, *dignitas*, *decus*—have strong connotations of reputation as well as of simple virtue. The reward of courage is not merely virtue itself but the glory of being seen to be virtuous, while the deterrent against cowardice is shame ('thou *durste* not syghe'). It is very hard—especially in Cicero's Rome—to distinguish honesty from honour, praiseworthiness from being praised.

Cicero's approach to the problems of public opinion is complicated by his double role—a Stoic/sceptic philosopher, but also a practising politician, lawyer, and orator. The Stoics, following Plato, traditionally condemned oratory: it is to philosophy as opinion is to knowledge, an art devoted not to seeking truth but to moulding opinions by appealing to passion, prejudice, and inconstancy of mind. Cicero in his philosophical works is well aware of this distinction: oratory 'is an arte appliable to the commen voyce of the people, and the verye ende and perfection of eloquence, is the prayse and commendacion of the hearers', whereas 'philosophy sekes not the judgement or prayse of manye, but of purpose flyes the preace [press] of the commen people' (*Tusc.* 2. 3–4, sigs. I2^{v}–I3^{r}).

As a theorist of oratory, on the other hand, he attempts to break down the distinction between philosopher and orator. *De oratore* (a popular work in the Renaissance) develops the ideal of the orator-statesman: the public speaker who is also a good and wise man, learned in philosophy and the arts and sciences, experienced in practical politics, wisely guiding public opinion for the good of the state. The speaker Crassus explicitly disagrees with Plato's condemnation of oratory, and exalts his ideal orator over the philosophers with their aridly technical and airily theoretical arguments.[11] In *De finibus* Cicero argues that the philosopher too needs oratory if he is to persuade people to virtue, as the Stoics, neglecting the art, discover: 'Their meagre little syllogisms . . . may convince the intellect, but they cannot convert the heart, and the hearer goes away no better than he came' (*Fin.* 4. 7). It seems an apt comment on Brutus' oration in the Forum.

Even more revealing, however, is Cicero's criticism of Stoic doctrines on the grounds that they could not convincingly be

[11] *De oratore* 1. 45–57.

defended at a public meeting. If an enemy army was at the gates of Rome, how could the Stoic stand up to argue that, after all, death and slavery are not really evils? Such views 'could not possibly be produced in public life, in the law-courts, in the senate!' (*Fin.* 4. 21). This is to equate truth with what an audience can be made to believe. A passage like this suggests how easily Cicero, in spite of his Stoic and sceptical awareness of the problems of knowledge, can slip into treating public opinion as the criterion of truth—an identification very easily made in a society as dominated by 'public life' as Cicero's Rome.

The scepticism of Cicero's philosophy is reflected in Shakespeare's characterization of him in *Julius Caesar*, as he responds with a cool suspension of judgement to Casca's account of the storm, refuses to be drawn into giving an opinion of its meaning, and concludes,

> But men may construe things after their fashion,
> Clean from the purpose of the things themselves.
>
> (1. 3. 34–5)[12]

It is a vital choric comment, for the difficulty of construing things correctly and the destructive power of 'hateful Error' (5. 3. 67) are major themes of *Julius Caesar* and the other Roman plays. These moral problems are sharpened by the nature of Shakespeare's Rome as a society dominated by 'opinion', echoing with oratory and rhetoric, preoccupied with honour and the making and moulding of public judgements, neglectful of self-knowledge. In this society, as in Cicero's thought, public opinion tends to displace truth, so that even the philosopher Brutus believes that the way Caesar's assassination is conducted 'shall *make* | Our purpose necessary' merely by 'so appearing to the common eyes' (2. 1. 177–9; my emphasis). Shakespeare's Roman heroes are entangled in the judgements of Roman society: Brutus is 'wrought' by Cassius' forged version of public opinion and his own desire for honour to murder Caesar; Coriolanus finds that the honour he seeks is defined by the 'voices' and 'stinking breath' of the mob he despises. And so, as Cicero says of his blind seekers of honour,

[12] This point is made by Vawter in 'After Their Fashion', but he limits its relevance to Cicero's criticism of Stoic views on fate and divination; I see its significance in the play as wider.

'some have [almost] rased theyr owne cities and some have slayne them selves.' It is a peculiarly Roman kind of tragedy.

The offices of virtue

Cicero's public concept of Roman virtue is most clearly developed in *De officiis*. Perhaps the best approach to the book is through its title. *On Duties*, as most commentators point out, is not quite an adequate translation; the Elizabethan rendering 'Tully's *Offices*', if cryptic, points by its very oddity to what is distinctive in Cicero's Roman concept of 'duties'.[13]

De officiis is based on a lost work, *Peri tou kathêkontos*, by the influential second-century BC Stoic Panaetius of Rhodes.[14] *Kathêkonta* are 'appropriate acts', those proper actions which arise out of a correct choice between 'indifferent' objects. *Kathêkon* means 'appropriate', or as Hicks glosses it '"becoming to man", suitable to his nature and being'.[15] It implies, that is, the central Stoic idea of *homologia*: correct action is action which is consistent with human nature.

To translate Panaetius' Greek term Cicero borrows a term from Roman politics. The *officia* of a public official or a military officer are the actions he is required by his office to perform, the duties appropriate to his role.[16] The meaning is similar, but the connotations are significantly different. In his whole approach to the nature of virtue and duty, as well as in his specific treatment later of decorum, Cicero tends to interpret Stoic *homologia* in terms of the performing of a public 'office' or social role.

This is characteristic of the Roman 'public temper' (in Eliot's phrase) of Cicero's ethics. Adapting Greek Stoicism for a Roman audience, he repeatedly invokes the similarity between Greek theory and Roman practice:

[13] Douglas, 'Cicero the Philosopher' 149; Hicks, *Stoic and Epicurean*, 93; Long, *Hellenistic Philosophy*, 188–9.

[14] On Panaetius, see Long, *Hellenistic Philosophy*, 211–16; Arnold, *Roman Stoicism*, 100–4; Griffin and Atkins, *On Duties*, pp. xix–xxi. How closely Cicero's work is based on Panaetius' is hard to say, since the source is lost; I shall refer for the sake of brevity to 'Cicero's ideas', but it should be noted that they are presumably in large part Panaetius'.

[15] Hicks, *Stoic and Epicurean*, 93.

[16] Long, *Hellenistic Philosophy*, 188. Cicero defends his use of the word in *Letters to Atticus*, 16. 11 and 16. 14: 'Don't we say the *officium* of consuls, of the Senate, of generals?'

For in maners, orders of livinge, and maynteyning of householde: We truly behave our selves both farre better than they, and also more liberall. And as for the comen wealth, our forefathers have governed it, with much more politike orders and lawes.... [W]hat so greate gravitye? what so notable constancye? stoutenesse of stomacke [*magnitudo animi*], honestye? or truste, what so passinge vertue in all kynde of poyntes, hath bene found in any nation? that it maye for the same be compared with oure auncesters? (*Tusc.* 1. 2, sigs. B1ᵛ–2ʳ)

Gravitas, *constantia*, *magnitudo animi*—the Greeks may have written more eloquently of such virtues, but the Romans have practised them. So Cicero continually supports his moral arguments with Roman exempla. Regulus, for instance, is cited in support of the Stoic position that pain is not an evil,

as no meane witnes, but (I beleve) the gravest of all. For what more substantiall wytnesse do we looke for, than a pere of the commonweale [*principem populi Romani*], who, for the continuinge of hys duetie, did wyllinglie enter into tormentes? (*Off.* 3. 105, sig. V8ʳ)

Cicero's code of Roman virtue is essentially a morality for 'peers of the commonwealth'. Public life is the arena of morality, and the good of one's country is the supreme goal. This is made most explicit in the *Somnium Scipionis* (a popular work in the Renaissance), in which Scipio dreams of an afterlife reserved for statesmen and patriots:

all those who have preserved, aided, or enlarged their fatherland have a special place prepared for them in the heavens, where they may enjoy an eternal life of happiness. For nothing of all that is done on earth is more pleasing to that supreme God who rules the whole universe than the assemblies and gatherings of men associated in justice, which are called States.[17]

Cicero's insistence that virtue can only be fully expressed in public life is not necessarily un-Stoic. It does, however, involve the rejection of a more private, individualistic, and unworldly strain which is also a part of Stoic thought, and which will emerge more clearly in Seneca.

We see Cicero dealing rather uneasily with this other strain in

[17] *De re publica* 6. 13. The *Somnium* is part of the last book of *De re publica*, but survived independently through the Middle Ages and was included in the standard school collection of Cicero's shorter works (Baldwin, *Small Latine*, ii. 581, 590).

his discussion of courage or fortitude (*magnitudo animi*), the third of the four cardinal virtues around which Book 1 of *De officiis* is organized. Courage is of course a central Stoic virtue, very close to constancy (steadfastness). It is also, as Cicero points out, a specifically Roman virtue:

> specially the people of Rome did excede in greatnesse of corage [*animi magnitudine*]. And theyr desyre of martiall glorie is declared, in that we see theyr images of honoure be set up, for the moste parte, in warlike aray. (1. 61, sigs. $D3^{v}$–$D4^{r}$)

The Roman assumption that 'valour is the chiefest virtue' (*Cor*. 2. 2. 84) is made explicit by Cicero in the *Tusculans* (2. 43): the word *virtus* means both 'virtue' in general and 'valour' in particular, and is the pre-eminent virtue of a man (*vir*).

Cicero immediately qualifies this ancient Roman view, however, by insisting that courage must be linked with justice, the primary social virtue. Without justice, courage is merely '*lewd hardinesse*', dangerously likely to grow into 'wilfulnesse . . . and an overseekinge of rule', and so produce ambitious and seditious disturbers of the commonwealth (1. 62–4, sigs. $D4^{r}$–$D5^{r}$).[18] It must also be directed towards true achievement rather than honour and fame—though 'scarce there is anie manne founde, who when he hathe sustained travailes, and aventured daungers, dothe not desire glorie, as rewarde [*mercedem*] of his doinges' (1. 65, sigs. $D5^{r-v}$). We may think of Coriolanus, the man of *magnitudo animi* who refuses to take 'a bribe to pay [his] sword' (1. 10. 38), yet 'pays himself with being proud' (1. 1. 31), and so falls into wilfulness and overseeking of rule. Cicero, like the Roman state of *Coriolanus*, is attempting to tame the individualistic and immoderate virtue of heroic valour into the service of the commonwealth.

At the same time, Cicero is equally wary of the Stoic concept of courage as *constantia*. He defines courage as having two aspects. The first is a mental attitude: the firm belief that nothing is to be valued but virtue, and a refusal to be subject to any external force or passion or accident. The second, which results from the first, is courage in action, the performing of great and useful deeds, even at the cost of extreme pain, toil, and danger.

> All the glorye, & honour of these two thinges, I adde thereto the profite [*utilitatem*], standes in the latter, but the cause, and meane, that makes

[18] As commentators note, Cicero presumably has Caesar in mind.

man[l]y menne, is in the former. For in it is that, whyche maketh excellent courages, and such as despise the worldes vanities. (1. 66–7, sigs. D5^{v}–D6^{r})

Though Cicero gives equal praise to both aspects of courage, the effect of his definition is to make Stoic *constantia* a means to an end, rather than an end in itself. It is valued for its *utilitas* in encouraging men to perform brave deeds for the common good.

The pursuit of philosophical enlightenment for its own sake, indeed, can be as selfish and anti-social as the pursuit of power and glory. Philosophers who withdraw from public life in their desire for tranquillity of mind, Cicero alleges, are as selfish as those driven by ambition, for—as the Stoic paradox of the *sapiens* as king suggests—they 'shoote at the same marke, that Kynges doo': absolute power and self-sufficiency (1. 70, sigs. D7^{r-v}).[19] Such retirement is, in most cases, a sign more of laziness and cowardice than of courage and constancy. Public life is the proper sphere for such virtues: the statesman, amid the passions and dangers of public life, needs constancy and tranquillity more than the ivory-tower philosopher:

And of suche as take uppon them the common weale, no lesse than of Phylosophers, yea and I wot not whether more, muste be used bothe a majestie [*magnificentia*], and a contempte of worldly thinges . . . and also a quietnesse of mynde, and voydnesse of care: for so thei shal not be thoughtful [*anxii*], and with gravitie, and stedfastnesse [*constantia*] they shall leade theyr lyfe. (1. 72, sig. D8^{v})

Cicero's ideal is a politician who has the moral qualities of a Stoic *sapiens*, but uses them for the good of the commonwealth rather than for his own self-perfection.

Cicero thus attempts to bring together the Stoic ideal of constancy (steadfastness) with the traditional Roman 'chiefest virtue' of valour, and to redefine both as a public-spirited civic virtue. He is, however, uneasily aware that both ideals, that of the aristocratic warrior and that of the Stoic *sapiens*, involve aspirations to individual self-advancement and self-perfection that may not be easy to reconcile with the common good of the state. In his

[19] Cicero here anticipates (though without explicit reference to Stoicism) the central point of Braden's argument about Stoicism's 'imperial self': 'Throughout Stoicism the operative values are, time and again, power and control: we restrict our desires less because they are bad in themselves than in order to create a zone in which we know no contradiction' (*Renaissance Tragedy*, 20). Braden does not cite the Cicero passage.

treatment of decorum, under the head of the fourth cardinal virtue, temperance, Cicero defines a more moderate form of constancy.

Decorum

Decorum is a difficult word to define or translate.[20] Grimalde renders it as 'comelinesse' (that which 'becomes'); Miller as 'propriety'; Griffin and Atkins as 'seemliness'. It means that which is fitting and appropriate for, or consistent with the nature of, a person or thing. It is, in other words, another aspect of the concept of *homologia*, harmony or consistency, which is for the Stoics the basic principle of morality. Early in *De officiis* Cicero describes as characteristically human our ability to perceive and follow this principle:

> And that truely is no smal power of nature & reason, that this creature onely perceves what is order: what it is, that becommeth [*deceat*] in dedes, and words: & what is measure. And therfore, of those same things which bee discerned by sight, no other creature perceiveth the beautie, the grace, and the proportion of parts[.] Which f[or]me, nature and reason conveying from the yies to the minde, dothe more juge a beautie, a stedfastnes [*constantiam*], & an order in counselles, & dedes fit to bee observed. (I. 14, sigs. A6^{v}–A7^{r})

Panaetius, Cicero's source, was particularly interested in decorum; his discussion of this topic 'is generally regarded as representing the most elaborate and innovative part of [his] work.'[21] His main innovation seems to have been the emphasis he placed, not only on consistency with Nature in general, but also on consistency with one's own individual nature. It is this double focus on the general and the individual, and the tensions it creates, which makes Cicero's decorum a dramatically fruitful concept.

Cicero admits that the nature of decorum is easier to grasp than explain. It is inseparably linked with virtue: 'both what becommeth is honest and also what is honest, becommeth' (I. 94, sig. F1^{v}). In general, it is whatever is appropriate to or in harmony with the

[20] Cicero's rendering of the Greek *prepon*, it derives from the impersonal verb *decet*: 'it is fitting, suitable, proper'.

[21] Christopher Gill, 'Panaetius on the Virtue of Being Yourself', in Anthony Bulloch *et al.* (eds.), *Images and Ideologies: Self-definition in the Hellenistic World* (Berkeley, 1993), 330–53 (339)—a useful discussion of the nature, limits, and problems of Panaetius' 'individualism'.

nature of a human being, and so can be applied to any of the virtues. Specifically, it is the quality

which is so to nature agreable, as it may appere both in mesurablenesse, and temperaunce, with a certaine honest show.

[*quod ita naturae consentaneum est, ut in eo moderatio et temperantia appareat cum specie quadam liberali.*] (1. 96, sig. F2^{v})

This rather cloudy definition suggests the range of meaning that decorum can embrace, from the grand concept of life in harmony with nature, down to *specie quadam liberali*—which Miller renders prissily but accurately as 'a certain deportment such as becomes a gentleman'. It can be seen as a fundamental principle of moral order, or as a matter of keeping up appearances and observing social conventions.

Cicero makes its nature much clearer by an analogy with the literary sense of the word. The classic account of literary decorum is Horace's in the *Ars poetica*, here quoted in Ben Jonson's translation:

Or follow fame, thou that dost write, or faine
Things in themselves agreeing [*sibi convenientia*]:
  If againe
Honour'd *Achilles* chance by thee be seiz'd,
Keepe him still active, angry, un-appeas'd,
Sharpe, and contemning lawes . . .
If something strange, that never yet was had
Unto the *Scene* thou bringst, and dar'st create
A meere new person, looke he keepe his state
Unto the last, as when he first went forth,
Still to be like himselfe, and hold his worth [*sibi constet*].[22]

So, Cicero explains, in a play we would be jarred if a good man were to utter wicked sentiments, but if a tyrant such as Atreus utters them, we applaud, because the lines are in character, 'the speache is fitte for the person' (Cicero's word is *persona*, which can mean 'mask', 'role', or 'person'). Literary decorum means the writer's maintenance of appropriateness and consistency of

[22] 'Horace, His Art of Poetrie', lines 169–82, in Ben Jonson, *Works*, ed. C. H. Herford and Percy and Evelyn Simpson, viii (Oxford, 1947), 312–13. It is interesting that Horace, describing literary decorum, slips into Stoic terminology (*convenientia, sibi constare*), while Jonson's phrase 'like himself' is one that we will meet again in Stoic contexts.

character: 'then, we saye, the poets keepe that grace, whiche becommeth: when it, that to eche person is fittinge, bothe is doone, and sayde' (1. 97, sig. F3ʳ).[23] Moral decorum, similarly, means the consistent playing of one's proper role.

In defining our proper role, however, we must distinguish between the two kinds of role which we have been assigned: the general role of a human being, and our individual roles.

> We muste understand . . . that wee be cladde by nature (as it were) with twoo parsons [*personis*], whereof the one is commune, bicause we al be partakers of reason, and the preeminence, whereby wee surmounte beastes, from whiche reason, all honestye, and comelinesse is deryved, and oute of the whiche, the waye of findinge duetie is soughte[;] the other is that whiche proprelie to echeman is assigned. (1. 107, sig. F7ʳ)

In the first place, simply by virtue of our humanity, we have been assigned 'a personage of gret excellence'; we have been given the 'partes' (the theatrical metaphor is implicit in Cicero's *partes*) of constancy, temperance, self-control, concern for others (1. 97–8, sig. F3ʳ⁻ᵛ). We are required to act in a way consistent with the dignity of human (as opposed to animal) nature: to act rationally, to control our passions and sensual appetites, to follow nature and right reason (1. 100–6). This is the universal aspect of Stoic *homologia*, life in harmony with the natural order. The result of such a life is a spiritual state analogous to physical beauty:

> For as the beutifulnesse of the bodye wyth proportionable makynge of the limmes moveth a mans eies and delyteth them even with this, that al the parts with a certain grace agre togither: right so this comelinesse that shyneth abroade in our life, winneth their likinge wyth whome we live, by an ordre, stedfastnesse, and mesurablenesse in all oure wordes, and deedes. (1. 98, sig. F3ᵛ)

The man who observes decorum has 'a daily beauty in his life' (*Oth.* 5. 1. 19), the kind of beauty which Antony sees in Brutus:

> His life was gentle, and the elements
> So mixed in him that nature might stand up
> And say to all the world 'This was a man'.
>
> (*JC* 5. 5. 72–4)[24]

[23] On the literary sense of decorum, see Madeleine Doran, *Endeavors of Art* (Madison, 1954), 77–9 and 217–32.

[24] An even closer analogy is Cicero's statement of the same idea in *Tusc.* 3. 30–1, which makes it explicit that the health and beauty of the soul, as of the body, arises from the harmonious mixing [*temperatio*] of its various parts.

The elements of Brutus' life, Antony claims, are so perfectly in harmony with one another and with nature that he fulfils with perfect decorum the role of 'a man'.

Decorum cannot be truly observed, however, without taking into account its second aspect: the nature of the individual. Human character varies as much as physical appearance: some people are naturally serious, some cheerful; some straightforward, some devious; some gracious, some harsh. Such differences are perfectly natural and not to be criticized; indeed, so long as they are not vicious, they should positively be cultivated.

But every mans owne guiftes, not such as be faultie [*vitiosa*], but natural [*propria*], ar ernestly to be maintained, wher[e]by the sooner may that comlinesse be kepte, whiche wee do seeke. For in such wise we muste worke, as againste all nature [*universam naturam*] wee never strive: which thing avoided, let us folow our own proper nature [*propriam naturam*]. (1. 110, sigs. F8^{v}–G1^{r})

So long as it is not in conflict with nature in the universal sense, with right reason and virtue, you should follow your own individual nature. It is impossible, however desirable it might seem, to act successfully against your own nature. Even though other courses may appear 'graver, and better' you must still follow those that you yourself are fitted for:

For neither is it to anye purpose to fight againste nature nor to ensue [i.e. pursue] any thynge that ye can not atteine. . . . [N]othing becommeth, *mawger Minerva*, as they say, that is, nature withstanding, and resistynge it. In brieefe, if ought bee comely, of trouth ther is nothing more seemely, than an evennesse [*aequabilitas*] in all [a] mans lyfe, and everye of hys doinges: which you can not keepe, if you counterfette an others nature, and lette passe your owne. (1. 111, sig. G1^{r})

The essence of decorum is self-consistency, and it is impossible to be self-consistent when you are playing an artificial and inappropriate role.

This view leads Cicero to a kind of ethical relativism. Right and wrong may be different for different people; to take an extreme example, suicide may be the right action for one person and wrong for another in the same situation. The companions of Cato at Utica were probably right to save their lives by surrender, but

when nature hadde geven Cato an uncredible gravitie, and the same hee hadde strengthened wyth a continuall stedfastnesse [*constantia*]: and alwayes hadde remayned in his intent, and determined purpose, it was meete for him rather to dye, than too looke upon the tyrauntes face. (I. 112, sig. G1v)[25]

It was in keeping with decorum, and therefore right, for Cato to kill himself; but such *constantia* would not necessarily have been right or decorous for another. Self-consistency does not necessarily mean the heroic constancy and 'continuall stedfastnesse' of a near-*sapiens* like Cato. The inflexibility of Ajax would not have been appropriate for the slippery and adaptable Ulysses.

Which diversities when wee beholde, it shal bee necessary to weye, what eche man hath of his owne, and to order those giftes, and not to have a mynde to trye, howe other mens graces woulde become hym. For that becommeth eche man, whiche is moste of all eche mannes owne [*id ... maxime quemque decet, quod est cuiusque maxime suum*]. Let every man therfore know his owne disposition [*Suum quisque igitur noscat ingenium*], and let him make him selfe a sharpe judge both of hys vyces, and of his vertues ... (I. 113–14, sig. G2r)

Cicero's echo of the ancient precept 'Know thyself' (*Nosce teipsum*) serves, rather surprisingly, to reintroduce the analogy of theatrical roles. We ought to know our own characters 'lest players may seeme too have more discretion than wee'. Actors choose 'not the best enterludes, but the fittest for them selves'—a point Cicero backs up with a lovingly well-informed roll-call of Roman actors and the parts in which they specialized:

For who upon theyr voices be bolde, they take Epigones, and Medea, who upon gesture, doo take Menalippa and Clytemnestre. Ever more Rutilius, whome I remember, tooke Antiopa, not often Esopus toke Ajax. Shall a player then see this in the stage, that a wise man shall not see in his lyfe?

The actor, more obviously a figure of flexible and changing identity, here paradoxically becomes an emblem of consistency. As Roman actors consistently play the parts which suit them, so we should each strive in life to play the most appropriate part. Of course, this is not always possible, and sometimes we have to perform a role which is uncongenial.

[I]n case necessitie shall drive us sometime, to those thinges, which shall not be for our disposition, all care, studie, and diligence, must bee em-

[25] The ambiguity of *constantia* is well illustrated by this passage: Grimalde translates it as 'stedfastnesse', Miller and Higginbotham as 'consistency'; both ideas are probably present.

ployed, that, if we do them not comlye, yet wyth as lyttle uncomlynesse as may be . . . (I. 114, sigs. G2^{r-v})

In practice, in society, the playing of an appropriate role is complicated by other factors. To the kinds of decorum appropriate to human nature and individual character must be added two further *personae* or roles: the one imposed on us by 'fortune' (social and family environment), and the one which we ourselves choose in choosing a career (I. 115). This most important and difficult choice of our lives is normally made when we are young and inexperienced; we may follow inappropriate role models, or be unduly influenced by family expectations, or merely drift into a career on the current of public opinion (I. 117–18). Ideally, however, the choice should be made on a basis of true self-knowledge and an accurate judgement of one's character and abilities. The influence of fortune as well as innate nature must be taken into account, but nature is 'muche the surer, and the stedfaster [*firmior . . . et constantior*]' (G4^{v}) and should always prevail. An unwise choice can later be changed, but slowly and cautiously, and with care to demonstrate to the world that the change is for the better (I. 120–1).

What is vital, Cicero sums up, is the choice of a way of life which can be followed consistently, so 'that in the continuinge of our life wee may agree with our selves [*constare . . . nobismet*], and never haulte in any dutie' (I. 119, sig. G4^{v}). The essence of decorum is *constantia* (consistency):

Who so then wyll applye all the purpose of hys lyfe, accordinge to the kynde of his nature not corrupted, let him keepe a stedfastnes, for that becommeth moste of all [*is constantiam teneat (id enim maxime decet)*]. (I. 120, sig. G5^{r}; cf. I. 125, sig. G7^{r})

Cicero's account of decorum has been immensely influential, although—or perhaps because—it is a deeply ambiguous concept capable of quite diverse interpretations. Some scholars have stressed its externality, treating decorum as a mere matter of proper behaviour, *species liberalis*; so Herschel Baker suggests that Cicero's legacy to the Renaissance was the identification of virtue with a 'rather prissy decorum'.[26] Others, however, such as Janet Spens and Hiram Haydn, have stressed the individualism inherent in Cicero's insistence on following one's own nature. They thus trace

[26] Baker, *Dignity of Man*, 297.

a direct line between *De officiis* and the Renaissance tradition which Haydn calls 'bastard Stoicism' and which I would prefer to label 'amoral constancy': the principle that truth to oneself overrides all other moral or social obligations.[27]

This is in my view a misinterpretation, which ignores Cicero's overriding insistence throughout *De officiis* on the good of society. I see the origins of 'bastard Stoicism' in Seneca rather than Cicero. Nevertheless, it is significant that such a misreading is possible. Out of context, Cicero's doctrine of the importance of consistent truth to oneself *could* be developed into an amoral and anti-social individualism which would clearly have appalled him. There is little sign that Cicero is conscious of these implications, except perhaps for the warning that truth to one's own nature must not conflict with universal nature.[28]

At the same time, decorum could tip over in the opposite direction into mere public role-playing. There is clearly a tension between the ideal of truth to oneself and Cicero's metaphor of the *persona*, of wearing a mask or playing a role. A role is necessarily played for the benefit of others, and concern for staying decorously in character implies attention to the reactions of the audience as much as truth to oneself. As we have seen, Cicero's public-spirited morality is always in danger of identifying truth with public opinion. So here he passes lightly over the likelihood of being led by external pressures to play an inauthentic, hypocritical, or inappropriate role.

Though Cicero's concept of decorum has been so influential that it is hard to prove direct indebtedness, I believe that these passages are central to Shakespeare's Roman plays, the source of his conception of Roman virtue as consistent role-playing. In the plays, however, decorum appears not as a straightforward moral yardstick (as for instance McAlindon assumes in *Shakespeare and*

[27] Janet Spens, 'Chapman's Ethical Thought', *Essays and Studies*, 11 (1925), 145–69; Hiram Haydn, *The Counter-Renaissance* (New York, 1950), 477–8. Spens's argument is cogently criticized by Robert Ornstein, *The Moral Vision of Jacobean Tragedy* (Madison, 1960), 283 ('if Chapman derived a philosophy of individualism from Cicero he was guilty of a unique and almost incredible misinterpretation').

[28] Gill notes 'certain problems and incoherences' in Panaetius' theory as reported by Cicero: 'The emphasis, for instance, on maintaining one's individual nature . . . is not matched by an equal emphasis, in the same context, on the importance of maintaining our common human *persona*' ('Being Yourself', 342). His later comparison with Nietzsche (351–3) is illuminating.

Decorum) but as a problematic concept whose implications and contradictions the plays explore. The Romans of *Julius Caesar* are indeed 'Roman actors', preoccupied with playing their roles with decorum and 'formal constancy', but tending to neglect Cicero's insistence on choosing the most appropriate roles. *Coriolanus* develops the paradox of decorum summed up in the hero's words 'I play | The man I am' (3. 2. 14–15); Coriolanus is grimly determined to be true to his own nature, but finally runs devastatingly into the conflict which Cicero hinted at between *propria natura* and the stronger claims of *universa natura*. *Antony and Cleopatra*, on the other hand, explores an alternative concept of decorum in which truth to oneself is divorced from consistency; Antony and Cleopatra, abandoning the principle that 'stedfastnes . . . becommeth moste of all', claim instead that 'everything becomes' them (1. 1. 51).

Throughout the Roman plays, however, Ciceronian decorum is balanced by a rather different conception of Stoic constancy. This version of constancy emphasizes not so much consistency in ordinary life as steadfastness in extreme situations; focuses less on human society and more on the individual human soul in a largely hostile universe; and, rather than locating virtue in what is appropriate for a human being, aspires to transcend human limitations. It is the ideal of the Senecan Stoic hero.

3
Seneca and the Stoic Hero

When *The Workes of Lucius Annaeus Seneca*, translated by Thomas Lodge, were published in London in 1614, the allegorical title-page prominently featured the figure of Constancy.[1] She sits, her right hand clasping a pillar, her left hand grasping an upright sword and resting in a brazier of burning coals. Her face is calm and untroubled. In its implications of courage, tranquillity, immovability, invulnerability—and of the self-conscious display of these qualities—it is a very suggestive representation of what Lodge and his illustrator clearly saw as the central virtue of Senecan Stoicism.[2]

If Cicero defined Roman virtue for posterity, Seneca defined Stoic virtue. He has always been seen as 'the *Archestoike*', and his extravagant style and his own ambiguous character and career have made him a focus for both admiration and hostility towards the Stoic ideal.[3] In particular he is identified with the idea of

[1] On Senecan texts and references, see Bibliographical Note.

[2] Cf. Huston Diehl, *An Index of Icons in English Emblem Books 1500–1700* (Norman, Okla., 1986), 10 ('the act of sitting' signifies 'a constant mind'), 95 (the hand in the fire is associated with the legend of Scaevola and expresses 'nobility and courage'), 163 (the pillar as symbol of constancy).

[3] The phrase is Erasmus', in Sir Thomas Chaloner's 1549 translation of *The Praise of Folie*, ed. Clarence H. Miller, EETS os 257 (London, 1965), ch. 30 (39; boldface in original). To some extent the labelling of Seneca as Stoic is an over-simplification: like Cicero, he is eclectic, and makes a didactic point (especially in the *Letters*) of citing admirable sayings from all schools. Unlike Cicero, however, he never fundamentally disagrees with the Stoics, who are always *nostri*, our own school (as Long points out, *Hellenistic Philosophy*, 233); and in the later tradition, for most purposes, Senecan thought essentially *is* Stoicism. On Seneca's philosophy, apart from the works cited in Ch. 1, I am indebted to Miriam T. Griffin, *Seneca: A Philosopher in Politics* (Oxford, 1976); Norman T. Pratt, *Seneca's Drama* (Chapel Hill, NC, 1983), esp. ch. 3; Thomas G. Rosenmeyer, *Senecan Drama and Stoic Cosmology* (Berkeley, 1989). Anna Lydia Motto, *Seneca Sourcebook: Guide to the Thought of Lucius Annaeus Seneca in the Extant Prose Works* (Amsterdam, 1970), is a useful reference. On his influence, see G. M. Ross, 'Seneca's Philosophical Influence', in C. D. N. Costa (ed.), *Seneca* (London, 1974), 116–65 (though Ross, writing as a historian of philosophy, plays down his importance); and, on the English Renaissance, Palmer, *Seneca's 'De Remediis Fortuitorum'*.

constancy as a heroic virtue, and with the image of the *sapiens*, the Stoic hero-sage—courageous, passionless, immovably enduring in adversity, demonstrating his superiority to fortune by resolute death or suicide. It is an ideal of which Shakespeare and his Roman heroes are very conscious.

The long-standing debate over Seneca's influence on Shakespeare, and on the English Renaissance in general, has focused on Seneca's plays. His prose essays and moral letters, which one scholar has called 'a greater and more pervasive influence', have been neglected.[4] Most of these works were not translated into English until 1614, and T. W. Baldwin concludes that there is no reason to suppose Shakespeare read Seneca at school or indeed at any time, though he may have picked up 'some moral crumbs in the form of *sententiae*'.[5] Most critics have tacitly accepted T. S. Eliot's dismissal: 'I think it quite unlikely that Shakespeare knew anything of that extraordinarily dull and uninteresting body of Seneca's prose . . .'[6]

It is not my purpose to prove that Shakespeare read Seneca's prose; my concern is with Seneca as the ultimate source for the Renaissance of the concept of Stoic constancy. In the 1590s and 1600s Seneca was at a peak of his popularity and influence, and Shakespeare could scarcely have avoided encountering his doctrines and his memorable sayings on virtue, passion, suffering, and death.[7] Whether he encountered them directly, through reading Seneca's essays in Latin or his tragedies in English translation, or indirectly, from collections of *sententiae*, from Neostoic writers such as Montaigne, or simply from talk with admirers of Seneca such as Jonson or Chapman, is less important (I would argue) than the ultimate provenance of the ideas.

4 Palmer, *Seneca's 'De Remediis Fortuitorum'*, 1.

5 Baldwin, *Small Latine*, ii. 610. E. A. Sonnenschein, 'Shakspere and Stoicism', *University Review*, 1 (1905), 23–41, suggested some possible Senecan borrowings, and Alice Harmon, 'How Great was Shakespeare's Debt to Montaigne?', *PMLA* 57 (1942), 988–1008, argued that Shakespeare derived his Stoic *sententiae* from Seneca and others by way of anthologies and commonplace books. The only translations of Seneca's prose before 1614 were Whyttynton's version of the dubiously Senecan *De remediis fortuitorum* (London, 1547; reprinted in Palmer) and Golding's of *De beneficiis* (London, 1578).

6 Eliot, 'Shakespeare and the Stoicism of Seneca', 129.

7 According to Palmer, Seneca's influence 'began to be felt intensively among the Elizabethans in the period from 1595 to 1620' (*Seneca's 'De Remediis Fortuitorum'*, 1–2); Ross refers to a 'cult of Seneca' at this period ('Seneca's Philosophical Influence', 146).

Constantia sapientis

Seneca's conception of constancy is most clearly expressed in the essay *De constantia sapientis*, subtitled *Nec injuriam nec contumeliam accipere sapientem* ('That a wise man cannot feele any injurie'). Pierre Grimal, in his commentary on the essay, points out that its title and subtitle are not simply synonymous. *Constantia* is an internal quality: a state of 'cohérence intellectuelle', that is, self-consistency and consistency with nature in one's thoughts, feelings, and beliefs. Indifference to external injuries is the practical result, in the 'domaine de l'action', of such an inner state.[8] This distinction, however, is not quite so clear in the essay itself, which represents constancy in images of heroic action and suffering.

The heroic quality of Seneca's constancy is made clear at the beginning, as he compares Stoicism with other philosophies which pander to human weakness:

> The Stoicks entertaining a more constant [*virilem*] course, they care not whether their followers find the way pleasant or no, but labour to pull us presently out of danger, and to conduct us to so high a place, which is so farre raised above any humane miserie, that it over-looketh Fortune. (*Const.* 1. 1, p. 658)[9]

The rewards, however, are commensurate with the demands. The Stoic *sapiens* is invulnerable to harm either from other men or from fortune. 'A Wiseman is secure, neyther can he be touched with any injurie or contumelie' (2. 1, p. [659]).

At this point Seneca imagines a protest from a listener, in the spirit of Cicero's criticism of the Stoics, that these are merely fine words without substance: 'you promise great things, and such as neyther may be wished, nor can be believed.' Like the Stoic paradoxes of the wise man who is always rich and free, this claim of invulnerability is merely a hyperbolical metaphor for the commonplace idea that the *sapiens* will endure suffering patiently. 'Thus, after you have braved a long time, you fall into the condition of

[8] Pierre Grimal, *Sénèque 'De constantia sapientis': Commentaire* (Paris, 1953), 32.

[9] The phrase translated by Lodge as 'above any humane miserie' is *extra omnem teli iactum* ('beyond the reach of any missile'). The image is echoed in *Tit.* 2. 1. 1–2 ('Now climbeth Tamora Olympus' top, | Safe out of fortune's shot')—though the echo is ironic, since Tamora is no Stoic but a minion of fortune.

other men; and there is no difference betweene you, but in change of names' (3. 1, p. 660). But Seneca defends himself: 'my intent is not to dignifie a Wise man with an imaginarie honour of words, but to lodge him in such a place where no injurie may attaine unto him' (3. 3, p. 660). The wise man will certainly be attacked, but—quite literally—cannot be hurt.

Seneca expresses this invulnerability in two images which recur throughout his works. One is that of the wise man as a rock, hard and invulnerable:

Even as there are certaine hard stones which Iron cannot enter, and the Adamant will neither be cut, filed, or beat to powder, but abateth the edge of those tooles that are applied unto it: as there are certaine things which cannot be consumed by fire, but continue their hardnesse and habitude amidst the flames; and even as the rocks that are fixed in the heart of the sea, breake the waves, and although they have been assaulted, and beat upon many infinite times, retaine no impression of the stormes that have assailed them; even so the heart of a wise man is solid, and hath gathered such force that hee is as secure from injurie, as those I made mention of. (3. 5, pp. 660–1)

The second is that of the wise man as a god, raised beyond harm:

hee is so highly raised above all the attaints of worldly things, that there is no violence whatsoever, that can aime his attempts so hie . . . Even as celestiall things are not subject to humane hands, and they that overturne temples, and melt downe Images, doe no wayes hurt the Deitie: so whatsoever is attempted eyther crabbedly, immodestly, or proudly against a wise man, is done in vaine. (4. 1–2, p. 661)

The source of the wise man's rocklike or godlike invulnerability is his indifference to external things. He does not 'esteeme any thing his except it be himselfe, or in regard of that part of himselfe which maketh him vertuous' (6. 3, p. 663). The external world and everything in it is under the control of fortune, and is fickle and ever changing. Only the mind can be constant. Benefits granted by fortune are merely on loan, and the wise man must be prepared to surrender them at any time. The liberating power of this total self-reliance is illustrated by the story of the philosopher Stilbon, who, when his city was captured and sacked, and the conquering general asked him how much he had lost, replied that he had lost nothing: 'I carry all my goods with mee' (5. 6, p. 662).

Amidst so many naked weapons, amidst the tumult of so many boote-haling souldiers; betwixt fire & bloud, and the sacke of a Citie, surprised by assault, amidst the ruine of temples falling upon the gods; one only man remained quiet and constant [*uni homini pax fuit*]. (6. 2, p. 662)

He tells the conqueror, 'Thou must not thinke . . . that I am overcome, or thou art victorious. Thy fortune hath overcome mine' (6. 6, p. 663). Shakespeare's Cleopatra—an improbable Stoic—has the same idea when she calls Octavius Caesar 'but Fortune's knave' (5. 2. 3) and informs his emissary with conscious irony that 'I am his fortune's vassal' (5. 2. 29). Power granted by fortune is meaningless; the only true power is that of the *sapiens*, who, knowing the worthlessness of worldly success and failure, can meet those two imposters with an unmoved mind.

Seneca cites Stilbon as an exemplar of the constancy (*firmitas*) which this attitude makes possible. His example shows

that a mortall man may raise himselfe above all the accidents of this life, may regard with an assured eye the paines, losses, wounds and stroakes, and the hurliburly of infinite calamities that environ him; that hee may endure adversitie, content himselfe moderately in prosperitie, without relying on this, or grudging himselfe at that, but remaining alwaies like himselfe in good and evill fortune [*unus idemque inter diversa*], not to esteeme any thing his except it be himselfe, or in regard of that part of himself which maketh him vertuous. (6. 2–3, p. 663)

Such a *sapiens* is more invulnerable than the walls of Babylon or Carthage or the Roman Capitol. Physical fortresses can be invaded or overthrown, 'but the fortresses that defence the Wise man, cannot bee surprised, neither feare they fire, they cannot be entred or scaled, or undermined, they are impregnable like the nature of the gods [*diis aequa*]' (6. 8, p. 663).

Seneca's *constantia*, thus, is primarily the quality of remaining unchanged and unmoved in mind in all situations. The key phrase is *unus idemque inter diversa*, one and the same amid changing circumstances. Lodge here translates *unus idemque* with the same phrase he elsewhere uses more literally to translate *similis sibi* and *par sibi*: 'like himselfe'. It is a common Elizabethan formula for describing heroic virtue.[10] Shakespeare uses the same phrase, most

[10] According to Hereward T. Price, '"Like Himself"', *RES* 16 (1940), 178–81, the phrase derives from 'worthy of himself', and implies 'being what he is, he will be especially fine or great or noble' (180). Price does not discuss its connotations

notably in the lines in *Julius Caesar* (closely adapted from North's Plutarch) in which Lucillius predicts Brutus's suicide: 'When you do find him, or alive or dead, | He will be found like Brutus, like himself' (5. 4. 24–5). Shakespeare, North, and Lodge all draw on the same traditional formula to sum up the essence of Stoic constancy. There is, however, a subtle difference between *unus idemque* and 'like himselfe'. Where Seneca asserts that the wise man simply *is* always the same, Lodge suggests that he strives to resemble an ideal version of himself; where Seneca asserts identity, Lodge implies imitation. The suggestion of conscious role-playing is not necessarily untrue to Seneca's idea of constancy.

The phrase *unus idemque inter diversa* could also, of course, describe Cicero's ideal: the essence of decorum is 'an evennesse [*aequabilitas*] in all [a] mans lyfe, and everye of hys doinges'. Seneca draws as well on this more moderate Ciceronian and Panaetian ideal of constancy (consistency). He recurs to it especially in the Letters, using the terms *aequalitas* (uniformity) or *tenor* (steady course).[11] Perfect virtue requires 'an equalitie and tenour of life in every thing consonant unto it selfe' (*Ep.* 31. 8, p. 224). The 'greatest Office, and token of Wisdome' is 'that the actions bee correspondent to the words, and that hee which followeth her be alwaies equall and like unto himselfe [*ut ipse ubique par sibi idemque sit*]'. Wisdom itself can be defined as 'Alwaies to will one thing, and to nill the same' (that is, always to will X and always to reject Y). It is unnecessary, Seneca adds (making a very characteristic Stoic assumption), to specify that the 'one thing' should be good, since 'One and the same thing cannot alwaies please

of role-playing; nor does Brower, who alludes to the phrase throughout *Hero and Saint* (e.g. 121, 221, 233, 366), though one passage (233) implies he is aware of them. Shakespeare's consciousness of them is suggested by his witty exploitation of the phrase in *Henry V*, Prol. 5, in a context which is both heroic and theatrical: if the part of Henry V was played by a real king, he would really appear 'like himself'. Massinger plays similarly with the phrase in *The Roman Actor*, 1. 1. 51–8 (*The Plays and Poems of Philip Massinger*, ed. P. Edwards and C. Gibson, iii (Oxford, 1976)), where the words ''Tis spoken like yourself' are addressed to an actor when he proposes to emulate the courage of the stage heroes he plays.

[11] Compare Jonson's reference to 'Calme *Brutus*['] tenor' ('To my chosen Friend, the learned Translator of Lucan, Thomas May, Esquire': *Works*, ed. Herford and Simpson, viii. 395)—a sense which seems closer to Seneca's Latin than to any of those listed in *OED*. Significantly, Jonson is praising Lucan's maintenance of literary decorum: '. . . neither *Pompey's* popularitie, | *Caesar's* ambition, *Cato's* libertie, | Calme *Brutus* tenor start; but all along | Keepe due proportion in the ample song. . . .'

any man, except it bee right' (*Ep*. 20. 2, 5, pp. 201–2). Another passage begins like Polonius' advice to Laertes:

And above all things let this bee thy care, that thou be constant to thy selfe [*ut constes tibi*] . . . The change of the will betokeneth that the minde swimmeth in one place, and appeareth in another, even as the wind carrieth it. That which is firme and hath a good foundation varieth not. This perfectly happeneth to a Wise-man, and in some measure to a Proficient [i.e. one who is making progress toward wisdom] . . . What difference is there then? He that profiteth is in a manner moved, yet forsaketh he not his place, but returneth to his bounds; the perfect Wise-man is in no sort moved. (*Ep*. 35. 4, p. 228)[12]

The closeness of this *aequalitas* to *constantia* is underlined by Lodge's translation and his headnote (taken from Lipsius' Latin edition), which sums up the advice of the letter as '*to live conveniently, that is, constantly, that is, wisely*' (p. 228).[13]

The relationship between *aequalitas* and *constantia* is developed in a complex passage in Letter 120. Seneca is here praising the 'greater mind' who 'judgeth nothing of these things that are about him to bee his owne' but 'useth them as lent him'. Such *constantia*, he says, is a sign of exceptional greatness of soul, and all the more so when it is combined with *aequalitas*; for *tenor* demonstrates that virtue is genuine, whereas pretended virtue cannot last.[14] 'Inconstancie [*mutatio*] . . . is a great token of an evill minde.' He goes on to quote Horace's satirical description (in *Satires* 1. 3) of an inconstant man,

who was never himselfe, or eve[n] like himselfe [*numquam eundem, ne similem quidem sibi*]; so diversly changed he. . . . Hereby especially is an imprudent mind discovered, everie one betrayeth him, and that which in my opinion is most base, he is unlike himselfe [*impar sibi est*]. Repute thou it a great vertue for a man to be one. But no man but a wise man doth one thing, all the rest of us have many shapes. To day we will seeme to be modest and grave, to morrow prodigall and vaine: we ofttimes change our maske, and oftentimes take a contrarie to that we have put off. Exact thou therefore this of thy selfe, that to thy last breath thou maintaine thy selfe such, as thou hast resolved to shew thy selfe. (*Ep*. 120. 18–22, pp. 480–1)

[12] Cf. *Ham*. 1. 3. 78, and Harold Jenkins's note ad loc. in the Arden edn. (London, 1982).

[13] Lodge, 228. 'Conveniently' translates Latin *convenienter* (appropriately, consistently), echoing Cicero's use of *convenientia* as a translation of *homologia* (*Fin*. 3. 21).

[14] I paraphrase, since Lodge completely obscures the point here.

Seneca thus distinguishes yet links two kinds of constancy (essentially different, though both derived from the principle of *homologia*): *constantia*, the steadfastness of mind that comes from an indifference to external goods and evils, and *aequalitas* or *tenor*, the consistency and harmony of one's actions, which can be imaged as the playing of one role or wearing of one mask throughout one's life. In this passage, influenced by Panaetius, Seneca's rhetorical strategy makes *aequalitas* seem the superior quality: it is good to be steadfast, even better to be consistently so.[15]

Elsewhere his emphasis is different. Especially when dealing (as in *De constantia sapientis*) with the constancy of the wise man, Seneca is less concerned with sustained everyday consistency than with steadfastness in extreme situations; his characteristic images are not of 'steady course' but of motionlessness, of immovable objects triumphantly withstanding irresistible forces. Constancy becomes a heroic quality whose prime function is to face suffering and death: 'Constancie, which cannot be dejected from her place, and giveth not over her resolution by no feare of torture' (*Ep.* 67. 10, p. 289). Moreover, his vivid images tend to blur the theoretical distinction (as defined by Grimal) between 'constancy' as a mental state of 'intellectual coherence', and the courage and endurance which are its practical results. In effect, 'constancy' becomes a way of acting—the way embodied in Lodge's title-page figure, smiling with her hand in the flames.

Seneca in effect defined 'constancy' for later ages. He also made it a controversial ideal. Few moralists would dispute the desirability of consistency, but Seneca's more grandiose claims for the power and worth of constancy—as the debate with his listener in the opening pages of *De constantia sapientis* suggests—may be harder to accept.

The god and the rock

Much of the peculiar quality of Seneca's *constantia sapientis* is embodied in the recurring images of the god and the rock. These images have also served, in the hands of later critics, to focus attacks on Senecan Stoicism, for the hubris of its aspirations and

[15] On Seneca's debt to Panaetius in this passage, see Griffin, *Seneca*, 341–2.

the inhuman hardness of its denial of feeling. Stoic constancy, in the eyes of its critics, is either superhuman or subhuman, but not human.

The image of the *sapiens* as godlike, *diis aequa*, sums up the Stoic aspiration to absolute perfection and power over oneself. The comparison rests on the wise man's constancy and tranquillity of mind. 'He may be termed, and is wise, who is replenished with joy, glad and moderate, and that feeleth no passion [*est . . . inconcussus*], liveth equal with the gods' (*Ep*. 59. 14, p. 270). The *sapiens* is *inconcussus*, unshaken and immovable, far above being affected by anything that happens on earth. 'As the immortall gods neither desire to be aided, neither can bee hurt; no more also can a wise man, who is neighbor to the gods, and like unto God, except in this that he is subject to death' (*Const*. 8. 2, p. 665). The same comparison and qualification appear in *De providentia*:

> Vertue hath contracted an amiable friendship betwixt good men and God. Say I friendship? Nay rather a kindred and likenesse, because a good man onely differeth from God but in time [*bonus tempore tantum a deo differt*]; he is his scholler, his follower and his true childe. (*Prov*. 1. 5, p. 499)

Such aphorisms may lie behind Menenius' bitter comment on Coriolanus (who, though scarcely a *sapiens*, aspires to the wise man's absolute immovability): 'He wants nothing of a god but eternity and a heaven to throne in' (5. 4. 23–5).

The differences between *sapiens* and god may indeed be interpreted to the advantage of the *sapiens*. In *De providentia* Seneca suggests that the wise man is in a sense superior to God, because God is unable to suffer: 'he is without the patience of evill, you above the patience' (6. 6, p. 508). The idea is developed in Letter 73. After praising the tranquillity of the philosopher 'which wee partake with the gods, that maketh us become gods', Seneca demands, 'What advantage hath *Jupiter* over a good man? It is but onely this, he is more long time good. . . . That vertue is not greater which is longer.' On the contrary, the *sapiens* is superior in that, unlike Jupiter, he is capable of temptation but overcomes it by his own fortitude (*Ep*. 73. 11–13, p. 306–7).

The proper relationship between humanity and divinity is problematic in classical thought. Side by side with the idea that a good man should strive to emulate the gods went the equally traditional idea that such striving is hubris, which invites divine punishment.[16] Christianity is more unequivocal in setting an absolute gulf between the human and the divine. Lodge's side-notes suggest the uneasiness of even a sympathetic Renaissance reader on this issue: '*At length hee counselleth him to aspire unto vertue, that is, to God; for that (such is the Stoicks pride) they make a Wiseman equall with him*' (p. 305).[17] From an orthodox Christian point of view, Seneca makes unacceptably inflated claims for what merely human virtue can accomplish.

Seneca's conception of the godlike Stoic hero influences all three Roman plays. Julius Caesar 'is now become a god' (1. 2. 118) and compares himself in his immovable constancy to Mount Olympus (3. 1. 74)—an image which brilliantly fuses Seneca's images of god and rock; Coriolanus strives to 'imitate the graces of the gods' (5. 3. 151), and 'wants nothing of a god but eternity'; even Antony is insistently associated with divinity and with Seneca's demigod hero Hercules. One of the driving forces of Shakespeare's Roman heroes is the desire to rise above humanity and attain a godlike immovability, invulnerability, and superiority to earthly changes.

The second image, of the *sapiens* as rock, sums up the Stoic ideal of *apatheia*. The Greek word implies both absence of emotion and imperviousness to pain. For the Stoics these are linked: suffering is caused by our emotional reactions to events, and the eradication of emotions brings about a state of tranquillity unmoved by anything external. The *sapiens*, like Horatio, 'is not passion's slave' and therefore is 'not a pipe for Fortune's finger | To sound what stop she please' (*Ham.* 3. 2. 68–70).

The Stoic view of emotion rests, in a sense, upon a metaphor. Both in Latin and English, feelings are described in terms of movement (*motus*, 'emotion', being 'moved'), whereas 'constancy' literally means standing still. The constant *sapiens*, therefore, must not be moved by passion. Emotions are 'improbable,[18] sudden and violent motions of the mind'; if allowed to become frequent and habitual, they will develop into 'sicknesses of the soule' (*morbi animi*)—settled perversions of values such as cowardice, cruelty, or ambition (*Ep.* 75. 11–12, p. 314). Progress towards the status

[16] W. K. C. Guthrie, *The Gods of the Greeks* (London, 1950), 113–16; Passmore, *Perfectibility*, 28–30.

[17] Cf. his note on the *Prov.* passage (p. 499): '*A Stoicall Paradox, which cannot be understood . . . in the Schooles of humanitie, but in that of the holy Ghost.*'

[18] That is, 'blameworthy' (Lat. *improbabiles*)—a sense not in *OED*.

of *sapiens* requires the gradual elimination first of such mental illnesses, then of all emotions.

Seneca acknowledges that this ideal is hard to achieve, and that even the *sapiens* will retain 'certaine touches of suspition and shadowes of passion' (*Ep.* 75. 12–14; *Ira* 1. 16. 7, p. 524). Nevertheless, in principle, emotions must be not merely controlled but eradicated. Seneca scathingly rejects the more permissive Aristotelian view that moderate emotion can be harmless or beneficial: that is as absurd as saying that it is proper to be moderately mad or moderately ill (*Ep.* 85. 9, pp. 348–9). Because in Stoic psychology the mind of an angry or frightened person is wholly taken over and 'changed her selfe into passion' (*Ira* 1. 8. 2–3, p. 517), it is impossible for passion to be controlled by reason, and Aristotle was quite wrong to suggest that (for instance) a soldier may find anger a useful tool: 'Reason . . . will never take to her assistants, improvident and violent passions over whom she hath no authority, and whom she never may restrain except she oppose their equals and likes unto them, as feare to Anger, Anger to cowardise, desire to feare' (*Ira* 1. 10. 1, p. 518)

The wise man, therefore, must act out of a rational knowledge of what is right, not out of emotion.

What then (saith he) shall not a good man be angry, if he see his father strooken, his Mother ravished? Hee shall not bee angrie, but revenge and defend them. . . . A good man executeth his offices without confusion or feare, and in such sort will performe those things that are worthy a good man, that hee will doe nothing that is unworthy a man. (*Ira* 1. 12. 1–2, p. 520)[19]

The same principle justifies one of the most controversial Stoic doctrines, that pity is a vice. Seneca is aware that popular opinion regards this doctrine as excessively hard (*duram nimis*: *Clem.* 2. 4. 2), but insists that, while the good man will act charitably and mercifully, he must not allow his mind to be disturbed by the suffering of others, any more than by his own.

For a Wiseman neyther troubleth nor tormenteth himselfe, his understanding is alwayes cleere, neither can any thing happen that may obscure the light thereof. Nothing becommeth a man more than greatnesse of courage [*magnus animus*]; But he cannot have a noble heart, if eyther

[19] Compare *Macb.* 1. 7. 46–7: 'I dare do all that may become a man; | Who dares do more is none.'

> feare or griefe doe daunt the same, or any of these passions obscure or contract it. This shall not befall a Wiseman; no, not in his [sc. own] calamities, but he shall dart back againe all these Arrowes that Fortune hath shot against him, and shall breake them before her face. He shall retayne one and the same countenance, alwayes both peaceable and constant [*inconcussam*], which he might not doe if sorrow were lodged in his heart. (*Clem.* 2. 5. 5, p. 608)

The constant man must both be, and be seen to be, entirely 'unmoved' by emotion.

Shakespeare, of course, did not need to read Seneca to be aware of the Renaissance commonplace that uncontrolled passion is dangerous, or of the stereotypical view of Romans as rational and self-controlled. Nevertheless, as critics such as Vawter and Anson have argued, the Roman view of emotion in *Julius Caesar* seems more specifically indebted to Stoicism. Brutus in particular, in his determination to separate reason from affections, to kill Caesar without the confusion of anger or hatred, and to avoid being 'moved', seems a would-be *sapiens*; the self-deceptions and hypocrisies in which the attempt involves him, and the failure betrayed by his inner perturbations and the cracking of his front of Stoic impassivity in the quarrel scene, suggest some of the drawbacks in the Senecan ideal.

The implication of the image of the rock is that a person who is completely unmoved by emotion is also invulnerable to suffering, becoming not only as immovable but also as impervious as a rock. But is the *sapiens* really invulnerable?

Seneca himself betrays some uneasiness about the rock image and its connotations. In *De constantia*, as we have seen, he compares the wise man to 'certaine hard stones which Iron cannot enter', to adamant or asbestos, or to rocks in the midst of a stormy sea which 'retaine no impression of the stormes that have assailed them'. Later, however, he repudiates the metaphor.

> I deny not but a wise man hath some sence of these evils, for we say not that he is hard and stupide, like a flint or as a barre of Iron. There is no vertue that hath not a sence of that which she suffereth . . . I confesse that a wiseman receiveth some strokes, but he rebateth them, he healeth them, and maketh them without effect . . . (*Const.* 10. 4, p. 667)

The imperviousness of a rock is now seen as an impossible and undesirable insensibility. In rejecting this image Seneca humanizes his *sapiens*, but also undercuts the picture of superhuman invulnerability presented earlier in *De constantia*, and lays himself open to the objection in the opening chapters: that the Stoic wise man has no special power over fortune, merely a great deal of commonplace endurance.

Is the *sapiens* really invulnerable, then, or does he merely pretend to be? This question arises again in a difficult passage later in *De constantia*, in which Seneca draws a distinction between Stoic and Epicurean views of pain:

> The Epicure saith, that a wise man ought to endure injuries, but we say that a Wise man cannot be injured.
>
> Neither hast thou cause to conclude that this repugneth against Nature. We doe not denie but that it is an incommodious thing to be beaten, to be enforced, and to be maimed in some member; but we denie that these are injuries. We take not from them the sense of paine, but the name of injury which cannot bee admitted without empeachment of vertues reputation [*nomen injuriae, quod non potest recipi virtute salva*]. . . . Askest thou me wherein they differ? Such difference is there betweene them as betweene two stout sword-players, whereof the one [stoppeth] his wound[20] and standeth on his guard; the other, looking backe at the people that crie out, maketh shew that it is nothing, and will not endure to have them parted. (*Const.* 16. 1–2, p. 668)

Seneca here comes close to granting his objector's charge of being concerned only with 'an imaginarie honour of words' in his insistence upon denying only 'the *name* of injury'. The Stoic, it appears, feels as much pain as anyone else but refuses to call it 'pain'. In the image of the two gladiators, the Epicurean fights on in spite of being wounded, the Stoic pretends that he is not wounded. The Stoic hero is seen as a performer in the public arena, whose heroism consists in his public denial of his genuine pain. The subversive implication of this image is that all Stoics may in fact be like Shakespeare's Brutus, who suffers pain and perturbation but keeps it concealed, who refuses to display any public emotion even at his wife's death, though the Epicurean Cassius protests

[20] I have altered Lodge's translation of *premit vulnus* as 'dissembleth his wound', which obscures the point of the comparison. For the distinction, compare the Stoic image of the wise man smiling on the rack with Epicurus' claim that 'Even if he is put on the rack, the wise man is happy . . . But . . . he shrieks and groans' (Long and Sedley, *Hellenistic Philosophers*, 22Q).

I have as much of this in art as you,
But yet my nature could not bear it so.

(4. 2. 248–9)

The performance of constancy

The image of the two gladiators suggests Seneca's tendency to see virtue as a public performance. The Stoic hero, like a gladiator in the arena, must display his constancy; questions of truth or pretence are secondary to the effect of the performance on its audience.

So, in *De providentia*, Seneca describes the suicide of the Stoic martyr Cato of Utica in terms of a gladiatorial show. Just as we take pleasure at the games in watching 'a young man of a constant resolution' courageously fighting a lion, so the gods take pleasure in the 'spectacle' of human virtue in combat with fortune.

I see not, say I, what thing *Jupiter* hath more admirable upon the earth, if he would fix his mind upon the same, then to behold *Cato* remaining firme and resolute . . . and invincible amidst his countries ruines. . . . I assure my selfe, that the gods with great joy beheld, when this great and worthie personage, a powerfull protector of himselfe, travelled to save others, and gave them meanes to escape: who likewise, in that last night of his life, followed his studie, whilest he thrust his sword into his belly, whilest he scattered abroad his bowels.

The reason for the failure of Cato's first suicide attempt, Seneca suggests, was that the gods took such pleasure in the 'spectacle' that they demanded a repeat performance:

It sufficed not the immortal gods to behold *Cato* once, vertue was retained and revoked, to the end that in a greater difficultie shee might approve her selfe. For there is more greater resolution in dying the second or third time, then in dying at the first. (*Prov.* 2. 7–12, pp. 500–1)

(The theatrical imagery is stronger in the Latin, since *revocata* can mean 'encored', and *in difficiliore parte* is literally 'in a more demanding role'.)

Seneca seems untroubled by this appalling vision of the gods as sadistic voyeurs who 'kill us for their sport'. His aim is to justify the ways of God to man. If the gods allow good men to suffer, it is because virtue, to be virtue, must be seen in action.

Vertue hath no vertue, if it be not impugned; then appeareth [*apparet*] it how great it is, of what value and power it is, when by patience it approveth [*ostendit*] what it may. (*Prov.* 2. 4, p. 500)

Two ideas are here confusingly mingled: that virtue needs to be tested by suffering, and that it needs to be publicly displayed. 'Vertue hath no vertue' (literally, it withers away, *marcet*) if it is not exercised, but also if it is not shown. You may be a great man, Seneca tells his reader, 'but how shall I know it, if Fortune give thee not leave and meanes to make proofe of [*in qua . . . ostenderet*] thy vertue? . . . No man, no not thy selfe shall bee able to know thy value' (4. 2–3, pp. 503–4). A virtue which is not seen may as well not exist.

Such passages, with their recurrence of words like *apparere* and *ostendere*, suggest that for Seneca *esse est percipi*. Constancy is, at least partly, a matter of keeping up appearances. The Stoic must 'retayne one and the same countenance [*faciem*]'; he is told to 'maintaine thy selfe such, as thou hast resolved to shew [*praestare*] thy selfe'. He is a performer who, like the wounded gladiator, must keep a poker face and refuse to acknowledge pain or emotion.

T. S. Eliot summed up this quality of performance in a famous passage to which I have already referred:

the ethic of Seneca's plays is that of an age which supplied the lack of moral habits by a system of moral attitudes and poses. To this the natural public temper of Rome contributed. The ethic of Seneca is a matter of postures. The posture which gives the greatest opportunity for effect, hence for the Senecan morality, is the posture of dying: death gives his characters the opportunity for their most sententious aphorisms.[21]

In spite of its stress on the rock-hard invulnerable core of the individual soul, Seneca's Stoicism is in important ways a public and external morality. He celebrates grand scenes and heroic gestures; even Stilbon, the exemplar of inner tranquillity, is shown as a hero because his virtue was publicly demonstrated and summed up in a memorably 'sententious aphorism'. This is a theatrical ethic, and it has fittingly found its most striking expression in drama.

Seneca's 'postures', nevertheless, are not merely hollow; they

[21] 'Seneca in Elizabethan Translation', 72. Eliot's point about the theatricality of Seneca's ethics, and their reliance on the presence of an audience, is developed by Braden, *Renaissance Tragedy*, 25–7, and Rosenmeyer, *Senecan Drama*, 47–56.

can be defended by reference to the 'public temper of Rome'. Seneca was writing for Roman aristocrats in the time of Nero—men for whom exhortations to courage in the face of torture, imprisonment, and disgrace were very relevant. Miriam Griffin appositely cites the words in Tacitus of the Stoic Thrasea Paetus, who invited his friends to watch his suicide on Nero's orders, since 'you have been born into times when it is expedient to steel the mind with instances of firmness [*constantibus exemplis*]'.[22] It is such *constantia exempla* which Seneca provides in his frequent roll-calls of heroic martyrs—in *De tranquillitate*, for example, where he cites the deaths of Socrates, Pompey, Cato, and others, and urges the reader to 'Consider how every one of them behaved himselfe constantly [*quomodo quisque illorum tulerit*]' and say, '*The more constant, the more happy thou art*' (16. 3, p. 653). Such examples are inspirational: it is 'for the good of all men' that 'everie one of the better sort . . . beare armes and performe actions' (*Prov.* 5. 1, p. 506) to show that suffering and death are not to be feared. For this purpose it is necessary that constancy be publicly displayed; a cloistered and fugitive virtue has no exemplary value. In the words of Coriolanus to his son, the Stoic hero ought to stand 'Like a great sea-mark standing every flaw | And saving those that eye thee!' (5. 3. 74–5).

The posture of dying

Suicide is the ultimate act of Stoic constancy. It asserts an immutable virtue which would rather die than change or compromise, a rocklike invulnerability and a godlike superiority to fortune; it also, as Eliot wryly noted, provides in 'the posture of dying' the most spectacular public demonstration of these qualities. For Shakespeare, suicide—to die like 'an antique Roman' (*Ham.* 5. 2. 293) or 'after the high Roman fashion' (*Ant.* 4. 16. 89), or, in Macbeth's jeer, to 'play the Roman fool' (5. 10. 1)—is the quintessential Roman act. It is also, of course, the most clearly unchristian.[23]

[22] Tacitus, *Annals*, 16. 35; Griffin, *Seneca*, 388.

[23] As we can see from Lodge's anxious marginal protests whenever Seneca discusses it: e.g. '*this . . . is but a Paradox of the Stoickes, refuted expressely by Nature, by the law of Nations, and condemned by the expres word of God*' (*Workes of Seneca*, 500).

Suicide, for Seneca, is the last defence of the *sapiens* against fortune. For the wise man life itself is an 'indifferent' thing, to be willingly sacrificed if it comes to a choice between life and virtue. To possess this wisdom is to be entirely liberated: 'fortune can do nothing over him that knoweth how to die' (*Ep.* 70. 7, p. 294). You cannot be forced to endure any suffering or do any evil, since you always have a way of escape.

> [H]ee that hath learned to die, hath forgotten to serve, it is above all power, undoubtedly beyond all. What careth he for prisons, holds, or restraints? He hath alwaies free passage. There is but one chaine that holdeth us bound, that is the love of life. (*Ep.* 26. 10, p. 215)

Freedom from that chain makes the Stoic totally invulnerable, by enabling him to escape at will from the world of change and fortune.

This is orthodox Stoic wisdom; but Seneca's obsessive recurrence to the subject of suicide may seem to display a kind of death-wish. He puts into the mouth of God a eulogy of suicide as his greatest boon to mankind (*Prov.* 6. 7, p. 509), and seems at times positively to incite the reader to self-destruction: 'Seest thou yonder steepie place? from thence mayest thou descend to thy libertie .... Seest thou thy throat, thy wesand-pipe, thy heart? These are the meanes to escape servitude' (*Ira* 3. 15, p. 565). He even suggests that suicide may be justified by mere *taedium vitae*, quoting the words of a Stoic to an elderly friend:

> *Bethinke thy selfe for how long time together thou hast done the same thing. Meate, sleepe, lust, by this circle all the World commeth. Not only a valiant man, a strong man, a miserable man can have a will to dye, but he also that disdayneth life.* (*Ep.* 77. 6, p. 321)

It is hardly surprising that Christians have regarded such preachings as incitements to despair. Seneca's emphasis is exceptional, but his apparent death-wish is partly inherent in Stoicism; in preaching contempt both for life's pleasures and for the fear of death, it tends, as Miriam Griffin points out, to make death seem like an attractive escape.[24]

[24] Griffin, *Seneca*, 385. Griffin argues (ch. 11) that Seneca's position on suicide is essentially orthodox despite his rhetorical extravagance; other scholars (e.g. Rist, *Stoic Philosophy*, 247–9) see him as distorting Stoic doctrine by portraying suicide as peculiarly noble and recommending it indiscriminately.

This attraction is heightened by what R. J. Kaufmann has called the 'teleological fallacy' of Stoicism: the idea 'that because death is the "end" of life in the sense of its termination it is also the "end" of life in the sense of its proper goal'.[25] Death is therefore the most important act in life, indeed more important than life. '*It is no great matter to live*,' says the Stoic counsellor of Letter 77, '*as all thy slaves live, and all other beasts also. It is a great matter to dye honestly, prudently, and valiantly*' (*Ep*. 77. 6, p. 321). The moment of death is a uniquely authentic manifestation of the quality of one's soul, 'the day . . . which should pronounce the sentence of all my yeres'.

All that which hitherto I have either spoken or done, until this houre, is nothing, light and deceivable are those pledges of my mind, and enfolded with many deceits: death shall be the onely faithfull testimonie, whether I have profited or not. Thus prepare I my selfe couragiously for that day, wherein I will pronounce of my selfe and judge, (all crafts and subtilties laid aside) whether I speak or thinke constantly. . . . It then wil appeare [*apparebit*] what thou hast done when thou departest thy life. (*Ep*. 26. 5–6, pp. 214–15)

If the manner of your death determines the quality of your entire life, it becomes all the more appealing to choose when and how to die, and so ensure that your character will 'appeare' as you desire. 'It skils not whether a man die sooner or later: to die either well or ill, that importeth much; and to die well is to flie the perill of an evill life' (*Ep*. 70. 6, pp. 293–4). Seneca no doubt does not intend the implication that suicide may be a way of running away from the moral risks of life; his point is that a person who is willing to die cannot be corrupted or compromised, but can maintain his integrity to the end.[26]

This motive for suicide, the preservation of personal integrity, Seneca refers to as *dignitas*—'honour' in Lodge's translation (*Ep*. 14. 2 p. 189). As Griffin points out, Seneca is here drawing on Panaetius and the concept of decorum. *Dignitas* is related (both in etymology and in sense) to *decorum*: it likewise refers to that which is appropriate to or worthy of a person.[27] To die for the

[25] 'The Seneca Perspective and the Shakespearean Poetic', *CompD* 1 (1967), 182–98 (191).

[26] Cf. *Ep*. 65. 22, p. 280.

[27] Griffin, *Seneca*, 381–2. In Roman usage *dignitas* normally refers to public authority or rank; like Cicero in translating *officia*, Seneca chooses a Latin political term to translate a Greek moral one.

sake of *dignitas* is to ensure 'that to thy last breath thou maintaine thy selfe such, as thou hast resolved to shew thy selfe'—to play one's role consistently to the end, and to die 'like oneself'. The idea is perfectly exemplified in the suicides of Roman Stoics such as Thrasea Paetus and Seneca himself, who staged their own deaths as exhibitions of constancy designed to sum up and manifest the virtues by which they had lived.

Death itself is in a sense the ultimate form of constancy, which (in Cleopatra's words) 'shackles accidents and bolts up change' (*Ant.* 5. 2. 6). To die 'constantly' is not merely to face the moment of dying with unflinching resolution, but also to die in a way consistent with one's life, and so to fix one's virtue, perfect and unchanging, for posterity.

Nowhere are Shakespeare's Romans more Stoic than in their attitude to suicide. There are some ten suicides in the plays, and no character (except Brutus in a confused and self-contradictory passage) ever criticizes the act.[28] Cassius praises it in Senecan tones as an escape from tyranny (*JC* 1. 3. 92–6), and Cleopatra calls it 'great | To do that thing that ends all other deeds' (*Ant.* 5. 2. 4–5). Moreover, they kill themselves not from grief (like Romeo) or remorse (like Othello), but from motives of *dignitas*, to avoid doing or suffering what would destroy their self-respect. Brutus, like Cleopatra, 'bears too great a mind' (*JC* 5. 1. 113) to be led in triumph; Cassius is ashamed 'to live so long | To see my best friend ta'en before my face' (5. 3. 34–5); Eros kills himself to avoid having to kill Antony—all 'die well . . . to flie the perill of an evill life'. In the posture of dying they are able to show themselves to the world as they wish to be: Brutus is 'found like Brutus' (5. 4. 25); Coriolanus, throwing himself on the Volscian swords, proclaims himself still the hero of Corioli; Cleopatra's magnificent death immortalises her as queen and lover. Suicide, for Shakespeare's Romans, is the final assertion of identity, a way of remaining *unus idemque* to the end. As Shakespeare clearly saw,

[28] *JC* 5. 1. 100–13; the passage is discussed in Chs. 6 and 7 below. There are four suicides in *Julius Caesar* and six in *Antony* (if one includes Enobarbus, who clearly wills his own death: *Ant.* 4. 6. 35–6). *Coriolanus* contains none, but the hero's death can be read as a kind of suicide if one sees him as deliberately rather than blindly provoking his own murder (Alan Howard powerfully plays the scene this way in Elijah Moshinsky's BBC TV production), and it involves similar issues and emotions to the other Roman suicides.

the logical end of Senecan constancy is self-preservation through self-destruction.[29]

Amoral constancy: Seneca's tragedies

The theatricality of Senecan constancy makes it seem natural that it should find expression in drama; and discussion of Senecan influence on Shakespeare and the Elizabethans has tended to focus on Seneca's tragedies.[30] In fact, Stoicism is hard to locate in the tragedies. Their difference in tone from the philosophical works is so marked that they were long assumed to be the work of a different Seneca. Modern scholars accept that the tragedies were written by the philosopher, and—more tentatively—that they rest, in some sense, on a basis of Stoic thought.[31] Their Stoicism, however, is overwhelmingly negative. In their worlds of disordered passion, madness, violence, and cruelty, there is little place for *constantia sapientis*; virtuous characters may suffer bravely, but do not rise above suffering with the heroic invulnerability of the constant *sapiens*. Rather it is the evil characters who tend to have heroic stature and to be depicted as possessing a kind of amoral constancy.

The pattern is clear in *Thyestes*.[32] The nominal hero, though he at first speaks Stoic wisdom about the worthlessness of worldly

[29] On Shakespeare's suicides, see Rowland Wymer, *Suicide and Despair in the Jacobean Drama* (Brighton, 1986), esp. ch. 7, 'Stoicism and Roman Deaths' (133–55).

[30] The literature on the influence of Senecan tragedy is too extensive to list here, especially since much of it is peripheral to my concerns; the major items are listed in the Bibliography. For surveys of the debate see Frederick Kiefer's two articles, 'Seneca's Influence on Elizabethan Tragedy: An Annotated Bibliography', *RORD* 21 (1978), 17–34, and 'Senecan Influence: A Bibliographic Supplement', *RORD* 28 (1985), 129–42; and the first chapter of Miola, *Classical Tragedy*.

[31] On the 'two Senecas' theory, see Pratt, *Seneca's Drama*, 12; Monsarrat, *Light from the Porch*, 34–5. The presence of Stoicism in the tragedies is variously argued by Pratt, 77–81; Braden, *Renaissance Tragedy*, ch. 2 (who argues that, though the plays can be seen as 'mounting a systematic negation of Stoicism' (29), they in fact arise from the same impulses); and Rosenmeyer ('Stoic natural science is at the very heart of Seneca's tragic enterprise', *Senecan Drama*, 89).

[32] Quotations from *Thyestes* are from Jasper Heywood's version in *Seneca His Tenne Tragedies*; other translations are from Loeb. Shakespeare may have drawn on *Thyestes* in *Titus Andronicus*: see J. C. Maxwell, introd. to Arden edn. (3rd edn., London, 1961), pp. xxxi–xxxii; Miola, *Classical Tragedy*, 23–9.

power, betrays his lack of true constancy by his faltering step and shifting gaze (421–2); he lets himself be persuaded to abandon Stoic self-sufficiency and place his trust in 'things unsure | Thy brother and the kingdome' (424–5, p. 70), and so ends in misery. In contrast Atreus, the villain, shows a kind of insane constancy in evil. He is undeterred from his revenge even by the terrifying omens as he prepares to sacrifice his nephews:

The woode then quakt, and all at once from trembling grounde anone
The Pallace beckt, in doubt which way the payse thereof would fall,
And shaking as in waves it stood . . .
The sights amas'de all other men, but stedfast yet alway
Of mynde, unmoved Atreus stands, and even the Gods doth fray
That threaten him . . .

(696–705, p. 79)

Unmoved 'when all the sway of earth | Shakes like a thing unfirm' (*JC* 1. 3. 3–4), Atreus takes on the qualities of the *sapiens* whose steadfastness puts even the gods to shame.[33]

Other Senecan villains show the same perverse constancy. Medea speaks like a Stoic heroine:

MEDEA. Fortune fears the brave, the cowardly overwhelms.
NURSE. If there is place for courage, then should it be approved.
MEDEA. It can never be that for courage there is no place.
NURSE. No hope points out a way for our broken fortunes.
MEDEA. Whoso has naught to hope, let him despair of naught.

(*Medea* 159–63)

Told that she has lost her husband, her power, her wealth, and has nothing left, she replies, 'Medea is left'—*Medea superest* (166). Her selfhood, her integrity of soul, is outside the reach of fortune, and if that is intact, nothing else matters. She cuts off the nurse's protesting cry 'Medea' with the word *Fiam* (171), 'I will be': she will be truly herself when everything else is stripped from her. It is a claim that Stilbon might have been proud of, though it leads to madness and murder.[34]

[33] Cassius' defiance of the gods, later in the scene (1. 3. 46–56), also recalls Atreus.

[34] Brower (*Hero and Saint*, 159–64) analyses Clytemnestra in *Agamemnon* in similar terms, as showing 'Stoic consistency for non-Stoic ends' (164), and suggests that this 'ambiguous caricature of a noble Stoic attitude' (162) shows how Seneca's rhetoric could pervert his philosophy.

Seneca presumably did not intend to turn such characters into Stoic heroes. Atreus, Medea, Clytemnestra, Phaedra, and the rest are conceived as characters ruinously mastered by their passions. Yet he repeatedly depicts them in ways which recall the ideal of *constantia sapientis*. In Senecan Stoicism, as R. J. Kaufmann puts it, 'a concern for authenticity of self becomes primary, though this tendency . . . creates major structural tensions in its conflict with Stoic quietism.' The Stoic ideal of self-consistency 'makes the oblivious monomaniac as eligible for heroism as the more selfless man, perhaps more so'.[35] Seneca cannot resist glorifying characters who are constant in selfhood, even when they lack every other virtue.

No character in Seneca's tragedies approximates more closely to the ideal of the Stoic hero than Hercules in *Hercules furens* and *Hercules Oetaeus*.[36] The Stoics traditionally admired Hercules as 'Contemner of pleasures, Fortune, and circumstance, selfless benefactor *pro bono publico*, victor over all terrors, and exemplar of aspiration for the highest virtue'.[37] In the tragedies he displays these qualities, but he is a very different kind of Stoic hero from the *sapiens* of the prose works: not tranquil but passionate, not passively enduring but violently aspiring.

Hercules can be seen as a translation into literal terms of the qualities metaphorically attributed to the *sapiens*. In *Hercules Oetaeus* the chorus of his captives sing of him as rocklike—'What Scythian crag . . . begot thee?' (143)—and invulnerable:

> By no wounds may his limbs be assailed; iron he feels blunt, steel is too dull; upon his naked body swords are broken, and stones rebound; and so he scorns the fates, and with body all invincible defies mortality. (151–5)

He is invincible and omnipotent: 'With his bare hands did he o'erthrow Oechalia's walls, and naught can stand against him; for whate'er he plans to overcome is overcome already' (162–4). His

[35] Kaufmann, 'The Seneca Perspective', 189, 191.

[36] Seneca's authorship of *Hercules Oetaeus* is disputed, but was accepted in the Renaissance, and there is 'a growing tendency' today to regard it as authentic (Pratt, *Seneca's Drama*, 28 and notes).

[37] G. Karl Galinsky, *The Herakles Theme* (Oxford, 1972), 167 (cf. 101–8); see also Waith, *Herculean Hero*, 30–8 (who notes that 'the physical strength of Hercules is identified with moral strength', 30); Pratt, *Seneca's Drama*, 115–16 (on Hercules in Seneca's prose).

inflexible countenance terrifies enemies into surrender (165–6). The *sapiens*' invulnerability and invincibility are here made literal. The effect, however—especially as conveyed through the complaints of his victims—is grotesque and disturbing, like Shakespeare's similar picture of Coriolanus in battle.[38]

Turned from a metaphor of spiritual strength into a literal superman, the Stoic hero becomes a disturbingly ambiguous figure. *Hercules Oetaeus* opens with Hercules boasting in 'Ercles' vein'[39] of his benefactions to humanity and demanding admission to Olympus. This is the ultimate Stoic aspiration, the claim of the good man to become godlike through his own virtue. But in the following scenes his wife and his captives present a very different view of him as arrogant, lecherous, cruel, wantonly destructive. Both benefactor and criminal, he seems a figure beyond good and evil, to whom normal human moral judgements are not applicable.

Hercules attains a more orthodox kind of Stoic heroism in his enormously prolonged death scene. Poisoned by the shirt of Nessus, he first gives way to murderous rage, but then rises to a determination to 'choose a death glorious, renowned, illustrious, full worthy of myself [*me digna*]' (1481–2). Heroic death 'will make me seem worthy of the stars', for 'Worthless is all that has been done' (1713–14): death (in keeping with the teleological fallacy) far outweighs in significance everything done in life. His death in the pyre on Mount Oeta is a conscious exhibition of heroic constancy: '’Midst scorching heat and threat'ning flames, unmoved [*immotus*], unshaken [*inconcussus*], to neither side turning his tortured limbs, he encourages, advises, is active still, though all aflame' (1740–3)—until at last 'he deemed that courage enough had been shown in death' (1747–8) and strides into the heart of the flames to die.[40] Having shown his superiority to pain and his ability to remain like

[38] Compare *Cor.* 2. 2. 101–22, and also 4. 7. 23–4 ('does achieve as soon | As draw his sword'), 5. 4. 22–3 ('What he bids be done is finished with his bidding'). Waith, who discusses the godlike and Herculean imagery applied to Coriolanus (esp. 121–2), does not note these parallels.

[39] *MND* 1. 2. 36. Bottom's audition speech clearly parodies part of this speech in Studley's version; see Miola, *Classical Tragedy*, 180–1. (I restore the F spelling: Oxford's ''erc'les' suggests that this is Bottom's idiosyncratic mangling of the name, but in fact Studley too uses 'Ercles'.)

[40] Waith calls this passage 'a *locus classicus* of Stoic fortitude' (*Herculean Hero*, 37).

himself to the end, he is worthy to attain godhead, and the play ends with his ascent to the stars.

Hercules embodies in extreme form the aspirations of Senecan Stoicism: immovability, self-consistency, superiority to fortune, godlike self-perfection. He shows what happens when these aspirations are taken to their logical conclusion. In the process constancy becomes detached from normal Stoic moral values, and 'authenticity of self' becomes an end in itself.

This potential for this amoral constancy is perhaps inherent in Stoicism from the beginning, in the ambiguity of Zeno's *homologia*; it is there even in the carefully moderate, socially circumscribed rules of Ciceronian decorum. But it is much clearer in the hyperbolical rhetoric of Seneca's essays, and emerges full-blown in his tragedies, where the same rhetoric becomes attached to characters who are heroic in nothing but their constancy. This development is possible because Seneca's is essentially an individualistic philosophy: the Senecan Stoic's aim is self-consistency and self-perfection, the fact that this is ultimately 'for the good of all men' being only an added justification. Paradoxically, Cicero, apparently more interested in individual personality, is far more careful to subordinate individuality to the demands of society and nature. It is therefore in Seneca, rather than Cicero, that I see the roots of Hiram Haydn's 'bastard Stoicism', and of the amorally individualistic hero-villains of Renaissance drama—the 'Herculean hero', the 'senecal man', the 'tragedy of titanism'—whose paradoxical association with Stoicism has been traced by many earlier critics.[41]

Shakespeare's Romans can also be located in this tradition. They are shaped by the ideals of Senecan Stoicism when they strive to be (or at least appear) rational, passionless, invulnerable to suffering or the fear of death, constant as 'the rock . . . not to be windshaken' (*Cor.* 5. 2. 110) or as 'marble' (*Ant.* 5. 2. 235); and, most obviously, when they strive to 'imitate the graces of the gods' (*Cor.* 5. 3. 151) and attain a more than human immovability and self-sufficiency. The danger is that, as in Senecan tragedy, such superhuman aspirations may tip over into amoral self-assertion. This danger is hinted at in Caesar, overbearing the Senate with the

[41] The phrases quoted are those respectively of Waith, ibid.; Henry W. Wells, 'Senecan Influence on Elizabethan Tragedy: A Re-estimation', *Shakespeare Assoc. Bulletin*, 19 (1944), 71–84; and Hardin Craig, 'The Shackling of Accidents: A Study of Elizabethan Tragedy', *PQ* 19 (1940), 1–19.

claim that he alone of all humanity is 'unshaked of motion' (3. 1. 70); it emerges more clearly in Antony, scarcely at all Stoic, but emulating his 'ancestor' Hercules (4. 13. 44) in the pursuit of a kind of apotheosis through the passionate pursuit of his own desires, and in Coriolanus, the Herculean war-machine whose dedication to absolute constancy almost destroys Rome. Such kinds of Herculean heroism may seem bizarrely unlike the Stoic virtue of a Brutus, but they are equally Senecan and also grow, directly or crookedly, out of the fundamental Stoic ideal of constancy. They suggest the dangers facing a society which, like Shakespeare's Rome, sets up 'constancy' as an unambiguously desirable virtue.

4
Constancy and Opinion: Renaissance Neostoicism

The ambivalent tradition

Fifteen hundred years after the death of Seneca, Stoic constancy once again became a subject of debate. In the later sixteenth century 'Neostoic' or 'Christian Stoic' writers—Montaigne, Lipsius, Du Vair, and others—revived the ideals of classical Stoicism, with particular emphasis on the virtue of constancy and its opposition to the corrupting power of 'opinion'; and this Stoic revival in its turn led to an anti-Stoic reaction. Shakespeare, in making constancy a central issue in the Roman plays, must have been aware of the contemporary debate.[1]

In a sense it is misleading to say that Stoicism was 'revived' or 'rediscovered' in the sixteenth century, for it had never entirely been lost.[2] Throughout the Middle Ages Cicero and Seneca were known and valued as moral authorities, and elements of Stoicism had permeated Christianity itself.[3] Renaissance humanism brought

[1] For details of the Neostoic works by Lipsius, Du Vair, Cornwallis, and Hall discussed in this chapter, see Bibliographical Note.

[2] This introductory section is largely based on secondary sources, principally: Baker, *Dignity of Man*, esp. ch. 18; Haydn, *Counter-Renaissance*; Robert Hoopes, *Right Reason in the English Renaissance* (Cambridge, Mass., 1962); André Malan Hugo, 'The Spiritual and Intellectual Background' in *Calvin's Commentary on Seneca's 'De Clementia'*, ed. and tr. Ford Lewis Battles and André Malan Hugo (Leiden, 1969), 12*–62*; Rudolf Kirk, introd. to *Two Bookes of Constancie* by Justus Lipsius, tr. Sir John Stradling (New Brunswick, NJ, 1939), 13–32; Paul Oskar Kristeller, 'The Moral Thought of Renaissance Humanism', in id., *Renaissance Thought II* (New York, 1965), 20–68; Anthony Levi, *French Moralists: The Theory of the Passions 1585 to 1649* (Oxford, 1964), esp. chs. 1–4; Long, Hellenistic Philosophy, ch. 6; Palmer, *Seneca's 'De Remediis'*; Quentin Skinner, *The Foundations of Modern Political Thought* (2 vols., Cambridge, 1978), esp. i. 69–112 (on humanism) and ii. 275–84 (on Neostoicism); Gerard Verbeke, *The Presence of Stoicism in Medieval Thought* (Washington, 1983); R. M. Wenley, *Stoicism and Its Influence* [London, 1925?], ch. 4; Léontine Zanta, *La Renaissance du Stoïcisme au XVIe siècle* (1914; repr. Geneva, 1975).

[3] Verbeke, *Stoicism in Medieval Thought*, 1–19, documents the 'largely unconscious' (1) presence of Stoicism in medieval thought, and the use of Cicero and Seneca by thinkers like Aquinas, Abelard, and John of Salisbury.

a more intense and systematic interest in classical thought, and Stoicism absorbed part of this interest: the works of Cicero and Seneca were newly edited and translated, and lost authors such as Epictetus and Marcus Aurelius were rediscovered.[4]

The Renaissance, however, inherited an ambivalent attitude to Stoicism, based on the coexistence throughout the history of Christianity of two conflicting attitudes towards pagan thought, the 'Alexandrian' and the 'Augustinian'.[5] The theologians of the Alexandrian school, in the early years of Christianity, regarded pagan philosophy as a divinely inspired preparation for Christianity, and tried to assimilate its best aspects. Stoic ideas about natural law, providence, conscience, the unity of mankind, were thus incorporated into Christianity and 'even contributed in shaping [its] moral ideals'.[6] Classical Stoics were drafted into the fold as honorary Christians, and the legend grew up that Seneca had been converted by St Paul; Tertullian called him *saepe noster*—often one of us.[7]

The 'Augustinian' strand of Christianity, on the other hand, took up the qualifications implicit in Tertullian's pregnant phrase, and emphasized the differences between pagan and Christian thought. The classic statement of this point of view, Augustine's *City of God*, focuses at several points on Stoicism and the ideal of the pagan hero. Perhaps because the Stoics seem superficially akin to Christianity, Augustine is especially vehement in pointing out that they are in fact carnal and worldly, desiring 'with amazing folly, to be happy here on earth and to achieve bliss by their own efforts'.[8] Augustine, who attacked the Pelagian heresy, sees the Stoic idea of human perfectibility in this life as a dangerous temptation to Christians.

His attack concentrates especially on the ideals of *constantia* and *apatheia*. The idea that the wise man can be invulnerable to external evils, because he knows that they are not really evil, is for Augustine an arrogant denial of the real evils inherent in our fallen

[4] John Edwin Sandys, *A History of Classical Scholarship* (Cambridge, 1908), ii. 103–5; Long, *Hellenistic Philosophy*, 238–9.

[5] The distinction is Hugo's, 'Spiritual and Intellectual Background', 47*.

[6] Verbeke, *Stoicism in Medieval Thought*, pp. vii and 45 (quotation); Wenley, *Stoicism*, 123; Ross, 'Seneca's Philosophical Influence', 124.

[7] Tertullian, *De anima* 20, quoted by Hugo, 'Spiritual and Intellectual Background', 50*.

[8] *Concerning the City of God against the Pagans*, tr. Henry Bettenson (Harmondsworth, 1972), 19. 4 (subsequent references in text).

world. The Stoics' glorification of suicide exposes the flaw in their arguments: if suffering is not an evil, why kill yourself to escape it? 'Was it by patient endurance that Cato took his own life?' (19. 4). As for the ideal of *apatheia*, it is either unattainable or undesirable. If it means the control of unruly passions, 'it is clearly a good and desirable state; but it does not belong to this present life'; such moral perfection is only attainable in the next world. If, on the other hand, it means absolute freedom from emotion, 'who would not judge this insensitivity to be the worst of all moral defects?' (14. 9). For Christians, emotions are good or bad depending on the quality of the will engaged in them and the object to which they are directed (14. 6). To reject emotion entirely shows an arrogance that is as sinful as any passion: 'they rather lose every shred of humanity than achieve a true tranquillity. For hardness does not necessarily imply rectitude, and insensibility is not a guarantee of health' (14. 9). Augustine's criticisms of the Stoics were to be enormously influential, recurring again and again in anti-Stoic polemics.

The Renaissance humanists, in their conscious rediscovery of pagan thought, inherited both the sympathetic Alexandrian and the critical Augustinian attitudes towards pagan thought and Stoicism in particular. On the whole, however, their attitude could be characterized as Alexandrian. The primary concern of the humanists was with morality, and they turned to classical philosophy for practical, secular moral teachings which would complement rather than challenge Christianity.[9]

Though Stoic writers were prominent in this revival of pagan thought, it was only in the most general sense a revival of Stoicism. The humanists' 'eclectic Stoicism' (in Hiram Haydn's phrase) was a blend of Stoic, Platonic, Aristotelian, and Christian elements; their concern was not to draw academic distinctions but to 'extract . . . a kind of common wisdom that could be learned, imitated, and utilized'.[10] The dominant influence was not Seneca but Cicero, especially *De officiis*. The humanists were in sympathy with Cicero's 'tolerant and "reconciling" philosophical position',

[9] Kristeller, 'Renaissance Humanism', esp. 26–9. I am using 'humanist' in the sense defined by Kristeller: one concerned with the revival of classical learning in literature, history, philosophy, and education.

[10] Haydn, *Counter-Renaissance*, 55 and *passim*; Kristeller, 'Renaissance Humanism' 37.

his moderate public-spirited Stoicism, and his sense that it was possible to be both moral and successful in public life.[11] This Ciceronian school is well illustrated in Sir Thomas Elyot's *The Boke Named The Governour* (1531). Elyot's guide to the moral 'offices' of a member of the English ruling class offers advice by which 'governors' can exercise authority successfully while visibly preserving their moral integrity: 'they shall than seme to all men worthye to be in authoritie, honour, and noblesse, and all that is under their gouvernaunce shall prospere and come to perfection.'[12] The single chapter that Elyot devotes to 'constance or stabilitie' (3. 19) acknowledges its importance but gives no sense that constancy in suffering is the quintessential virtue.

The humanist attitude to Seneca's harsher and more extreme brand of Stoicism is more ambivalent, and more qualified by Augustinian objections. Erasmus' view of Seneca, for instance, is both divided and shifting. In an essay of 1515 he expresses almost unqualified enthusiasm; in the introduction to his 1529 edition of Seneca he is much more critical, arguing that Seneca must be read in his pagan context ('For if you read him as a pagan, he wrote Christianly; if as a Christian, he wrote paganly'), and attacking the Stoics' arrogant self-sufficiency in Augustinian tones: 'our faith tells us . . . that man has nothing good in himself'.[13] Earlier, in the *Praise of Folly* (1509), Erasmus launched a classic attack on *constantia sapientis*—admittedly through the somewhat unreliable mouth of Folly, but with a comic energy which suggests at least partial sympathy with her views. When Seneca forbids all emotion to his wise man, Folly declares,

> he leaveth man, no man, but rather a newfounde god without bodily sence, such as never was, nor never shall be. Yea, to speake plainlier, he dooeth naught els than fourme a stone image of a man, without fealyng, or any maner inclinacion perteinyng to a man in deede. . . . For whiche of you woulde not lothe, and blisse you from the company of suche maner a man, *as were mortified, and benummed in all those sensis and understandynges, that naturally other men are ledde by? that had no affections reignyng in him? nor woulde no more bee sterred with love, or*

[11] Haydn, *Counter-Renaissance*, 53–4 (53); Palmer, *Seneca's 'De Remediis'*, 2, 17–18.

[12] Everyman's Library (London, 1907), 3. 30.

[13] Quoted in Margaret Mann Phillips, 'Erasmus and the Classics', in T. A. Dorey (ed.), *Erasmus* (London, 1970), 15–16; see also Ross, 'Seneca's Philosophical Influence', 143–5; Hugo, 'Spiritual and Intellectual Background', 58–9*.

compassion, than if he were a flint stone? . . . [W]ho woulde not sooner preferre any one chosen evin amonges the thickest of the people? who beyng a foole, could aptly either governe, or obey fooles, please the myndes of suche as be lyke unto hym, whiche is the moste parte, be treatable to his wyfe, gladly seen of his friendes, mearie in companie, and lastly woulde thinke nothyng unbecomyng hym, that other men use commenly to dooe. But I wene, ye be werie now of this theyr wyseman, as I, for my part, was a good whyle agoe.[14]

Erasmus's divided attitude to Seneca is echoed on the Protestant side by Calvin, who in his youth admired Seneca sufficiently to publish a commentary on *De clementia* (1532) which nevertheless criticizes Seneca's views on pity and glory.[15] In the *Institutio Christiana* (1559) he declares that 'patiently to bear the cross is not to be utterly stupefied and to be deprived of all feeling of pain', like the Stoic *sapiens*, 'one who, having cast off all human qualities, was affected equally by adversity and prosperity . . . nay, who like a stone was not affected at all'. He goes on:

Now, among the Christians there are also new Stoics, who count it depraved not only to groan and weep but also to be sad and care ridden. . . . Yet we have nothing to do with this iron philosophy which our Lord and Master has condemned not only by his word but also by his example.

. . . I decided to say this in order to recall godly minds from despair, lest, because they cannot cast off the natural feeling of sorrow, they forthwith renounce the pursuit of patience. This must necessarily happen to those who make patience into insensibility, and a valiant and constant man into a stock.[16]

Both Erasmus and Calvin take over the Senecan image of the *sapiens* as stone or iron—the Stoic as stock, to use the traditional pun—and turn it against him as an emblem of inhumanity or subhumanity. Calvin's distancing of himself from Seneca is particularly interesting, since Calvinism has often been likened to Stoicism on the score of pitilessness.

The 'new Stoics' criticized by Calvin in 1559 only rose into real

[14] *The Praise of Folie*, tr. Chaloner, 39–40. Anson's discussion of this passage (13–14) does not note that the images Erasmus is playing with are themselves Stoic.

[15] Calvin, *Commentary*, on 1. 3, 2. 4, 2. 5.

[16] *Institutes of the Christian Religion*, ed. John T. McNeill, tr. Ford Lewis Battles (2 vols., London, 1961), i. 709–10 (3. 8. 9–10). I owe this reference to Zanta, *Renaissance du Stoïcisme*, 68.

prominence from the 1570s onwards, with the rise of what has become known as the Neostoic movement. The main figures of the movement were Michel de Montaigne (in his early essays, written in the mid-1570s, published 1580), Justus Lipsius (*De constantia*, 1584; *Manuductio ad Stoicam philosophiam*, 1604), Guillaume du Vair (*La Philosophie morale des stoiques*, 1585; *De la constance*, 1604), and Pierre Charron (*De la sagesse*, 1601). These works began to appear in English in the 1590s and 1600s (Lipsius' *Two Bookes of Constancie* in 1595, Du Vair's *Moral Philosophie of the Stoicks* in 1598, Montaigne's *Essayes* in 1603), and were followed by English works in the same vein, such as Joseph Hall's *Heaven upon Earth; or, Of true Peace and Tranquillitie of Minde* (1606), and Sir William Cornwallis's *Essayes* (1600–1, revised and expanded 1606 and 1610).

The intellectual origins of the new movement are obscure and debated; it has been variously linked with humanism, with Protestantism, and with the growing rationalist tradition which led to the Enlightenment.[17] The most obvious explanation, however, is political. As ancient Stoicism originated in the disorder of the Hellenistic world, so Neostoicism arose as a response to the warfare, social disorder, and natural disasters afflicting France and the Low Countries in the last decades of the sixteenth century, and found a muted echo in the *fin de siècle* insecurities of late Elizabethan England. This is the explanation given, for example, by Montaigne:

> True-perfect liberty, is, for one to be able to doe and work all things upon himselfe. *Potentissimus est qui se habet in potestate* (SEN. *Ep.* ix). *Hee is of most power, that keepes himselfe in his owne power.* In ordinary and peacefull times, a man prepares himselfe for common and moderate accidents: but in this confusion, wherein we have beene these thirty yeeres, every French man, be it in generall or in particular, doth hourely see himselfe upon the point of his fortunes overthrow and downefall. By so much more ought each one have his courage stored, and his minde fraughted, with more strong and vigorous provisions. (3. 12, pp. 300–1)

[17] Levi (*French Moralists*) stresses continuity with earlier humanist and 'Alexandrian' traditions; Kirk (introd. to Lipsius) stresses connections with Protestantism (though, as Hoopes points out (*Right Reason*, 135), several leading Neostoics were Catholic); Zanta's pioneering study (*Renaissance du Stoïcisme*) placed Neostoicism in the rationalist tradition of *la morale indépendente*.

With humanist practicality, Neostoics like Montaigne, Lipsius, and Du Vair set out to provide such 'strong and vigorous provisions' for those suffering in 'public evils'.

What, then, was new in the Neostoic movement? Some historians, like Anthony Levi, stress continuity with earlier humanist traditions, seeing a shift in emphasis rather than substance: 'a more frequent and more general recourse to the moral maxims and principles of the stoics, a more systematic attempt to adapt them to orthodox Christian sentiment'.[18] But the new emphases are significant. The Neostoics were interested in reviving Stoicism as a school of thought in its own right, rather than quarrying it in search of materials for the humanist synthesis; Lipsius in particular returned to the fragments of the Greek Stoics in an attempt to reconstruct the full range of ancient Stoic thought (physics, logic, and epistemology as well as ethics). Most importantly, the Neostoics made a determined bid to reconcile Stoicism with Christianity, and to defend doctrines, such as the extirpation of the passions and the ideal of the *sapiens*, which the Augustinian tradition had regarded as indefensibly unchristian.

The most obvious feature of the new movement is its stress on Seneca rather than Cicero. Ralph Graham Palmer sums up the change with reference to England:

> Sixteenth-century Englishmen had loved Cicero for his humanity, his broad view, his participation in great events, his normality, his conception of duties. Englishmen of the early seventeenth century, on the other hand, were attracted by a moralist who possessed a finely-developed critical sense, who stood serene and aloof, who depended on himself against outer circumstance.[19]

The philosophical shift goes along with a change in literary fashions: a preference for 'Senecan' styles of writing and argument (abrupt, pointed, paradoxical, deliberately inelegant) over the Ciceronianism of the earlier humanists. In the hands of Montaigne, Lipsius, and the English Neostoics, the new style reflects a shift from the public, oratorical stance of the humanists to a way of writing which can mirror individual personality and experience.[20]

[18] Levi, *French Moralists*, 54.

[19] Palmer, *Seneca's 'De Remediis'*, 24–5.

[20] The Senecan style is discussed in Morris W. Croll's classic essays of 1914–29, collected in his *Style, Rhetoric, and Rhythm*, ed. J. Max Patrick *et al.* (Princeton, 1966), esp. 110–25 on its philosophical implications.

The result of this change of allegiance from Cicero to Seneca is a new stress on the harsher and more individualistic doctrines of Stoicism, on the endurance of suffering and death, and on the heroic virtue of the *sapiens*. In particular there is a new stress on constancy as—to cite the English title of Du Vair's work on the subject—*The True Way to Vertue and Happinesse*.[21] Neostoic constancy clearly derives from Seneca's *constantia sapientis*; it is also opposed, even more starkly than in the classical Stoics, to the corrupting force of opinion. In the following sections I shall look in more detail at the ways in which 'constancy' and 'opinion' are defined in some representative Neostoic texts.

To be immovable: Neostoic constancy

The nature and the appeal of Neostoic constancy are best summed up in Lipsius' *De constantia*, a work which was translated into every major European language and went through eighty editions over three centuries.[22] Justus Lipsius (1547–1606), a Belgian, was one of the leading scholars of his age, editor of Tacitus and Seneca (his 1604 edition 'was the chief instrument of the extraordinary diffusion of Seneca's influence throughout the seventeenth century'), author of treatises on politics, Stoicism, and Stoic physics, and (in Léontine Zanta's words) 'le fondateur du néo-stoïcisme'.[23] The discrepancy between Lipsius' theory and practice (as he tried to evade political unrest by continual travel and several politic changes of religion) was not lost on his contemporaries: Joseph Hall satirically attributed to the natives of 'Fooliana the Fickle' a coin bearing the inscription 'CONST[antia] LIPS[ii]' and the image of a chameleon. But those most drawn to Stoicism are not necessarily constant by nature.[24]

[21] Levi (*French Moralists*, 55) notes the 'vogue', towards the end of the sixteenth century, for discourses on constancy; he cites the works of Lipsius and Du Vair, and an anonymous treatise *De la constance requise aux afflictions des misères de ce temps* (Paris, 1589).

[22] On the popularity of *De constantia* see Kirk, introd. to Lipsius, 9, 34; Croll, *Style, Rhetoric, and Rhythm*, 176.

[23] Croll, *Style, Rhetoric, and Rhythm*, 173; Zanta, *Renaissance du Stoïcisme*, 164.

[24] On Lipsius' life and work, see Croll, *Style, Rhetoric, and Rhythm*, esp. 168–77; Kirk, introd. to Lipsius, 3–12, 33–56; Levi, *French Moralists*, 63–73; Jason Lewis Saunders, *Justus Lipsius: The Philosophy of Renaissance Stoicism* (New York, 1955); Zanta, *Renaissance du Stoïcisme*, 151–240. Hall's gibe is quoted by Kirk, 12.

De constantia is a dialogue between the young Lipsius, who wants to flee his war-torn country to escape its miseries, and his older friend Langius, who warns him that he is lost in 'the smoake of OPINIONS' (p. 73). You cannot run away from suffering, for its source is within the mind.

Would you faine change countries? nay rather change your owne mind wrongfully subjected to affections, and withdrawne from the naturall obedience to his lawfull Ladie, I mean REASON. . . . Above all things it behooveth thee to be CONSTANT: For by fighting many man hath gotten the victory, but none by flying. (pp. 77–8)

From the start, thus, Lipsius reminds us of the root meaning of 'constancy': standing firm. Constancy is defined as '*a right and immoveable strength of the minde, neither lifted up, nor pressed down with externall or casuall accidentes*'. It arises out of patience ('*voluntarie sufferance without grudging*'), which, 'being regulated by the rule of *Right Reason*, is the verie roote whereuppon is setled the high and mighty bodie of that fair oake CONSTANCIE' (p. 79).

Also from the first Lipsius links the struggle for constancy with the fundamental opposition between 'REASON' and 'OPINIONS'. Right Reason ('*A true sense and judgement of thinges humane and divine*') and Opinion ('*A false and frivolous conjecture of those thinges*') are for Lipsius mighty opposites, linked to the Platonic dichotomy of soul and body, the heavenly and earthly part of man. Soul and body are joined in 'jarring concord', perpetually fighting for mastery, from which conflict arise all the disturbances of the human mind; and in this conflict 'The captains are, REASON and OPINION' (pp. 79–80).[25]

Reason, 'the perfection of the soule', derives from the divine fire of God, and its sparks in man naturally rise up towards heaven. It is constant in virtue, 'resolute and immoveable in a good purpose, not variable in judgment, ever shunning or seeking one and the selfe same thing' (p. 81). Opinion, on the other hand, derives from 'the filth of the bodie and contagion of the senses' (p. 81), which gradually corrupt the soul's original goodness. Tending always downward to its origin in the earth, it is

vaine, uncertaine, deceitfull, evill in counsell, evill in judgement. It depriveth the mind of Constancie and veritie. To day it desireth a thing, to morrow

[25] As Saunders (*Justus Lipsius*, p. xv) and Levi (*French Moralists*, 67) point out, the idea that matter is evil is Neoplatonic rather than Stoic.

it defieth the same. It hath no respect to sound judgment, but to please the bodie, and content the senses. (p. 83)

To be in bondage to opinion is to be like Coriolanus' plebeians, whose 'affections are | A sick man's appetite':

> With every minute you do change a mind,
> And call him noble that was now your hate,
> Him vile that was your garland.
>
> (I. I. 175–6, 180–2)[26]

To live a virtuous and happy life you must cast out opinion, or else be in the condition of an unballasted ship, 'continuallie floting on the waves of doubtfulnes, without any certain resolution, murmuring, troublesome, injurious to God & men' (p. 83).

What precisely Lipsius means by 'opinion' is a question I shall return to in the next section; but what does emerge powerfully from these passages is the contrast between stability and change. It is the changeableness of opinion that makes it the arch-enemy of constancy, the prime virtue. To be constant is to be stable in convictions, unmoved by emotion, '*neither lifted up nor pressed down*' by external events, and, hence, steadfast and immovable in adversity. Langius urges young Lipsius to drink from the cup of constancy,

> whereof when thou hast once taken a taste, being firmelie setled against all casualties, bearing thy selfe upright in all misfortunes, neither puffed up nor pressed downe with either fortune, thou maist challenge to thy selfe that great title, the neerest that man can have to God, *To be immooveable*. (p. 83)

God (as Lipsius later says) is 'stayed, resolute and immutable, alwaies one, and like himselfe, not wavering or varying in those thinges which once he willed and foresawe. For, *The eternall God never changeth his minde*, saith *Homer*' (p. 112). In this sense, as well as in the Senecan sense of being tranquil and unperturbed by earthly things, Lipsius' constant man is like God. The passage reproduces exactly, without concessions to Augustinian Christianity, the tone of Seneca's *De constantia sapientis*, and makes it easy

[26] Peter Ure, 'A Note on "Opinion" in Daniel, Greville, and Chapman', in his *Elizabethan and Jacobean Drama*, ed. J. C. Maxwell (Liverpool, 1974), 209–20, notes this similarity (218–19).

to see the tradition on which Shakespeare was drawing when he made Caesar boast of being 'constant as the Northern Star'.

The power of constancy is defined in a slightly different way in the *De la constance* of Guillaume du Vair (1556–1621), French politician, diplomat, bishop of Marseille, and translator of Epictetus.[27] Du Vair's dialogue (clearly influenced by Lipsius', at times to the extent of plagiarism)[28] is likewise set at a time of political turmoil (the seige of Paris in 1590), and likewise presents its author as an unhappy vacillator argued by wiser friends into recognizing the necessity of 'constancy in public evils'. Du Vair represents constancy in a memorably paradoxical image, of a soldier who was pierced by so many arrows that they held his corpse standing stiffly upright, and terrified the enemy into flight in the face of his apparent invulnerability. Constancy converts defeat into victory:

> The afflictions that are borne constantly, and with the counterpoyse of reason, doe maintayne us straight and strong: and whereas without them, we should bow too much to the earth, they set us up againe, and lift us to heaven. For wee have nothing that giveth us so sure a testimonie of the immortalitie of our soules, and a glance more evidently of the hope of eternall life, then the courage that is infused into us by constancie; which exhorting us to brave and generous actions, and unto patience, seemeth forthwith to propose unto us the reward, and give us a secret feeling of the place, where we ought to expect it. Which is not in this wretched and mortall world ... But above in heaven in a permanent Cittie ... (*True Way*, pp. 110–11)

The association here of Stoic constancy with the Christian heaven is taken up in the concluding discussion of the immortality of the soul. Du Vair, like Lipsius, uses the image of the soul as a divine fire (p. 149) whose sparks aspire to rise upwards. Man strives to emulate the qualities of God, and so

> unite and conforme himselfe as much as hee can, to that eldest incomprehensible Divine Essence. Which caused the Auncient *Zoroaster* to crie out in amazement,
>
> *O mortall man, thy boldnesse is extreame.*

[27] On Du Vair's life and thought see Kirk, introd. to *The Moral Philosophie*, 7–14, 25–37; Levi, *French Moralists*, 74–95; Zanta, *Renaissance du Stoïcisme*, 241–72.

[28] The second half of Book 2 follows Lipsius' discussion of providence and destiny (2. 8–17) almost word for word.

As beeing not able to comprehend that in this low and mortall World, amongst Filth and Dust; there could be found so strong a nature, that should rayse her selfe above the Heavens, and by the knowledge of so many things, and imitation of divine actions, should almost Deifie her selfe in this life. (p. 156)

Audaciously, Du Vair fuses Christian salvation with the Senecan ideal of self-perfection through Stoic virtue. Du Vair's is more clearly a Christian Stoicism than Lipsius';[29] for both, nevertheless, 'constancy' is not just patient submission to external evils, but a supreme virtue by which the human mind can imitate the perfection of God, become superior to all earthly things, and 'almost Deifie her selfe in this life'.

Why constancy, though? Why should this particular quality be chosen by Lipsius and Du Vair as the quintessential virtue? The imaginative appeal of constancy becomes clearer in a powerful passage in *De constantia*, where Langius is arguing that political upheaval is natural and necessary and therefore should not cause us grief. Pointing out that 'it is a naturall propertie to all things created, to fall into mutabilitie and alteration' (p. 106), he launches into a tremendous rhetorical set-piece on the subject of universal mutability. Novas, tides and floods, earthquakes, the rise and fall of islands, all show that nothing in the natural world is permanent, for God 'would have nothing firm and stable but himself alone' (p. 106). In the human world, too, cities and empires continually rise and fall; even Rome, '(falsly tearmed everlasting) where is she? Overwhelmed, pulled downe, burned, over-flowed: Shee is perished with more than one kinde of destruction' (p. 109). Langius rises to an apostrophe to the necessity which governs these changes:

O the law of NECESSITY, woonderfull, and not to be comprehended: All things run into this fatall whirlepoole of ebbing and flowing: And some things in this world are long lasting, but not everlasting. . . . [B]eholde the alterations of all humaine affares: and the swelling and swaging of them as of the sea. Arise thou: fal thou: rule thou: obey thou: hide thou thy head: lift thou up thine and let this wheel of changeable things run round, so long as this round world remayneth. (pp. 110–11)

[29] As Monsarrat puts it, 'Whereas Lipsius gives the impression of introducing Christian elements into a basically Stoic vision of the world the process is reversed with Du Vair' (*Light from the Porch*, 65).

Young Lipsius weeps, overcome by a sense of the vanity of human life: 'What is it to be some bodie? what is it to be no bodie? Man is a shadowe and a dreame.' This is not, however, the moral Langius intends:

> But thou young man doe not onely contemplate on these things; but contemne them. Imprint CONSTANCIE in thy mind amid this casuall and inconstant variablenesse of all things. (p. 111)

The immediate qualification that this inconstancy is only 'in respect of our understanding and judgment: for that if thou looke unto God and his providence, all things succeed in a steddy and immoveable order' (p. 111) does not negate the effect of the preceding pages. More clearly perhaps than any classical Stoic, Lipsius conveys the need for constancy in a world of continual change where nothing is stable but the rocklike strength of the human mind. The apocalyptic imagery of the passage and its dreamlike sense of universal dissolution are reminiscent of *Antony and Cleopatra*, especially the passage in which Antony, facing death, feels his identity dissolving like the clouds, like 'a shadowe and a dreame'. It is in such a world, where even 'everlasting' Rome proves unstable, that Shakespeare's Romans clutch at Stoic constancy for support.

'Opinion that is constant never'

For Lipsius, as we have seen, the arch-enemy of constancy is opinion. The idea is a traditional Stoic one; it derives from the fundamental principle that, in Epictetus' words, 'What disturbs men's minds is not events but their judgements on events'; ultimately it derives from Plato's dichotomy of knowledge and opinion. The Neostoics, however, place a peculiar emphasis on this doctrine, and turn Opinion into a personified abstraction which is made responsible for all human ills.[30]

What does Lipsius mean by 'opinion'? Since it is associated with the body rather than the soul, and its 'seat is the Sences', it seems primarily to mean judgements based on sense-perceptions and instinctive responses to physical pleasure and pain, rather than on the moral consciousness which we derive from right reason. Judging

[30] Ure's 'Opinion' is a very useful discussion of the concept.

on this basis, opinion endorses our instinctive but false beliefs, for instance, that pain is an evil or wealth desirable. Responding to external stimuli which are continually changing, it is changeable and unstable, and so 'depriveth the mind of Constancie and veritie'.

As well as an internal force in the mind, however, opinion is also the external power of public opinion—that is, the beliefs held by the 'foolish' majority of humanity who are guided by opinion rather than reason and whose judgements are therefore false and fickle. Thus, when Langius tells young Lipsius that he is befogged by the 'smoake of OPINIONS', he means both that he is being guided by instinct rather than reason, and that he is foolishly accepting popular fallacies.[31]

Du Vair's acount in *De la constance* makes clear the connection between opinion as a psychological process and public opinion. Our senses, the 'Sentinels of the Soule', perceive 'not the true and internall Nature, but onely the superficiall and externall forme of things'. Therefore

> they present their *Idea's* unto the Soule with favour, and even with a fore-judgement of their qualitie, according as they appeare severally pleasing and gracefull to them; and not as they are profitable and necessarie to the universall well-fare of man: and moreover, let in with the *Idea's*, the fond opinion of the Vulgar; from whence is framed, that inconsiderate Opinion we have of things, that they are good or bad, profitable or hurtfull, to be imitated, or to be shunned, which certainly is a dangerous guide, and rash mistresse to follow, and justly such as our *Belleau* hath set it forth.
>
> *Opinion that is constant never,*
> *That workes in vaine, and striveth ever:*
> *That buildes her selfe a firme assurance,*
> *Upon the sands of light inconstance.*
>
> (*True Way*, pp. 11–12)[32]

As a result, Opinion is enabled to seize the citadel of the mind and tyrannize over it.

This emphasis on 'the fond opinion of the vulgar' as a power which corrupts moral judgement leads the Neostoics to a preoccupation with problems of public opinion, reputation, and honour.

[31] Kirk's gloss of 'opinion' as 'prejudice' is thus, I think, an over-simplification.

[32] Quoting the French poet Rémy Belleau (1528–77). Compare the account in Middleton and Rowley's *The Changeling*, I. i. 72–6 (ed. N. W. Bawcutt, Revels, 2nd edn., London, 1961).

Du Vair's discussion of honour in *La Philosophie morale des stoiques* is closely based upon Cicero's in the *Tusculans* and *De officiis*, and shows the same moral ambiguities. True honour is 'the glittering & beaming brightnes of a good and vertuous action', which is reflected back to us from the reactions of others, 'and so by a reflexion in our selves, brings us a testimonie from others of the good opinion which they have of us' (*Morall Philosophie*, p. 78). As Cassius argues to Brutus, 'the eye sees not itself | But by reflection' (1. 2. 54–5). We can only see ourselves as we are reflected in the opinions of others; nevertheless, true honour is an accurate reflection and a genuine form of self-knowledge. The danger is that we will come to act for the *sake* of others' opinions; then

> wee doe but embrace a shadowe instead of a bodie, and fasten the rest of our minds upon the opinion of the vulgar sort of people, and so voluntarily renounce our liberties, to serve the humours and passions of other men ... and wee love not vertue, but as the common people doe love and favour it ... (pp. 78–9)

We must remember that virtue is its own reward, 'that the fruit of noble actions is to bee sayd to have performed them most nobly, and that vertue cannot finde out of her selfe any recompence sufficient to guerdon her selfe withall' (p. 81). Nevertheless, this formulation ('to bee *sayd*') returns us to the opinions of others.

The problems and paradoxes in both Cicero's and Du Vair's discussions are no doubt inherent in the concept of 'honour' itself. It is a straightforward concept only so long as it is agreed that moral standards are absolute, that right reason leads infallibly to correct moral judgements, and that the standards of one's own society are identical with these moral absolutes. As soon as these certainties are questioned, when it is suggested that moral judgements may be subjective and the standards of a society relative rather than absolute, then 'honour' becomes problematic. Such questions, of course, are inevitably raised when Shakespeare depicts ancient Rome in a historical perspective, as a society with its own moral code which is not identical with that of his audience.

The Neostoic preoccupation with opinion and honour is seen especially clearly in the *Essayes* of Sir William Cornwallis (?1579–1614). Cornwallis, a country gentleman's son, knighted on Essex's

Irish campaign and later a member of Parliament, wrote (and continually revised) his essays under the influence of Montaigne and Seneca. As a Neostoic moralist who is also a young Elizabethan gentleman, he recurs with particular intensity to the moral problems of honour and reputation.[33]

For Cornwallis, knowledge, which 'without admiration sees, and without sorrow feeles all the shapes and apparitions of the world' (Essay 36, 'Of Knowledge', p. 132), leads to happiness and godlike constancy:

> To know himselfe and the appurtenaunces to himself is the use of knowledge, and this knowledge unmaskes his eyes & shews him wonders in himselfe. He becomes in this like unto God . . . To know himselfe, is to know before hand what may happen to himselfe; so shall he in despight of the apparitions of the world stand unmoveable . . . (Essay 41, 'Of Sorrow', pp. 165–6)

On the other hand, opinion—'the straungest thing of the world, and yet it is nothing'—is 'the mother of Hipocrisie'; its followers 'often goe like vertue, speake like Vertue, doo like Vertue, but that is where Vertue is in fashion; for as it alters, they alter; they love not her, but Opinion.' They are absurd and pitiable, continually tormented by anxiety as they rely on something that is fickle and unreliable. Those who seek Stoic wisdom and tranquillity should 'not beleeve any thing rashly', and should, like Cato, prefer to be rather than be thought good (Essay 16, 'Of Opinion', pp. 54–5).

Cornwallis repeatedly stresses the moral and practical dangers of a concern for the opinion of others. A man who, instead of being guided by a true knowledge of his duty, is 'like a feather governed by the breath of men', is in an unstable position, since 'his foundation is the many headed multitude, a foundation both in respect of their number and nature uncertaine and, consequently, dangerous' (Essay 30, 'Of Popularitie', p. 102).[34] Such a man cannot be constant:

[33] On Cornwallis, see Allen's introd. to the *Essayes*, and Monsarrat, *Light from the Porch*, 109–17; on his debt to Montaigne, R. E. Bennett, 'Sir William Cornwallis's Use of Montaigne,' *PMLA* 48 (1933), 1080–9, and his own comments in Essay 12, p. 42. Shakespearian echoes in Cornwallis (e.g. the Shallow-like picture in Essay 24 of old men talking about their wild youth) are probably the result, as Allen suggests (p. xv), of Cornwallis's playgoing.

[34] Simmons, *Pagan World*, 41, cites this passage in connection with *Cor.* 2. 3. 15–24.

It is impossible that the motions of a minde led onely by fame should be otherwise then a trembling, unsetled thing . . . Inconstant they must bee, for they fetch all their determinations from the countenances of other men and upon them build either by scornefull lookes or the basest, basest dejections.

Among such fame-seekers Cornwallis singles out (in a passage which seems oddly to echo the opening scene of *The Merchant of Venice*) those who cultivate a reputation for gravity:

It is oddes, but they act their partes first by themselves and after get them by heart. They spitte all one way, and upon no occasion will alter the tune of their hemmes and coughes . . . Never laugh—let the occasion bee never so just; their eyes must never make a turne but gallop right forward. In a word, they are lockt up in formality, & barred is the chest, where they are inclosed with the eyes of men. Were there a more substantialnesse of Fame then there is, this were a deare earning of it to deny the course of nature in these indifferent thinges. (Essay 35, 'Of Trappes for Fame', p. 126)[35]

The behaviour here ridiculed could, of course, be interpreted as 'constant'. Cornwallis half-betrays a sense that constancy itself may become an act, directed towards being 'dressed in an opinion | Of wisdom' (*Merc.* I. I. 91–2) rather than towards wisdom itself. Unlike his mentor Montaigne, however, he does not develop the insight.

In their opposition of constancy and opinion (more explicit and emphatic than that of the classical Stoics), the Neostoics seem to anticipate the linking of these themes in Shakespeare's Roman plays. The plays too are concerned not only with Stoic constancy but, insistently, with problems of knowledge and judgement, the dangers of error, and the paradoxes of honour and fame. The Neostoics, however, draw a black-and-white contrast between the virtue of constancy and the evil of opinion. Shakespeare, perhaps drawing on Montaigne, suggests that the desire for constancy may lead not to liberation from opinion but to an increased dependence on it.

[35] See *Merc.* I. I. 50–6, 86–102, and compare especially 55–6 ('they'll not show their teeth in way of smile | Though Nestor swear the jest be laughable') with Cornwallis's 'Never laugh—let the occasion bee never so just'. If Cornwallis is echoing Shakespeare, it suggests intriguingly that his attention may have been caught by Stoic ideas in Gratiano's diatribe against 'this fool gudgeon, this opinion' (102), and perhaps in Antonio's image of life as a play.

Neostoicism and anti-Stoicism

It is not surprising that the vogue of Neostoicism led to an anti-Stoic reaction, which restated more forcefully the traditional Augustinian objections to Stoic pride and presumption, and emphasized the gap that must exist between Stoicism and Christianity. The anti-Stoic view was put violently in 1598 by John Marston, here at one extreme of his erratic love-hate relationship with Seneca:

> *I will*, cryes *Zeno*, ô presumption!
> *I can*, thou maist, dogged opinion
> Of thwarting Cynicks. To day vicious,
> List to their precepts, next day vertuous.
> Peace *Seneca*, thou belchest blasphemy.
> *To live from God, but to live happily*
> (I heare thee boast,) *from thy Phylosophie,*
> *And from thy selfe*, ô ravening lunacie![36]

James VI in *Basilikon Doron* (1599) advised his son to be constant in adversity, but 'not with that Stoick insensible stupiditie that proud inconstant LIPSIUS perswadeth in his Constantia'; revising four years later, he widened the attack to embrace 'many in our dayes' who, 'preassing to win honor, in imitating that auncient sect, by their inconstant behaviour in their own lives, belye their profession'. By the 1620s the very notion of constancy seems to have become suspect; so the preacher Thomas Gataker warned that 'this semblable tenor and constant carriage without any alteration at all either way, howsoever things goe' was 'an evill signe' of irreligion, and 'a sinne too-too rife in these times'.[37]

It is perhaps more surprising—though in keeping with the traditional ambivalence of Christianity towards Stoicism—to find a similarly critical attitude in a writer commonly categorized as 'Neostoic'. Joseph Hall (1574–1656), moralist, satirist, controversialist, later bishop of Exeter and of Norwich, was known as the

[36] *The Scourge of Villanie*, Satyre IV, lines 145–52, in *The Poems of John Marston*, ed. Arnold Davenport (Liverpool, 1961), 123.

[37] Both quotations are taken from Monsarrat (*Light from the Porch*, 106, 108), whose ch. 4 is a very useful discussion of anti-Stoicism. It appears (as Monsarrat hints, e.g. 107, 154) that 'Stoicism' and 'constancy' became code words for a certain fashionable pose of cynical and affectless 'cool'. See also Henry W. Sams, 'Anti-Stoicism in Seventeenth- and Early Eighteenth-Century England', *Studies in Philology*, 41 (1944), 65–78.

'English Seneca', the leading English exponent of Neostoicism and Senecan prose style.[38] His *Heaven upon Earth* sets out to teach the Senecan virtue of tranquillity, 'an even disposition of the heart' in which it is not elevated or depressed by good or bad fortune but like well-balanced scales 'hang[s] equall and unmoved betwixt both' (pp. 86–7).[39] Yet, while embracing Seneca's aim, Hall stresses the pagan philosopher's inability to achieve it. 'If *Seneca* could have had grace to his wit' he could have been wiser than any divine; as it was, he went as far as a man could possibly go by the light of nature.

> But this in truth is a taske, which Nature hath never without presumption undertaken, and never performed without much imperfection. . . . And if she could have truly effected it alone, I know not what employment in this life she should have left for grace to busie her selfe about, nor what privilege it should have been here below to be a Christian, since this that we seek is the noblest worke of the soule, and in which alone consists the only heaven of this world. . . . Not *Athens* must teach this lesson, but *Jerusalem*. (pp. 85–6)

Hall's position in this defensive preface is essentially Augustinian, but part of his argument strikes a more modern and sceptical note. Arguing that the Stoics' aims are noble but their methods are 'vaine', he declares that tranquillity cannot be found in 'a constant state of outward thinges' (not that Seneca ever claimed it could); nor can it be found in 'the naturall temper of the soule, so ordered by humane wisdome, as that it should not be affected with any casuall events', since the soul

> cannot ever by naturall power be held like to it selfe; but one while is cheerefull, stirring and ready to undertake; another while drousie, dull, comfortlesse, prone to rest, weary of it self, loathing his owne purposes, his owne resolutions. In both which since the wisest Philosophers have grounded all the rules of their Tranquillity, it is plaine that they saw it afarre off, as they did heaven it selfe with a desire and admiration, but knew not the way to it: whereupon alas, how slight and impotent are the remedies they prescribe for unquietnesse! (p. 88)

[38] On Hall, see Kirk's introd. to *Heaven upon Earth*, 19–65, and Monsarrat, *Light from the Porch*, 98–105, who argues that the nickname 'English Seneca' refers exclusively to Hall's prose style and not to his attitudes, which are Christian rather than Stoic.

[39] Compare Lipsius' definition of constancy; 'tranquillity' (derived from Seneca's *De tranquillitate animi*) is almost synonymous, but its connotations are less heroic and more everyday.

The idea that the human mind is too changeable ever to achieve constancy and 'be held like to it selfe' is for Hall an argument against the possibility of purely natural virtue: 'It must be, it can be none but a divine power, that can uphold the mind against the rage of main afflictions' (p. 90). Montaigne takes the same insight into 'the naturall temper of the soule' and develops it into an entire philosophy which questions whether it is either possible or desirable for human beings to '*bee immooveable*'.

Lipsius and the Neostoics, with their idealization of constancy and its capacity to make human beings divine, and their emphasis on the dangers of opinion as an enemy to constancy, provide a crucial background to Shakespeare's Roman plays: they set the issues that the plays deal with. It is Montaigne, however, in his deeply sceptical critique of constancy, who provides the most illuminating parallel with Shakespeare's treatment of those issues.

5
Montaigne and the Profitable but Absurd Desire

Michel de Montaigne (1533–92) began his *Essays* as a Neostoic, gradually distanced himself from the Stoic ideal, and ended by regarding it with a blend of admiration, repulsion, and ironic criticism. One of his running concerns is constancy and inconstancy; another is a sceptical analysis of reason, knowledge, and opinion. His relevance to the concerns of this book would be obvious even if we did not know, as we do, that Shakespeare knew and borrowed from the *Essays*, in John Florio's 1603 translation.[1]

The extent of Shakespeare's knowledge and borrowing is a long-debated question. Edward Capell first noted in 1781 that Gonzalo's account of his utopia in *The Tempest* (2. 1. 149–74) is based on a passage in Florio's version of Montaigne's essay 'Of the Caniballes' (1. 30, p. 220)—a parallel which has been almost universally accepted.[2] In the nineteenth century there were suggestions of a broader influence, and in 1897 John M. Robertson attempted to show that Montaigne was Shakespeare's sole intellectual mentor.[3] E. R. Hooker (1902) and G. C. Taylor (1925) extended the list of parallels, though with a more moderate view of their significance, Hooker seeing the *Essays* as 'a mere storehouse of material' from which Shakespeare could draw (for instance) Stoic sentiments on death to assign to his Romans. She also made the important suggestion that, since Shakespeare probably knew Florio (they shared Pembroke's patronage), he could have read Florio's translation in manuscript before 1603.[4] In 1942,

[1] On Montaigne texts and references, see the Bibliographical Note.

[2] An attempt to question it by Margaret T. Hodgen, 'Montaigne and Shakespeare Again,' *Huntingdon Library Quarterly*, 16 (1952–3), 23–42, was unconvincing.

[3] *Montaigne and Shakespeare* (2nd edn., London, 1909; first pub. 1897).

[4] Hooker: 'The Relation of Shakespeare to Montaigne', *PMLA* 17 (1902), 312–66 (quotation, 347; on Florio, 349–50). Taylor: *Shakspere's Debt to Montaigne* (New York, 1925).

however, Alice Harmon pointed out that most of the ideas shared by the two writers were commonplaces derived ultimately from Cicero, Seneca, and Plutarch, and to be found in any number of Renaissance anthologies and handbooks.[5] She thus raised fundamental questions about Montaigne's influence on Shakespeare (and indeed about the whole concept of 'influence' among Renaissance writers), which remain unresolved. Eleanor Prosser commented in 1965 on the 'interesting paradox' that '[a]lmost all critics accept Montaigne's influence on Shakespeare as established, yet very few regard the supporting evidence as conclusive'; of hundreds of proposed parallels only Capell's was generally felt to be proven.[6] Recent critics have produced further parallels but have noticeably shied away from a comprehensive discussion of the relationship.

My intention in this chapter is to focus not so much on Montaigne as a source of Stoic doctrines as on his more original critique of the ideal of Stoic constancy. His final view of that ideal, as 'a profitable desire; but likewise absurd' (2. 12, p. 325), seems to me close to that implied in Shakespeare's Roman plays—closer than those of either the Neostoics or the Augustinian anti-Stoic tradition. Of course, this may be a 'parallel' rather than an 'influence', showing only that Montaigne and Shakespeare responded in similar ways to their reading of Cicero, Seneca, and Plutarch.

[5] 'How Great was Shakespeare's Debt to Montaigne?', *PMLA* 57 (1942), 988–1008. George Coffin Taylor, 'Montaigne–Shakespeare and the Deadly Parallel', *PQ* 22 (1943), 330–7, is a reply.

[6] 'Shakespeare, Montaigne, and "the Rarer Action"', *ShakS* 1 (1965), 261–4 (261); Prosser's parallel (*Temp*. 5. 1. 25–30/*Essays*, 2. 11, p. 108) has also been generally accepted. On the early history of the debate, see Robertson, *Montaigne and Shakespeare*, 31–7; Hooker, 'Relation of Shakespeare to Montaigne', 313–14; Harmon, 'Shakespeare's Debt to Montaigne', 988–9. The only comprehensive recent discussion, Tetsuo Anzai's *Shakespeare and Montaigne Reconsidered*, Renaissance Monographs 12 (Tokyo, 1986), starts from the plausible premiss that 'Shakespeare responded in his basic interests to Montaigne's basic preoccupations' (4), but his attempt to show that Shakespeare's development paralleled Montaigne's, from Stoicism (*Hamlet*) through radical scepticism (*Lear*) to an 'ideal of Nature redeemed' (63) in the last plays, is less compelling. Two articles relevant to my concerns are Robert Ellrodt, 'Self-consciousness in Montaigne and Shakespeare', *ShS* 28 (1975), 37–50, who sees both writers' treatment of inconstancy and self-dramatization as signs of an interest in the psychology of 'self-consciousness', and Joan Lord Hall, '"To Play the Man Well and Duely": Role-playing in Montaigne and Jacobean Drama', *Comparative Literature Studies*, 22 (1985), 173–86, a wide-ranging discussion which emphasizes (as I do) Montaigne's suspicion of the histrionic, but characterizes Shakespeare by contrast as 'the one playwright who does consistently explore the positives of role-playing' (179) as a means of moral discovery and growth.

Nevertheless it seems plausible, given the evidence that Shakespeare read the *Essays*, that it was Montaigne who focused and shaped his interest in the theme of constancy.

Any discussion of the influence of Montaigne's thought is complicated by the difficulty of defining just what Montaigne thought. This is partly a result of the nature of the *Essays*, which were in a state of continual change over more than twenty years: from the first two Books written in the 1570s and published in 1580, through the major expansion of these essays and the addition of a third Book in 1588, to the further expansions which Montaigne made in the margins of his personal copy, posthumously published in 1595. As a rule Montaigne did not cut or change what he had written but simply added new passages, so that any essay, or even paragraph, may contain material from different dates expressing quite contradictory views. Montaigne's acceptance of this state of confusion and self-contradiction is characteristic. He was deeply influenced by the sceptical philosophy of Pyrrhonism, and had painted on the ceiling of his library the Pyrrhonistic maxim that 'to any reason an equal reason can be opposed'. R. A. Sayce, quoting this, adds

> it is impossible (or at least not easy) to make any statement about him without immediately stating the contrary, to such an extent is his thought . . . made up of antitheses, ambiguities, contradictions of every kind, to such an extent does it endeavour to grasp the full diversity of things.[7]

Inconsistency is part of the very fabric of Montaigne's thought, and for that reason any attempt to summarize it (including my own) is bound to oversimplify. This is true of the most influential account, that of Pierre Villey, who distinguished three periods: conventional Neostoicism, a sceptical 'crisis' in the mid-1570s, and finally a tolerant, quasi-Epicurean *philosophie de la nature*.[8] Subsequent scholars have with some justification criticized this account as overly schematic. Nevertheless, as Peter Burke says, 'it is difficult to disagree with Villey about the general direction of Montaigne's development,' and I shall use his three periods as

[7] *The Essays of Montaigne: A Critical Exploration* (London, 1972), 1.

[8] *Les Sources et l'évolution des Essais de Montaigne*, (2 vols. 1908; 2nd edn., Paris, 1933); developed in his commentaries in *EMM*.

a rough guide through the windings, backtrackings, and self-contradictions of Montaigne's changing attitude to constancy.[9]

The Stoic Montaigne

Montaigne began as an orthodox Neostoic, and it is impossible to isolate a point at which he ceased to be one.[10] Throughout his writings Seneca is the writer he quotes most often; and even after his death, eulogists called him 'Magnanime Stoïque' and praised his 'philosophie courageuse et presque stoique'.[11] His Stoicism is purest, however, in the early essays. Short, aphoristic sermons in the Senecan manner, often a mosaic of Senecan quotations, they show a Neostoic preoccupation with the need for (in the words I quoted in the previous chapter) 'strong and vigorous provisions' against the fear of death and ruin.

Death is the dominant motif. The early Montaigne subscribes wholeheartedly to the Stoic teleological fallacy.[12] In 'That to Philosophie [*sic*], Is to Learne how to Die' (1. 19)[13] he argues, quoting Cicero (*Tusc.* 1. 30), that the philosopher's life is a preparation for death. We cannot be happy if we fear death; to attempt to ignore it would be 'brutall stupiditie' (p. 76); rather we must continually meditate on it until we have overcome the fear of it. The essay is a tissue of Stoic quotations and themes which, as commentators have noted, often find echoes in Shakespeare's 'Stoic' passages on death: Cassius on suicide ('He who hath learned to die, hath unlearned to serve'); Caesar on the folly of fearing death ('what matter is it when it commeth, since it is unavoidable?'); Edgar on enduring our going hence even as our coming hither ('*Depart . . . out of this world, even as you came into it*'); Hamlet defying augury ('no man dies before his houre. The time you leave

[9] Sayce, *Essays of Montaigne*, 327–9; Donald M. Frame, *Montaigne: A Biography* (London, 1965), 147; Peter Burke, *Montaigne* (Oxford, 1981), 64–6 (65).

[10] On Montaigne as Neostoic, see Skinner, *Foundations*, ii. 275–84; on his connections with Lipsius and other Neostoics, see Frame, *Montaigne*, 86, 249, 303.

[11] Quoted in Sayce, *Essays of Montaigne*, 163. Montaigne's use of Seneca is documented in the index to *EMM*.

[12] See e.g. 2. 13, p. 331 (quoting Seneca, *Ep.* 77. 6); 1. 18, p. 72 (quoting *Ep.* 26. 6).

[13] 1. 20 in modern editions (Florio followed the 1595 French edition, which shifted 1. 14 to 1. 40 and renumbered the intervening essays: Sayce, *Essays of Montaigne*, 14).

behinde was no more yours, than that which was before your birth, and concerneth you no more').[14] Shakespeare may indeed have borrowed aphorisms such as these from Montaigne, though as Harmon pointed out it is hard to establish ownership in such commonplaces.

To overcome the fear of death and other supposed evils, the Stoic Montaigne relies on will, standing firm to 'oppose and bandy against' them (1. 40, p. 278), and reason, which teaches that they are not truly evils. The Stoic doctrine of moral knowledge is expounded in 1. 40, 'That the Taste of Goods or Evils Doth Greatly Depend on the Opinion We Have of Them,' and in 1. 50: 'Therefore let us take no more excuses from externall qualities of things. . . . Our good, and our evill hath no dependancy, but from our selves' (p. 343). Or in Hamlet's words, 'there is nothing either good or bad but thinking makes it so' (2. 2. 250–1). This is familiar Stoic teaching, but Montaigne seems to push it in the direction of complete relativism. The essence of the Stoic theory is that our false opinions blind us to clear moral truth; Cicero and Seneca would insist that virtue, at least, was good in itself. Montaigne, like Hamlet, omits the qualification: '*no* dependancy', '*nothing* either good or bad'. In this respect one can trace a direct line of development between Montaigne's Stoicism and his later scepticism.[15]

Montaigne's Stoic values are summed up, inevitably, in the term 'constancy'. In 'Of Constancie' (1. 12)—originally focused on the literal question of steadfastness versus tactical retreat in battle, but later extended to more metaphorical senses—he defines constancy in moderate terms as courageous endurance of the inevitable, and control (not eradication) of human emotions. This is the steadfast state of mind in which Montaigne wishes to face pain and death. He quotes Seneca on the importance of dying '*honestly,*

[14] 1. 19, p. 80 (*JC* 1. 3. 88–99); p. 86 (*JC* 2. 2. 32–7); p. 87 (*Lear* (F version) 5. 2. 9–11); p. 89 (*Ham.* 5. 2. 165–70). For opposing views of these parallels, see Hooker, 'Relation of Shakespeare to Montaigne', 317–21, and Harmon, 'Shakespeare's Debt to Montaigne', 999–1001. Hooker argues convincingly that the last-quoted passage explains and justifies the F reading of Hamlet's speech ('since no man has ought of what he leaves . . .').

[15] The close connection between Stoicism and scepticism in much Renaissance thought is emphasized by Levi. He indeed argues (e.g. *French Moralists*, 11, 56–7) that the two philosophies were virtually identified; but this blurs the crucial distinction between the Stoic and Neostoic view that we are blinded to clear truth by the 'smoake of OPINIONS', and the sceptical view that truth is unattainable.

wisely and constantly' (2. 13, p. 331, quoting *Ep.* 77. 6), and declares that 'my chiefest study is, I may well demeane my selfe at my last gaspe, that is to say, quietly, and constantly' (1. 18, p. 73).[16] Constancy also embraces consistency; Montaigne quotes Seneca's dictum that the essence of virtue is 'at all times to will, and not to will one same thing' (2. 1, p. 8, quoting *Ep.* 20. 5), and declares that to join constancy (consistency) to virtue is the 'last perfection' of the human mind (2. 2, p. 23). (We must return to these two passages, however, to see the ironic qualifications with which they are hedged in their context.)

The exemplar of constancy in both senses is Cato: 'a patterne, whom nature chose to shew how farre humane vertue may reach, and mans constancie attaine unto' (1. 36, p. 245), and a man whose life was 'an harmony of well according tunes . . . which cannot contradict it selfe' (2. 1, p. 9). In 'Of Crueltie' Montaigne eulogizes Cato's suicide, suggesting that he died not with stoical 'impassibilitie' but with 'a kinde of unspeakable joy' and that one might almost think that he welcomed defeat for the chance to perform such a glorious act, simply for the sake of 'the beautie of the thing it selfe in it selfe' (2. 11, pp. 111–12). The imaginative warmth of such a passage suggests that Montaigne's early Stoicism was not merely (in Villey's phrase) an 'affaire de mode', though Villey may be right in suggesting that its appeal was more emotional than intellectual. Montaigne was strongly attracted to the 'beauty' of the ideal of Stoic heroism.[17] Yet implicit in his praise of Cato's joyful plunge towards death is a hint of his developing reservations about that ideal.

A diverse and wavering subject

Even in the earliest essays, Montaigne's Stoicism is counterbalanced by a powerful sense of the inconstancy of the world and (especially) of human nature. This keynote is sounded at the

[16] In the 1588 edition Montaigne changed *seurement* ('constantly') to *sourdement* ('quietly'), marking a significant chance of outlook which Florio elides (*EMM* 80 n.).

[17] *Sources*, ii. 51–66 (61). Later critics rightly stress the continuing influence of Stoicism on Montaigne: e.g. Sayce, *Essays of Montaigne*, 328; Skinner, *Foundations*, ii. 276; C. A. Mayer, 'Stoïcisme et purification du concept chez Montaigne', *Studi Francesci*, 70–2 (1980), 487–93.

beginning, middle, and end of the original two-Book *Essays*.[18] The first essay, 'By Divers Meanes Men Come unto a Like End', declares

> Surely, man is a wonderfull, vaine, divers, and wavering subject: it is very hard to ground any directly-constant and uniforme judgement upon him. (1. 1, p. 19)

The theme is developed at length in 2. 1, 'Of the Inconstancie of Our Actions':

> *There is nothing I so hardly beleeve to be in man, as constancie, and nothing so easie to be found in him, as inconstancy.* (2. 1, p. 8)

> What we even now purposed, we alter by and by, and presently returne to our former biase: all is but changing, motion, and inconstancy. . . . We goe not, but we are carried: as things that flote, now gliding gently, now hulling violently; according as the water is, either stormy or calme. . . . We float and waver betweene divers opinions: we will nothing freely, nothing absolutely, nothing constantly. (p. 9)

> We are all framed of flaps and patches and of so shapelesse and diverse a contexture, that every peece and every moment playeth his part. And there is as much difference found betweene us and our selves, as there is betweene our selves and other. (p. 14)

And the last words of the last essay of Book 2 underline the point: '*Diversity is the most universall quality*' (2. 37, p. 523).

Montaigne repeatedly stresses the inconsistency and inexplicability of human behaviour, and criticizes those who seek to simplify it into a neat pattern. The theme of 1. 1 is that the same action can lead on different occasions to directly opposite results. Montaigne wryly notes the flaw in his own method: collecting historical examples in order to generalize about human behaviour, he finds that its most predictable quality is unpredictability. 'Of the Inconstancie of Our Actions' criticizes biographers who attempt to impose a 'constant and solid contexture' on their subjects: 'They chuse an universall ayre, and following that image, range and interpret all a mans actions; which if they cannot wrest sufficiently, they remit them into dissimulation' (2. 1, p. 8). Such over-tidy explanations ignore our inconsistency, swayed from moment to

[18] *EMM*, headnote to 1. 1; Sayce, *Essays of Montaigne*, 107. Villey (*Sources*, 7) believes 1. 1 is a later essay, placed first in order to stress the 'idée capitale' of inconstancy. Burke, *Montaigne*, ch. 8, has an excellent brief discussion of Montaigne's sense of change.

moment by the most trivial impulses, and the perversity which leads us to do good deeds from bad motives. Montaigne concludes that to pronounce upon human character requires a far more subtle science of psychology, which must be based upon self-knowledge:

It is no part of a well grounded judgement, simply to judge our selves by our exteriour actions: A man must thorowly sound himselfe, and dive into his heart, and there see by what wards or springs the motions stirre. (p. 15)

Montaigne develops the point in 'How We Weepe and Laugh at One Selfe-same Thing' (1. 37), where he criticizes historians who 'remit . . . into dissimulation' the grief of men at their enemies' deaths. We must recognize the complexity of human emotions: 'our mindes are often agitated by divers passions', and although one may be predominant, 'it is not with so full an advantage, but for the volubilitie and supplenesse of our minde, the weakest may by occasion reobtaine the place againe, and when their turne commeth, make a new charge' (p. 248). So we can weep and laugh almost simultaneously at the same thing, and it is quite possible 'to mourne for him dead, whom a man by no meanes would have alive againe' (p. 249). As Antony comments on the death of Fulvia,

What our contempts doth often hurl from us
We wish it ours again. The present pleasure,
By revolution low'ring, does become
The opposite of itself. She's good being gone . . .

(*Ant.* 1. 2. 117–20)

Here and elsewhere in *Antony and Cleopatra* Shakespeare seems to be reading Plutarch through Montaigne's eyes, with a sense of the 'volubilitie and supplenesse' of human emotions which is taken from Montaigne.[19]

Of course, a sense of human inconstancy is not incompatible with Stoicism. Such a sense is one of the driving motives of the classical Stoics and the Neostoics. For them, it leads to a renewed insistence on the need for constancy. Montaigne, however, goes fur-

[19] Antony's response to Fulvia's death is not in Plutarch (the same motif appears at 3. 2. 54–60 and 5. 1. 26–30). On Montaigne's love for Plutarch, especially for his psychological insight, see esp. 2. 10, pp. 102–3; and, for a comparison with Shakespeare, Anzai, *Shakespeare and Montaigne*, ch. 1.

ther. For him, inconstancy seems to be so ingrained in human nature that Stoic constancy may be impossible, and even undesirable.

In 'Of the Inconstancie of Our Actions' Montaigne sets his vision of universal flux, of human beings floating back and forth 'lackeying the varying tide' (*Ant.* 1. 4. 46), against the Stoic ideal of constancy epitomized in Cato. Montaigne approves the ideal, yet stresses how ambitious it is and how rarely achieved:

View all antiquity over, and you shall finde it a hard matter, to chuse out a dozen of men, that have directed their life unto one certaine, setled, and assured course; which is the surest drift of wisdome. For, to comprehend all in one word, saith an ancient Writer [Seneca, *Ep.* 20. 5], and to embrace all the rules of our life into one, it is at all times to will, and not to will one same thing. (2. 1, p. 8)

To be genuine, such constancy must show itself under all circumstances and in every action, great or small, and therefore 'to judge a man, we must a long time follow, and very curiously marke his steps; whether constancie doe wholy subsist and continue upon her owne foundation in him' (p. 13). It depends upon an ability to see one's life steadily and see it whole.

It is impossible for him to dispose of his particular actions, that hath not in grose directed his life unto one certaine end. It is impossible for him to range all peeces in order, that hath not a plot or forme of the totall frame in his head.

But, Montaigne immediately adds,

No man makes any certaine designe of his life, and we deliberate of it but by parcels. (pp. 13–14)

This could be taken merely as a complaint that we fail to live up to the ideal of constancy. In context, however, it looks more like a fundamental objection to the ideal: that it depends upon a perfect rationality and a perfectly integrated view of life which, given the fragmented nature of our existence and the fact that we are all 'framed of flaps and patches', is inherently impossible. Montaigne sums up, somewhat equivocally, by quoting Seneca (*Ep.* 120. 22): '*Esteeme it a great matter, to play but one man*' (p. 14). It is indeed 'a great matter', but is it too great to be achieved?

In the next essay, 'Of Drunkennesse' (2. 2)—another early essay, also written around 1572—Montaigne, improvising around the theme of drunkenness, directs two even more searching criticisms at the Stoic ideal. The first arises out of the 'old and pleasant question, whether a wisemans mind were like to yeeld unto the force of wine'. Montaigne mocks this question for the 'vanity' implied in its confidence in the power of the mind.

Of a thousand there is not one perfectly righteous and setled but one instant of her life, and question might be made, whether according to her naturall condition she might at any time be so. But to joyne constancie unto it [is] her last perfection: I meane if no thing should shocke her: which a thousand accidents may doe. (2. 2, p. 23)[20]

Our vauntedly immovable minds are enclosed in flesh and at the mercy of a thousand physical accidents: drink, drugs, humours, reflexes—'Nature having purposed to reserve these light markes of her aucthoritie unto herselfe, inexpugnable unto our reason, and to the Stoicke vertue: to teach him his mortalitie, and our insipiditie' (p. 23). This Augustinian insistence on the vulnerability of the mind to the body anticipates much of Montaigne's later criticism of Stoicism (as well as much of the emphasis of *Julius Caesar*).

Here, however, it is only a preparation for a more startling criticism: that the virtue of the Stoic hero is in itself a kind of drunkenness or madness. Moral doctrines which attempt to exempt the wise man entirely from human weakness or emotion are unnatural and dangerous, and based upon self-deception. When we see (for example) Lucius Brutus putting his sons to death, we must wonder, with Plutarch, if he was not in fact 'moved by some other passion', pride, anger, or cruelty; '*All actions beyond the ordinarie limits, are subject to some sinister interpretation*' (p. 24). Or when we read of Stoic martyrs boasting of their indifference to pain upon the rack or in the flames, 'Verely wee must needs confesse there is some alteration, and some furie (how holy soever) in those mindes' (p. 25). Such 'constancy' must arise from a kind of madness, akin to poetic or prophetic fury.

Our minde cannot out of her place [i.e. while remaining in her normal place] attaine so high. She must quit it and raise her selfe aloft, and taking the bridle in her teeth, carry and transport her man so farre, that afterward hee wonder at himselfe, and rest amazed at his actions. (p. 25)

[20] Taylor, *Shakspere's Debt to Montaigne*, notes an echo of this in Hamlet's 'the *thousand* natural *shocks* | That flesh is heir to' (3. 1. 64–5); 'flesh' perhaps sharpens the parallel, since Montaigne's point is the power of the 'flesh' over the mind.

And Aristotle was right

to call any starting or extraordinarie conceit (how commendable soever) and which exceedeth our judgement and discourse, folly. For somuch as *wisdome, is an orderly and regular managing of the minde, and which she addresseth with measure, and conducteth with proportion*... (p. 26)

Montaigne suggests a startling paradox: Stoic wisdom is folly. True wisdom consists in order, balance, and regularity, whereas the inordinate virtue of the Stoic hero can only be shown in bursts and transports of heroic insanity. To be wholly unaffected by external things, wholly detached from the body, is not a normal state but a kind of madness. We may achieve it for brief heroic moments, but we cannot be like that *constantly*. Stoic constancy, in other words, cannot be constantly (consistently) practised.[21]

Montaigne is, I believe, the first writer in the tradition to suggest that there is an inherent contradiction in the concept of 'constancy': the two senses, heroic steadfastness and consistency, are not merely distinguishable but in fact incompatible.

The 'Apologie' and the repudiation of Stoicism

Montaigne's most comprehensive attack on Stoicism comes in 'An Apologie of *Raymond Sebond*' (2. 12, written *c.*1573–9), the longest by far of the essays (two hundred pages in the Everyman edition) and the most belligerently sceptical. Villey no doubt exaggerated in claiming that the 'Apologie' marks a 'sceptical crisis', a sudden and traumatic loss of faith; as I have argued, scepticism is part of Montaigne's thought from the first, even tinging his brand of Stoicism.[22] Nevertheless the essay marks a decisive rejection of the Stoic faith in reason, constancy, and human perfectibility.

The immediate source of Montaigne's new scepticism was Sextus Empiricus' handbook of Pyrrhonism, a sceptical philosophy of the first century AD which traces its origins to the semi-legendary

[21] M. A. Screech, *Montaigne and Melancholy: The Wisdom of the 'Essays'* (London, 1983), 153–4, has an interesting discussion of this passage from a different point of view, in relation to 'ecstasy' and heroic madness.

[22] Villey, *Sources*, ii. 143–223; Richard H. Popkin, *The History of Scepticism from Erasmus to Spinoza* (Berkeley, 1979), 43. For criticism of Villey's view, see Sayce, *Essays of Montaigne*, 328; Frame, *Montaigne*, 175; Burke, *Montaigne*, 65.

doubter Pyrrho.[23] Its central tenet is that we can have no knowledge beyond appearances (for instance, the fact that this page appears white to me). Pyrrhonians thus reject all philosophies claiming certain knowledge of truth: the Platonic-Stoic distinction between knowledge and opinion is illusory, since all is opinion. They also reject more moderate brands of scepticism, such as Cicero's Academic theory of probability: since everything is uncertain, any proposition is as probable as any other, and 'to any reason an equal reason can be opposed'. The Pyrrhonian ideal is complete suspension of judgement, refusing to affirm or deny any proposition, while following for practical purposes the common assumptions and customs of one's own society. Montaigne, as a Christian sceptic or fideist, qualifies the pagan doctrine by allowing just one source of absolute truth: divine revelation. Paradoxically, the only things we can believe with certainty are those for which there is no rational evidence.[24]

Montaigne wrote the 'Apologie' in response to a request by a Catholic patroness to defend the *Natural Theology* of the twelfth-century theologian Raymond Sebond against its Protestant critics. The result was a back-handed defence which, as a French critic has remarked, supports Sebond as the rope supports the hanged man.[25] Montaigne defends Sebond's rationalistic arguments for Christianity against their rationalistic critics by a thorough-going assault on human reason, demonstrating its impotence not only to refute Sebond but to know or prove anything whatsoever. He describes the purpose of his argument as

> to crush, and trample this humane pride and fiercenesse under foot, to make them feele the emptinesse, vacuitie, and no worth of man: and violently to pull out of their hands, the silly weapons of their reason; to make them stoope, and bite and snarle at the ground, under the authority and reverence of Gods Majesty. (2. 12, p. 137)

'They' are ostensibly Sebond's Protestant critics; but in the course of the argument it becomes clear that to a large extent, as Donald

[23] My account of Pyrrhonism is largely based on the lucid summary by Popkin, *Scepticism*, Preface, pp. xiii–xvi, and on Montaigne's own account in 2. 12, pp. 203–8; other sources include Long, *Hellenistic Philosophy*, 75–88; Bevan, *Stoics and Sceptics*, lecture 4; *OCD*, s.v. 'Pyrrhon', 'Scepticism'.

[24] 2. 12, p. 200, 277. I assume, like most modern critics, that Montaigne's fideism is genuine rather than an ironic cover for religious scepticism: see Popkin, *Scepticism*, 54–5 and notes; Sayce, *Essays of Montaigne*, ch. 9; Burke, *Montaigne*, ch. 4.

[25] Frame, *Montaigne*, 170–2 (quoting Louis Cons, 170).

Frame argues, the real target of Montaigne's attack is the Stoics and their faith in human perfectibility through reason.

The last quarter of the essay is dedicated to Montaigne's most radical assertion, that we cannot possibly know reality; and the proof is entirely based on the inconstancy of our perceptions and beliefs.[26] Montaigne argues that human opinions, like human character, are both 'divers' and 'wavering'. The diversity of opinions, the fact that 'no proposition is seene, which is not controversied and debated amongst us' shows 'that our judgment doth not absolutly and clearly seize on that which it seizeth' (p. 276) as Stoic epistemology would have it. Nor do we even agree with ourselves: our opinions change from moment to moment, swayed by 'the bodies motions and alterations' (pp. 277–8) and by the violent gusts of our emotions (p. 281). Our senses, too, are wholly unreliable (pp. 306–22).

The accepted opinions of mankind—laws, customs, and creeds—are similarly diverse and changeable, and so betray their arbitrary nature. '*Truth ought to have a like and universall visage throughout the world*' (p. 296), but there is nothing universal in human beliefs except diversity. There is no custom so silly or so horrible that some society has not prescribed it as a moral or legal duty.

> It is credible that there be naturall lawes; as may be seene in other creatures, but in us they are lost: this goodly humane reason engrafting it selfe among all men, to sway and command, confounding and topsi-turving the visage of all things, according to her inconstant vanitie and vaine inconstancy. (p. 298)

Casually Montaigne kicks aside the Stoic distinction between reason and opinion: 'this goodly humane reason' (as he sarcastically terms it) is no more than our old friend, vain and inconstant opinion.

Montaigne sums up what may be called his 'uncertainty principle':

> In few, *there is no constant existence, neither of our being, nor of the objects*. And we, and our judgement, and all mortall things else do uncessantly rowle, turne, and passe away. Thus can nothing be certainely established, nor of the one, nor of the other; both the judgeing and the judged being in continuall alteration and motion. We have no communication with being; for every humane nature is ever in the middle

[26] I am indebted to Frame's analysis (ibid. 163–70) and tabular summary (172–3).

between being borne and dying; giving nothing of it selfe but an obscure apparence and shadow, and an uncertaine and weake opinion. And if perhaps you fix your thought to take its being; it would be even, as if one should go about to grasp the water... (p. 323)

The only being exempted from this universal flux is God, whose '*immoveable and immutable eternity*' (p. 325) Montaigne praises (in words taken from Plutarch). Rather than concluding on this note, however, he turns instead on the Stoic claim that man can be like God. He quotes Seneca (*Quaestiones naturae* 1)—'*Oh what a vile and abject thing is man... unlesse he raise himselfe above humanity!*'—and comments:

Observe here a notable speech, and a profitable desire; but likewise absurd. For to make the handfull greater then the hand, and the embraced greater then the arme; and to hope to straddle more then our legs length; is impossible and monstrous: nor that man should mount over and above himselfe or humanity; for, he cannot see but with his owne eyes, nor take hold but with his owne armes. He shall raise himselfe up, if it please God extraordinarily to lend him his helping hand. He may elevate himselfe by forsaking and renouncing his owne meanes, and suffering himselfe to be elevated and raised by meere heavenly meanes. It is for our Christian faith, not for his Stoicke vertue to pretend or aspire to this divine Metamorphosis, or miraculous transmutation. (pp. 325–6)

The conclusion of Montaigne's massive argument is thus, as Frame puts it, 'not an affirmation of Pyrrhonism but a repudiation of Stoicism'.[27] The Stoic ethic is based upon the belief that truth is accessible, and that human beings, by reason and will, can attain godlike perfection. In response Montaigne insists upon the weakness of human reason, unable to perceive truth, dependent on the body, emotions, and senses, adrift in a sea of flux, utterly alien to the perfect constancy of God.

Montaigne's divided feelings in this repudiation are summed up in his brief comment on Seneca's dictum. It is 'notable' (memorable and worth pondering), and expresses 'a profitable desire' (for who would not wish to rise above the condition described in the 'Apologie'?); but it is 'absurd', because inherently impossible. This sentence was added by Montaigne in his final revisions of the *Essays*, and the complexity of its judgement (not, I think, simply

[27] Frame, 175; cf. 179–80.

ironic) suggests the complexity of Montaigne's final attitude to Stoicism: admiration for its aspirations, coupled with a half-mocking, half-sad sense of their impossibility.[28]

Self-knowledge and sceptical constancy

Montaigne's rejection of Stoic constancy does not mean that he ceases to want some kind of stability amid the world's flux. In the essays written shortly after the 'Apologie', he seeks to find such stability in an ideal of consistent selfhood based on self-knowledge—the only kind of knowledge in which he now sees any possibility of certainty. The later essays attempt to carry out the project proposed in 'Of the Inconstancie of Our Actions': to 'dive into his heart, and there see by what wards or springs the motions stirre'.

The opening paragraphs of 'Of Repenting' (3. 2, written *c.*1586?) define this aim, and the difficulty of achieving it in a world of flux. The essay begins with Montaigne's most famous evocation of mutability, a passage in which Lipsius' lament for 'this wheel of changeable things' is transposed into a key of humour and exhilaration:

> The world runnes all on wheeles. All things therein moove without intermission; yea the earth, the rockes of *Caucasus*, and the Pyramides of Ægypt, both with the publike and their own motion. *Constancy it selfe is nothing but a languishing and wavering dance.*

In the midst of this dance Montaigne attempts to observe himself, though the experiment is made difficult by the fact that both observer and subject are continually changing:

> I cannot settle my object; it goeth so unquietly and staggering, with a naturall drunkennesse. I take it in this plight, as it is at th'instant I ammuse my selfe about it. I describe not the essence, but the passage; not a passage from age to age . . . but from day to day, from minute to minute. . . . I may soone change, not onely fortune, but intention. It is a

[28] Vawter, 'Division', 182–3, relates the conclusion of the 'Apologie' to *Julius Caesar*, but oversimplifies the attitudes of both Montaigne and Shakespeare to Stoicism. On the possible influence of Montaigne's scepticism on *Julius Caesar*, see J. S. M. J. Chang, '*Julius Caesar* in the Light of Renaissance Historiography', *JEGP* 69 (1970), 63–71, and Julian C. Rice, '*Julius Caesar* and the Judgement of the Senses', *SEL* 13 (1973), 238–55.

counter-roule of divers and variable accidents, and irresolute imaginations, and sometimes contrary: whether it be that my selfe am other, or that I apprehend subjects, by other circumstances and considerations. Howsoever, I may perhaps gaine-say my selfe, but truth . . . I never gaine-say: Were my mind setled, I would not essay, but resolve my selfe. (3. 2, p. 23)

The central idea of these essays is 'Know thyself.' This ancient maxim has two traditional interpretations, depending which 'self' (or *persona*, to use Cicero's term) it refers to: one's self as a member of the human race, or one's individual self. In the first sense, the phrase is a warning against *hubris*; it means 'Know you are a human being, recognize your human limitations.' In the second sense, it means 'Know yourself as an individual, be guided by knowledge of your own qualities and faults.' Montaigne's ideal of self-knowledge embraces both senses. At the same time, he is aware that the maxim is 'a paradoxall commandement', for there is nothing we are less inclined to do (3. 9, p. 252). As human beings, we are denied self-knowledge by 'vanity', an unrealistically lofty notion of human nature and its capacities; as individuals, we are tempted from it by a preoccupation with role-playing and the opinions of others.

On the first ground Montaigne criticizes philosophers, and especially the Stoics, for the faults attacked in 'Of Presumption' (2. 17) and 'Of Vanity' (3. 9). Circling in the latter essay around the biblical text that 'all is vanity' (Ecclesiastes 12: 9), Montaigne unexpectedly turns to attack, not the inevitable vanity of our everyday lives, but that of the philosophers who seek to transcend it. This is 'vain' in both senses of the word, both arrogant and futile.

Life is a materiall and corporall motion, an action imperfect and disordered by its owne essence: . . . To what purpose are these heaven-looking and nice points of Philosophie, on which no humane being can establish and ground it selfe? And to what end serve these rules, that exceed our use and excell our strength? (3. 9, p. 237)

Wee are farre enough from being honest according to God: For, wee cannot be such according to our selves. Humane wisedome could never reach the duties . . . it had prescribed unto it selfe. And had it at any time attained them, then would it doubtlesse prescribe some others beyond them, to which it might ever aspire and pretend. So great an enemy is our condition unto consistence. (p. 239)

The examples which follow, of the ludicrous hypocrisies into which our impossible pretensions to virtue lead us, may have struck Shakespeare. The adulteress railing against fornication (p. 237) suggests Lear on Goneril (*Lear*, 4. 5. 116–21); the judge who scribbles a note to his mistress on the back of an adulterer's sentence (p. 237) looks like a hint for Angelo; and the comment that '*No man is so exquisitely honest or upright in living . . . that ten times in his life might not lawfully be hanged*' (p. 239) is echoed by Hamlet's 'Use every man after his desert, and who should scape whipping?' (2. 2. 531–2).[29]

In his final additions Montaigne adds to this passage (p. 237) a quotation from *De officiis* (1. 110) on the necessity for following both universal Nature and one's own nature. The point, I think, is that Cicero's warning against taking on roles for which one is not suited is as true for mankind in general as for individuals.[30] It is philosophers such as the Stoics, with their insistence that man must '*raise himselfe above humanity*', who drive us to such absurd hypocrisies in our attempts to pretend to be better than we are, and to play a role in which we are (like Sir Nathaniel playing Alexander the Great) hopelessly 'o'erparted'.

Montaigne, in fact, sees Stoicism in general as tainted by its concern with public performance. His test case is the story of the Stoic Posidonius, who insisted on continuing to lecture during the throes of a painful illness, declaring, '*Paine, doe what thou list, I shall never be drawne to say, that thou art an evill.*' Even in an early Stoic essay Montaigne objected (in the vein of Seneca's critic in *De constantia sapientis*) that this defiance 'contends but for the word' (1. 40, p. 275). Now he extends the criticism: 'Why doth Philosophy, which onely respecteth livelinesse and regardeth effects, ammuze it selfe about these externall apparances? Let her leave this care to Mimikes, to Histrions, and to Rhetoricke Masters, who make so great accompt of our gestures' (2. 37, p. 493). Similarly, he now rejects the Stoic desire 'to make either triall or shew of my constancy' on his deathbed, for 'then shall the right

[29] This parallel was noted by Robertson (*Montaigne and Shakespeare*) and Taylor (*Shakspere's Debt to Montaigne*).

[30] An example of the fact that 'the context from which [Montaigne] borrows is often more relevant to his immediate text than the line or lines he actually incorporates' (Mary B. McKinley, quoted by Terence Cave, 'Problems of Reading in the *Essais*', in I. D. McFarlane and Ian Maclean (eds.), *Montaigne* (Oxford, 1982), 133–66 (151)).

and interest I have in reputation cease' (3. 9, p. 224); and he praises those ancient Romans like Petronius who died casually, without ceremonies or sermons or 'ambitious affectation of constancie' (p. 231). Why should self-reliant virtue be so concerned about how others perceive it?

The same concern for role-playing and public opinion is responsible for the failure of self-knowledge in the second sense: knowledge of one's individual self. This, of course, is an orthodox Neostoic idea. 'In going about to frame apparances according to the common opinion, wee defraud our selves of our owne profits. Wee care not so much, what our state, or how our being is in us, and in effect, as wee doe how and what it is, in the publike knowledge of others' (3. 9, p. 195). In 'Of Repenting' Montaigne recommends judging by one's own consistent 'touch-stone':

Such as we especially, who live a private life not exposed to any gaze but our owne, ought in our hearts establish a touch-stone, and there to touch our deedes and try our actions. . . . None but your self knows rightly whether you be demiss and cruel, or loyal and devout. Others see you not, but ghesse you by uncertaine conjectures. They see not so much your nature as your arte. Adhere not then to their opinion, but hold unto your owne. (3. 2, p. 26)

Every one may play the jugler, and represent an honest man upon the stage; but within, and in bosome, where all things are lawfull, where all is concealed; to keepe a due rule or formall decorum, that's the point. (p. 27)

The phrase 'formall decorum' is Florio's addition, but it correctly suggests a similarity between Montaigne's ideal of consistent selfhood and Cicero's decorum. There are, however, important differences. Montaigne insists on the complexity and mysteriousness of what goes on in the individual human mind, and hence the irrelevance of external judgements of character. More fundamentally, whereas Cicero stresses the playing of an appropriate role, Montaigne sees a fundamental dichotomy between person and role, 'apparance' and 'essence'. This idea is expressed in a passage which may have caught Shakespeare's eye, for it quotes a version of the Latin tag which was the motto of the Globe theatre:

Mundus universus exercet histrioniam. All the world doth practise stage-playing. Wee must play our parts duly, but as the part of a borrowed personage. Of a visard and apparance, wee should not make a real essence, nor proper of that which is another. Wee cannot distinguish the skinne from the shirt. It is sufficient to disguise the face, without deforming the breast. I see some transforme and transubstantiate themselves, into as many new formes and strange beings, as they undertake charges: and who emprelate themselves even to the heart and entrailes; and entraine their offices even sitting on their close stoole. (3. 10, pp. 262–3)

All role-playing, for Montaigne, is to some extent a betrayal of the integrity of the personality. Above all one must not allow one's personal identity to be swallowed up in one's role—as, arguably, happens to Caesar or Coriolanus.

This difference in outlook may partly explain Montaigne's distaste for Cicero as a writer and a person, and his reluctance to acknowledge the debt of his ideas to Cicero's, though he quotes him with increasing frequency in Book 3.[31] Jeffrey M. Green, in a perceptive article, argues that Montaigne's basic objection is to the externality of Cicero's concept of virtue:

Cicero seems not completely to grasp the difference between speaking and doing; Montaigne was always acutely aware of it. Cicero treats virtues as important as patriotism and firmness in the face of death as parts of a public performance. For Montaigne, they could not be performed before an audience; they had to be demonstrated in action, when an occasion called for them.[32]

For Montaigne, Cicero's ideal of consistent selfhood is hopelessly bound up with concern for public performance. Montaigne is anxious to dissociate himself from what he sees as a shabby and second-rate version of his own ideal. It is only in his final revisions of the *Essays* that, by inserting some quotations from *De officiis* 1, he partially acknowledges his debt to Cicero.[33]

In two of the essays of Book 2 Montaigne develops an idea of consistent selfhood which is very similar to Cicero's decorum, but with one crucial exception: whereas Cicero's concept is based on the Stoic idea of *homologia* with right reason, Montaigne's is explicitly based upon scepticism and arbitrary, irrational choice. Montaigne recommends being true to one's own character because

[31] The index to *EMM* lists fifteen citations in Book 3, as against four in Book 1 and six in Book 2.

[32] 'Montaigne's Critique of Cicero', *JHI* 36 (1975), 595–612 (606). Green does not specifically discuss decorum. See also George M. Logan, 'The Relation of Montaigne to Renaissance Humanism', *JHI* 36 (1975), 613–32 (623).

[33] Higginbotham's judgement that Montaigne's ideas of truth to oneself are 'largely prompted' by Cicero (introd. to *Cicero on Moral Obligation*, 28) is thus in my view overstated.

it is one's own, and there is no rational reason for judging that any other course would be better. In Coriolanus' words, he will follow 'mine own truth' (3. 2. 121)—not because it is 'truth' but because it is 'mine own'. The possibility of such 'sceptical constancy' may indeed be latent in Stoicism from its beginnings, if *homologia* is interpreted (against the orthodox grain) as internal self-consistency with no reference to an external *logos*.[34]

The idea of constancy arising from scepticism first appears in the 'Apologie':

> Now by the knowledge of my volubilitie, I have by accidence engendred some constancy of opinions in my selfe; yea have not so much altered my first and naturall ones. For, what apparance soever there be in novelty, I do not easily change, for feare I should lose by the bargaine: And since I am not capable to chuse, I take the choise from others; and keepe my selfe in the seate, that God hath placed me in. Else could I hardly keepe my selfe from continuall rowling. (2. 12, pp. 284–5)

In its context this is a plea for loyalty to Catholic orthodoxy. The idea can, however, be given a more relativistic slant, to suggest that we should stick to our own opinions because they are our own. In 'Of Presumption' (2.17, written *c.*1578–80), Montaigne confesses that his besetting fault is indecisiveness. Easily swayed by argument, conscious of the weak foundations of his own beliefs, he is nevertheless 'not very easie to change, forsomuch as I perceive a like weaknesse in contrary opinions' (p. 381). Scepticism can serve as a bulwark for stability of opinion: if it shows you the doubtfulness of your own convictions, it also shows the doubtfulness of other points of view—and why exchange one uncertainty for another? At least his own opinions are based on self-knowledge:

> This capacitie of sifting out the truth, what, and howsoever it be in me, and this free humour I have, not very easily to subject my beliefe, I owe especially unto my selfe, for the most constant, and generall imaginations I have are those, which (as one would say) were borne with me: They are natural unto me, and wholy mine.

They have been strengthened 'by the authoritie of others, and by the sound examples of ancients'; but the essential fact about them

[34] Braden suggests something like this: 'The self aspires to be an imitation of the order of the cosmos, but it might as well be an arbitrary stand taken against a meaningless reality that has value only as an opportunity for proving ourselves' (*Renaissance Tragedy*, 21).

is that they are his own. That is why he has remained firm in them, and, if he cannot lay claim to brilliance, can at least claim the merit of consistency: 'the order, correspondencie, and tranquillitie of opinions and customes' (p. 385).

In his final revisions, Montaigne here inserts from *De officiis* (1. 111) Cicero's statement that the essence of decorum is consistency (*aequabilitas*), which can only be achieved by being oneself. Montaigne's originality lies in the sceptical and relativistic turn he gives the concept of decorum: *because* nothing is certain, you may as well be consistent in following your 'own truth', whether or not it is true for anyone else.

The opening pages of 'Of Vertue' (2. 29, also written around 1578–80) present a model of sceptical constancy, in a passage as complex and problematic as any in the *Essays*. The opening sentences rapidly sketch the distinction made more clearly in 'Of Drunkennesse' between 'the sodaine fits and fantasies of the soule, and a resolute disposition and constant habitude' (p. 430). He concedes, in a manner so offhand that it sounds ironic, that we can attain any degree of virtue, even godlike virtue, even (echoing Seneca's most hyperbolical claim) a virtue greater than God's. 'But it is by fits.' We may be raised by 'a kinde of passion' above our normal selves for a brief moment; but such fits cannot last, and we soon subside from the heights back into our normal state of trivial inconstancy, 'so that upon every slight occasion, for a bird lost, or for a glasse broken, wee suffer our selves to be mooved and distempered very neere as one of the vulgar sort.' After all, anyone can be godlike for a few minutes; it is constancy (consistency, *aequabilitas*) which is the rare and truly valuable quality.

> *Except order, moderation and constancie, I imagine all things may bee done by an indifferent and defective man.* Therefore say wisemen, that directly to judge of a man, his common actions must specially be controuled, and he must every day be surprised in his work-day clothes. (p. 431)

At this point, rather unexpectedly, Montaigne turns to Pyrrho, the sceptic 'who framed so pleasant a Science of ignorance', and takes him as an exemplar of constancy.

> And forasmuch as he maintained the weakenesse of mans judgement, to be so extreame, as it could take nor resolution, nor inclination [i.e. neither certainty nor even probability]: and would perpetually suspend it, ballancing, beholding and receiving all things, as indifferent: It is reported of

him, that he ever kept himselfe after one fashion, looke and countenance ... (p. 431)

He retells some of the traditional anecdotes about Pyrrho: how he would continue a conversation even after the departure of the person he was talking to, or keep walking in a straight line even if there was a wall or a ditch in his path—since, sense-perceptions being unreliable, he saw no reason to let them affect his behaviour. More seriously, he would submit to surgical operations 'with such constancy' that he was never even seen to twitch.[35] Montaigne comments

> It is something to bring the minde to these imaginations, but more to joine the effects unto it, yet is it not impossible. But to joine them with such perseverance and constancy, as to establish it for an ordinary course; verily in these enterprises so farre from common use, it is almost incredible to be done.

Then comes a deflating conclusion: Pyrrho was on one occasion seen to defend himself against being bitten by a dog, and had to apologize for this lapse in principle: '*It is ... very hard, altogether to dispoile and shake off man*' (p. 432).

The tone of this passage is mercurial: at one moment Pyrrho seems absurd, falling into ditches on stubborn principle; the next moment, on the operating table, he shows the heroism of a Stoic *sapiens*, and Montaigne's admiration of such 'almost incredible' constancy seems sincere. Montaigne portrays Pyrrho as a man who actually succeeded in uniting the two senses of 'constancy', practising heroic steadfastness not 'by fits' but almost consistently; who was always the same, *unus idemque inter diversa*, unmoved by outside influences, to the point both of superhuman heroism and of comic imperviousness to the realities of everyday life. The equivocal tone, wavering between laughter and admiration, captures more clearly than any summary Montaigne's equivocal response to such constancy.

It is unexpected, however, that Montaigne's epitome of constancy should be not a Stoic but the founder of scepticism. He suggests, moreover, that Pyrrho's constancy is a logical consequence of his scepticism: 'And *forasmuch as* he maintained the

[35] For the ancient sources of these stories, see Long and Sedley, *Hellenistic Philosophers*, 1A–C.

weakenesse of mans judgement . . . he ever kept himselfe after one fashion' (my emphasis). Pyrrho carries to its logical conclusion (almost *ad absurdum*) the principle of sceptical constancy suggested in the 'Apologie' and 'Of Presumption': that, since everything is uncertain, you may as well stick consistently by your own opinions.

The principle, carried as far as Pyrrho carries it, is almost an existentialist one: in the absence of an objective or absolute truth, one can only make an arbitrary choice of certain attitudes, beliefs, and principles, and then maintain them rigidly. It is a philosophy of desperation. Shakespeare's Antony and Coriolanus each, in the later acts of their tragedies, make something like this kind of *acte gratuit*, arbitrarily committing themselves to a consistent course in order to maintain identity in an unmeaning world. Montaigne's Christian scepticism, however, will not go quite so far, and his half-comic treatment of Pyrrho suggests a drawing back from the implications of sceptical constancy. In the last essays of Book 3 he develops a philosophy which does not require one to '*shake off man*', one based not upon constancy but upon 'the benefit of inconstancy'.

The benefit of inconstancy

In Montaigne's final essays, the ideal of self-knowledge is allied not so much with constancy as with a cheerful acceptance of inconstancy. '*Life is a motion unequall, irregular and multiforme*' (3. 3, p. 38), and we must move with it:

> WE must not cleave so fast unto our humours and dispositions. Our chiefest sufficiency is, to apply our selves to divers fashions. It is a being, but not a life, to bee tied and bound by necessity to one onely course. The goodliest mindes are those that have most variety and pliablenesse in them. (3. 3, pp. 37–8)

Where Montaigne once mourned 'the Inconstancie of Our Actions' and the fact that 'there is as much difference found betweene us and our selves, as there is betweene our selves and other' (2. 1, p. 14), he now sees such variety as preferable to Stoic rigidity. In Shakespearian terms, he rejects the self-destructive inflexibility of Coriolanus' determination '[n]ot to be other than one thing', and chooses instead, like Antony (though in a far more balanced and moderate way), to pursue 'infinite variety'.

Montaigne now finds his 'provisions' against pain and death in change rather than constancy. In 'Of Diverting and Diversions' (3. 4) he suggests that the most effective way of dealing with sorrow is not to face it down in the Stoic manner, but to distract the mind to less painful thoughts.

> A sharpe conceit possesseth, and a violent imagination holdeth me: I finde it a shorter course to alter and divert, then to tame and vanquish the same: if I cannot substitute a contrary unto it, at least I present another unto it. *Change ever easeth, Varietie dissolveth, and shifting dissipateth.* If I cannot buckle with it, I flie from it: and in shunning it, I stray and double from it. . . . Nature proceedeth thus, by the benefit of inconstancy. (3. 4, p. 57)

Instead of facing adversity like the Senecan rock, storm-battered but immovable, Montaigne prefers to slip away. Inconstancy can be a benefit, not a fault. On the same principle he defends the habit of travel against Stoic critics like Lipsius who object that one cannot run away from one's own disordered mind.[36] If in practice he finds comfort in 'varietie and the possession of diversitie', why should he not take advantage of the fact? It may be 'a testimony of unquietnesse and irresolution', but these, 'to say truth, are our mistrisse and predominant qualities' (3. 9, p. 236). The very word 'diversion' echoes Montaigne's earlier characterization of human nature as 'divers and wavering'. It is this diversity and changeableness of both the world and our minds which allows us to find comfort in change, rather than in a single-minded confrontation with the worst.

Montaigne similarly criticizes the Stoic treatment of death in 'Of Physiognomy' (3. 12, *c.*1585–8). Quoting again Cicero's dictum that the philosopher's life is a preparation for death, he explicitly rejects the teleological fallacy: death 'is indeede the end [*bout*], yet not the scope [i.e. aim, *but*] of life. It is her last, it is her extremity, yet not her object. Hir selfe must be unto hir selfe, hir aime, hir drift and her designe' (p. 307; *EMM*, p. 1051). To spend one's life preparing for death is a waste of time; peasants who have never given death a thought can die with exemplary constancy. Montaigne, who once condemned such unconcern as

[36] Villey (*Sources*, ii. 399–401) suggests the connection with Lipsius' *De constantia*.

'brutall stupiditie', now exclaims, 'In Gods name . . . let us henceforth keepe a schoole of brutality' (p. 308). As in the 'Apologie', he mocks and rejects the Stoic emphasis on reason as the one true way to virtue. Human reason is so 'adulterated' and 'sofisticated' that it has become merely opinion, 'variable and peculiar to every man, and hath lost her proper, constant and universall visage' (p. 305). We must look to animals or to simple uneducated people to learn true, natural virtue.

'Of Experience' (3. 13), the final essay and probably the last written (*c.*1587–8), may be seen as the nearest thing to a conclusion to the *Essays*.[37] In this imperfect world our task is, not merely to endure, but as far as possible to enjoy life. We must accept our human condition for what it is, taking pleasure in the commonplace pleasures of life, not despising but accepting the body. We must recognize that 'all is vanity', and, in recognizing that, accept it as the nature of our condition.

My selfe, who brag so curiously to embrace and particularly to allow the commodities of life; whensoever I looke precisely into it I finde nothing therein but winde. But what? we are nothing but winde. And the very winde also, more wisely then we loveth to bluster and to be in agitation: And is pleased with his owne offices, without desiring stability or solidity; qualities that be not his owne. (3. 13, p. 374)

Our chief task is to recognize what qualities or 'offices' (Montaigne echoes Cicero's term) are proper to our human nature, and to live by these fully and cheerfully:

There is nothing so goodly, so faire and so lawfull as to play the man well and duely: Nor Science so hard and difficult, as to know how to live this life well. And of all the infirmities we have, the most savage, is to despise our being. (p. 379)

The conclusion of 'Of Experience' (and thus of the *Essays*) is, like that of the 'Apologie', an attack on those who refuse to accept our human condition and seek to 'escape man'. Such excessive desire for perfection is, paradoxically, 'savage': 'insteade of transforming themselves into Angels, they transchange themselves into beastes' (p. 385).

[37] '[O]n y peut chercher, sinon à proprement parler la conclusion de Montaigne, du moins quelques idées sur lesquelles . . . il tient à prendre congé de son lecteur' (Villey, *EMM* p. 1064).

> *It is an absolute perfection, and as it were divine for a man to know how to enjoy his being loyally.* We seeke for other conditions because we understand not the use of ours: and goe out of our selves, forsomuch as we know not what abiding there is. *Wee may long enough get upon stilts, for be wee upon them, yet must we goe with our owne legges. And sit we upon the highest throne of the World, yet sit we upon our owne taile.* The best and most commendable lives, and best pleasing men are (in my conceit) those which with order are fitted, and with *decorum* are ranged to the common mould and humane model: but without wonder or extravagancy. (p. 386)

Montaigne's conclusion thus returns to Cicero's ideal of decorum, in its universal sense.[38] Our hardest and most important task is to recognize what is appropriate to the role of a human being, and to fulfil that role with grace and decorum—'*to play the man well and duely*'.

Montaigne and Shakespeare

The similarity between Montaigne and Shakespeare on the theme of constancy goes well beyond an echoing of commonplaces about death and suffering. They share a preoccupation with the theme: Montaigne, who calls constancy the 'last perfection' of the mind, would echo the cry of Shakespeare's Proteus: 'O heaven, were man | But constant, he were perfect.' Yet both see this 'profitable desire' as 'likewise absurd', because the ineradicable inconstancy of things and of human nature, which makes us desire constancy, also makes it impossible to achieve. Montaigne throughout his later essays analyses why the failure is inevitable; Shakespeare, depicting a society which is identified with the ideal of constancy, dramatizes its failure. His Roman heroes repeatedly fail to achieve the 'miraculous transmutation' into perfection through constancy. *Antony and Cleopatra*, his most Montaignian play, shows a world in which Roman constancy dissolves in flux, and the mutability of the outside world is matched by the mercurial changes of the characters' minds.

Some of the criticisms of Stoic constancy which Montaigne and Shakespeare share are traditional, going back to Augustine or even

[38] The word '*decorum*' is Florio's addition (Montaigne simply has '*avec ordre*'), but I think a legitimate one.

to Cicero: its arrogance, its ignoring of the demands of the body, its concern with role-playing and 'ambitious affectation', its perverse attraction towards death. Others are more original. I would single out three insights which they seem to share.

First, a sense of the possible contradiction between constancy (steadfastness) and constancy (consistency). Montaigne in 'Of Drunkennesse' is, I have suggested, the first person to articulate the point that the heroically exorbitant virtue of the *sapiens* may be incompatible with Ciceronian *aequabilitas*. These contradictions are central to the Roman plays, and Montaigne's point is especially relevant to the heroic but un-Stoic constancy of Coriolanus.

Second, the idea of sceptical constancy. Montaigne inverts traditional Stoicism by associating constancy with scepticism rather than knowledge: in a world where nothing is certain, we can achieve stability by following an arbitrary but consistent code. Shakespeare, insistently linking Roman constancy with opinion, implies that it is just such a code. The point is clearest, once again, in Coriolanus, who (like Pyrrho) pursues his 'own truth' with a fanatical and irrational consistency.

Third, the idea of 'the benefit of inconstancy'. Montaigne's late suggestion that there may be positive value in an embracing of diversity and mutability is, I think, sympathetically embodied by Shakespeare in *Antony and Cleopatra*. Nevertheless the disastrous results of Antony's pursuit of 'varietie and flexiblenesse' suggest that for Shakespeare this ideal may be no more adequate than that of Stoic constancy in dealing with a mutable world.

6

A Constancy Triptych: North's Plutarch and the Roman Plays

In the last five chapters I have argued that the conception of Romanness in the Roman plays derives largely from the Stoic tradition. In doing so I have virtually ignored the one indisputable source of the plays: Sir Thomas North's translation (1579) of Jacques Amyot's translation (1559) of Plutarch's *Parallel Lives*.[1] To what extent did Shakespeare find his constant Romans in Plutarch? In this chapter I shall suggest that one reason for his choice of Brutus, Antony, and Coriolanus as protagonists is that their Lives can be read as a kind of triptych on the theme of constancy.[2]

Plutarch, of course, did not design such a triptych: he did not write these three Lives as a group, was not a Stoic (indeed he was something of an anti-Stoic), and was not especially preoccupied with constancy.[3] It is the Renaissance translators, Amyot and North, who make it into a central issue by using the words 'constancy' and 'constant' to translate a variety of Greek expressions, and by introducing them as moral glosses without warrant in the original text. Shakespeare, reading with his ear attuned to the recurrences of these words, could have seen the figures of Brutus, Antony, and Coriolanus as linked and contrasted in terms of their relation to the virtue of constancy. What emerges from the Lives, in North's

[1] For details of texts and references, see Bibliographical Note. I have also consulted *Shakespeare's Plutarch*, ed. T. J. B. Spencer (Harmondsworth, 1964). Most studies of the Roman plays pay some attention to Plutarch; M. W. MacCallum's *Shakespeare's Roman Plays and their Background* (London, 1910; repr. New York, 1967) is still valuable. David C. Green, *Plutarch Revisited: A Study of Shakespeare's Last Roman Plays and Their Source* (Salzburg, 1979) is factually useful but critically simplistic.

[2] I pass over the 'Life of Julius Caesar', which Shakespeare seems to have used less than the other three (as Spencer suggests, *Shakespeare's Plutarch*, 14). The 'Life' stresses Caesar's resilience and adaptability rather than his constancy, and gives little hint for the Senecan poses of Shakespeare's character.

[3] On Plutarch's anti-Stoicism see D. A. Russell, *Plutarch* (London, 1972), 68–9; it does not emerge in the Lives which Shakespeare used.

translation, is an Aristotelian pattern of virtue as a mean between excess and defect: Brutus embodying the virtue of constancy, Antony its defect, inconstancy, and Coriolanus its excess, wilful obstinacy.

Though Plutarch did not plan this pattern, it is in harmony with the Aristotelian temper of his thought, with its assumption that (in Amyot's words) '*it is a vertue of the minde which teacheth a man the meane poynt betweene the two faultie extreamities of too much & too litle, wherein the commendation of all doings consisteth.*'[4] A judgement of Brutus as an ethical ideal, and of Antony and Coriolanus as representing various kinds of '*faultie extreamities*', is implicit in the three Lives. Shakespeare has a sharper sense, honed perhaps on Montaigne, of the paradoxes of constancy, and though the Roman plays retain the outline of the Plutarchan triptych, they considerably complicate its simple Aristotelian pattern.

Constant Brutus

The words 'constancy' and 'constant' appear nine times in North's translation of the 'Life of Marcus Brutus', and their shifting connotations sum up the whole range of Brutus' virtues. Constancy is associated at the start with the rational virtue of Brutus the philosopher.[5] This is emphasized by a comparison with his ancestor Lucius Junius Brutus, who drove the Tarquin kings out of Rome.

> But that *Junius Brutus* being of a sower stearne nature, not softned by reason, being like unto sword blades of too hard a temper: was so subject to his choller and malice he bare unto the tyrants, that for their sakes he caused his owne sonnes to be executed. But this *Marcus Brutus* in contrary maner . . . having framed his manners of life by the rules of vertue and study of Philosophy, and having imployed his wit, which was gentle and constant, in attempting of great things: me thinkes he was rightly made and framed unto vertue. (p. 1053; 'Brutus' 1. 1–2)

Implicitly, Plutarch rejects any analogy between Lucius Brutus' execution of his sons and Marcus Brutus' murder of his friend.

[4] North, sig. *5^{r}. This passage is quoted by Philip Brockbank in his introduction to the Arden *Coriolanus* (London, 1976), 28. On Plutarch's Aristotelian ethics see also Russell, *Plutarch*, 84–5.

[5] Plutarch's treatment of Brutus' philosophical allegiances is discussed in Ch. 7, pp. 125–7 below.

Where old Brutus was governed by irrational 'choller', young Brutus, naturally more gentle, was guided by reason and principle. North's 'constant' here translates Amyot's *grave* and Plutarch's *embrithê* (weighty, serious-minded, Latin *gravis*). North thus equates constancy (consistency) with Roman *gravitas*: moral seriousness, stability, and self-control. As Plutarch later describes him, Brutus 'would never be in any rage, nor caried away with pleasure and covetousnesse, but had ever an upright mind with him, and would never yeeld to any wrong or injustice' (p. 1066; 29. 2).[6]

The idea of constancy (*embrithes*) is developed in Caesar's comment on Brutus and Plutarch's gloss on it:

> They say also that *Caesar* sayd, when he heard *Brutus* plead: I know not, sayd he, what this young man would, but what he would, he willeth it vehemently. For as *Brutus* gravitie and constant minde would not graunt all men their requestes that sued unto him, but being moved with reason and discretion, did alwayes encline to that which was good and honest: even so when it was moved to follow any matter, he used a kinde of forcible and vehement perswasion that calmed not, till he had obtained his desire. For by flattering of him, a man could never obtaine any thing at his handes, nor make him to do that which was unjust. (p. 1055; 6. 4–5)

'Gravitie and constant minde' is North's expansion of Amyot's *gravité* (Plutarch's *embrithes*). Two ideas are implied: Brutus is careful not to be easily swayed by emotion but only by a rational decision about what is just; once resolved, however, he is unshakeably determined. The same concept of constancy underlies Cassius' warning to Brutus that Caesar's favours are designed 'not to honour his vertue, but to weaken his constant minde' (p. 1056; 7.4),[7] and North's side-note on a later passage in which Brutus refuses to accept Cassius' plea that absolute standards of honesty are out of place in wartime: '*The wonderfull constancy of Brutus, in matters of justice & equity*' (p. 1069; on 'Brutus' 35). Brutus will do what he knows to be right, unswayed by pressure or persuasion. 'Constancy' in these passages stands for an immovable moral rigour, such as Shakespeare's Caesar claims in the 'Northern Star' speech.

[6] In the Greek, he is *apathês* with respect to anger, pleasure, or greed.

[7] This 'constant' is North's; Amyot has *la force de son courage* (688[r]), translating Plutarch's *alkên* and *thumon* (both meaning spirit, courage). The effect is a shift in meaning from courage to moral principle.

As Plutarch proceeds to the conspiracy, 'constancy' shifts towards the more Senecan sense of steadfastness in the face of adversity; at the same time it takes on overtones of dissimulation. Both Brutus and Portia show a 'formal constancy' which disguises their inward perturbation. Brutus in public 'did so frame and fashion his countenaunce and lookes, that no man could discerne he had any thing to trouble his minde', yet appeared 'cleane chaunged' at home (p. 1058; 13. 1). Portia gives herself a voluntary wound to demonstrate that she can 'constantlie beare a secret mischaunce or griefe', and declares that 'now I have found by experience, that no paine nor griefe whatsoever can overcome me' (pp. 1058–9; 13. 4–5)—a claim ironically disproved by her hysterical collapse on the day of the murder (p. 1060; 15. 4–5). Brutus' self-control is more successful. Plutarch comments on 'the wonderfull assured constancie [*apathes*] of these conspiratours' (and North's side-note underlines their '*wonderfull constancie*') as they maintain their apparent calm through a series of near-betrayals (p. 1059; 14. 4) and, in Brutus' case, a false report of his wife's death (p. 1060; 15. 6).[8]

Steadfastness and dissimulation are again linked as Portia faces parting with Brutus: she 'did what she could to dissemble the griefe and sorrow she felt' and 'alwaies shewed a constant and patient minde', but finally broke down while looking at a painting of the parting of Hector and Andromache (p. 1063; 23. 2).[9] Brutus praises her because, although 'the weake constitution of her bodie' does not allow her to fight, 'for courage and constant mind, she shewed her selfe as stout in the defence of her country, as any of us' (p. 1063; 23. 4).[10] This contrast between bodily weakness and moral strength is a recurring motif in *Julius Caesar*.

The last explicit reference to constancy in the 'Life,' and perhaps the most interesting, is Brutus' reply to Cassius' question whether he will kill himself if defeated.

> *Brutus* a[n]swered him, being yet but a young man, and not over greatly experienced in the world: I trust, (I know not how) a certaine rule of Philosophy, by the which I did greatly blame and reprove *Cato* for killing

[8] This passage probably suggested the way Brutus receives the news of Portia's real death in 4. 2.

[9] This shattering of a character's precarious self-control by a trivial provocation may have helped to suggest Brutus' response to the Poet in 4. 2.

[10] These two references to 'constancy' derive from Amyot.

of himselfe, as being no lawfull nor godly acte, touching the gods, nor concerning men, valiant, not to give place and yeeld to divine providence, and not constantly & patiently to take whatsoever it pleaseth him to send us, but to draw back and flie: but being now in the middest of the danger, I am of a contrary mind. For if it be not the will of God, that this battell fall out fortunate for us: I will looke no more for hope . . . but wil rid me of this miserable world, and content me with my fortune. For, I gave up my life for my countrey in the Ides of March, for the which I shall live in an other more glorious world. (pp. 1071–2; 40. 4–5)[11]

As commentators have noted, North here obscures the meaning.[12] In the Greek Brutus clearly says that in his youth he disapproved of suicide, but now he has changed his mind. North, by changing a past to a present tense and punctuating 'being yet a young man . . .' as an authorial comment, makes it seem that Brutus performs a moral about-face in the middle of the speech. Shakespeare's version (5. 1. 100–13) sharpens the contrast: Brutus declares his disapproval of suicide, then, when Cassius asks if that really means that he is willing to be led in triumph, declares (without apparently recognizing his self-contradiction) that he would rather die.[13] Building on North's mistranslation, Shakespeare raises the question about suicide posed by Augustine: is it more 'constant' to stand fast and endure suffering, or to end it by suicide? Is suicide heroic or cowardly?

His treatment of Portia's death raises similar questions. Either deliberately, or misled by an unclear passage in North, he conflates two versions in Plutarch: one in which Portia killed herself after Brutus' death, another in which she died at an earlier point of illness complicated by depression (p. 1078; 'Brutus' 53. 4–5). Shakespeare's version suggests that Portia, out of '[i]mpatience' (*JC* 4. 2. 206)—the opposite of Stoic patience—takes what Brutus calls the 'cowardly and vile' course of killing herself '[f]or fear of what *might* fall' (5. 1. 103–5, my emphasis).

[11] 'Constantly' comes from Amyot (698^{v}), and, in conjunction with 'patiently', gives a Stoic turn to Plutarch's *adeôs* (fearlessly).

[12] e.g. MacCallum, *Shakespeare's Roman Plays*, 184–5. Amyot's version is correct but capable of being misread.

[13] Shakespeare's sharp awareness of dealing here with a pagan philosophy is suggested by his removal of North's Christian language: the suggestion of an afterlife in 'an other more glorious world' (a misinterpretation by North) is replaced by an 'everlasting farewell', and 'God' (which is in the Greek) is replaced by a vague 'some high powers'.

In the final sections of the 'Life,' though 'constancy' is not mentioned, a related idea emerges: that of being 'like oneself'. Plutarch suggests that Brutus is bound by the opinion others have of him: 'they had so great an opinion of *Brutus* vertue, that the common voice & opinion of the world would not suffer him, neither to overcome, nor to save himself, otherwise then justly and honestly' (p. 1075; 46. 3). When Lucillius is captured impersonating Brutus, some of the onlookers criticize Brutus, 'saying it was not done like himselfe so cowardly to be taken alive . . . for feare of death'; but Lucillius declares that Brutus will never be taken alive, 'For wheresoever he be found, alive or dead: he will be found like himselfe' (p. 1076; 50. 2–3).[14] Shakespeare relates this exchange to the Renaissance use of 'like oneself' as a formula for constancy, and draws out the implications of role-playing and of living up to others' opinions of oneself.

'Constancy' in the 'Life of Brutus' has a range of meanings: integrity, resolution, rationality, endurance of suffering, concealment of feelings, willingness to die—or to live. Plutarch, Amyot, and North give Shakespeare the hint to see constancy as the keynote of Brutus' character. But it is Shakespeare who relates constancy to other motifs only briefly or not at all present in Plutarch: acting, opinion, Romanness. And it is Shakespeare who extends the virtue of constancy to Caesar, and gives him a Senecan boast on the subject for which there is no basis either in the 'Life of Brutus' or the 'Life of Caesar'.

Inconstant Antony

Constancy is far less prominent in the 'Life of Marcus Antonius' than in that of Brutus. Nevertheless, the two 'Lives', read in conjunction (as Shakespeare must have read them in preparing for *Julius Caesar*), may be seen as inverted mirror images. Plutarch's Antonius is an antitype of his constant Brutus: emotional, unscrupulous, intemperate, vacillating, impatient, capricious, repeatedly flying from one extreme to another. He is capable of great virtues —courage, magnanimity, generosity—but never of practising them consistently or carrying out any purpose with resolution.

[14] Plutarch's phrases are *tês doxês anaxion* (unworthy of his reputation) and *axiôs . . . eautou* (worthy of himself).

His unstable opportunism is seen after the murder of Caesar, as 'the opinion he conceived of him selfe after he had a litle felt the good will of the people towards him . . . did easily make him alter his first minde' (p. 975; 'Antony' 14. 3). Lacking a moral direction of his own, he is easily carried away by the influence of others, as he is, literally, at Actium:

There *Antonius* shewed plainly, that he had not onely lost the courage and hart of an Emperor, but also of a valiant man, & that he was not his owne man: (proving that true which an old man spake in myrth, that the soule of a lover lived in another body, and not in his owne) he was so caried away with the vaine love of this woman, as if he had bene glued unto her, & that she could not have removed without moving of him also. (p. 1000; 66. 4)

The only explicit, and surprisingly positive, reference to constancy in the 'Life' comes in the account (which Shakespeare closely followed in *Ant.* 1. 4. 56–71) of Antony's harrowing retreat from Modena:

Howbeit he was of such a strong nature, that by patience he would overcome any adversitie, and the heavier fortune lay upon him, the more constant shewed he himselfe. Every man that feeleth want or adversity, knoweth by vertue and discretion what he should doe: but when in deede they are overlayed with extremity, and be sore oppressed, few have the hearts to follow that which they praise and commend, and much lesse to avoide that they reprove and mislike. But rather to the contrary, they yeeld to their accustomed easie life: and through faint heart, & lacke of corage, doe chaunge their first mind and purpose. And therefore it was a wonderfull example to the souldiers, to see *Antonius* that was brought up in all finenesse and superfluity, so easily to drinke puddle water, and to eate wild frutes and rootes: and moreover it is reported, that even as they passed the Alpes, they did eate the barkes of trees, and such beasts, as never man tasted of their flesh before. (p. 976; 17. 2–3)

'Constant' (North's interpolation) suggests both sheer endurance and the ability to stick to a course of action despite pressure to 'chaunge [one's] first minde and purpose'.[15] Antonius is capable of

[15] What Plutarch says (in the Loeb translation) is 'But it was his nature to rise to his highest level when in an evil plight, and he was most like a good and true man [*homoiotatos en agathoi*] when he was unfortunate.' (Amyot's phrase is *veritablement vertueux*, p. 635v.) North sacrifices Plutarch's neat antithesis (that Antony was at his best when things were worst) to the Stoic overtones of 'patience' and 'constant'.

this kind of constancy in hardship; his lack of it in the face of pleasure and flattery may be seen as the key to his tragedy.

The theme of constancy is thus implicit in the 'Life of Antonius'. There is, however, little hint in Plutarch for the continual play in *Antony and Cleopatra* with ideas of mutability and stability, constancy and variety; nor does Plutarch's account of the lovers' suicides suggest the shadows of Stoic heroism with which Shakespeare surrounds their deaths. Shakespeare also suggests what is hardly implied in Plutarch, that there is a kind of moral principle involved in Antony's faults. The same reinterpretation is involved in his treatment of Plutarch's Coriolanus.

Obstinate Coriolanus

In 'The Life of Caius Martius Coriolanus' constancy is again a keyword. Plutarch, however, treats Coriolanus not as a constant man but as a man ruined by wilful obstinacy. It is Shakespeare, I believe, who sees a fundamental similarity between what Plutarch presents as Brutus' virtue and Coriolanus' vice.

Plutarch's opening description of Martius (as he calls him throughout) suggests the contradictions in his attitude to his anti-hero:

> This man also is a good proofe to confirme some mens opinions. That a rare and excellent witte untaught, doth bring forth many good and evill thinges together, like a fat soile bringeth forth herbes & weedes that lieth unmanured. For this *Martius* naturall wit and great hart did marvellously sturre up his courage to doe and attempt notable actes. But on the other side for lacke of education, he was so cholericke and impacient, that he would yeeld to no living creature: which made him churlish, uncivil, and altogether unfit for any mans conversation. Yet men marvelling much at his constancie, that he was never overcome with pleasure, nor money, and how he would endure easilie all manner of paines and travailles: thereupon they well liked and commended his stowtnes and temperancie. But for all that, they could not be acquainted with him, as one citizen useth to be with another in the cittie. His behaviour was so unpleasant to them by reason of a certaine insolent and sterne manner he had, which because it was too lordly, was disliked. And to say truly, the greatest benefite that learning bringeth men unto, is this: that it teacheth men that be rude and rough by nature, by compasse and rule of reason, to be civill and curteous,

& to like better the meane state, then the higher. (pp. 235–6; 'Caius Marcius Coriolanus' 1. 2–4)

In Plutarch's Greek this passage is an orderly series of balanced antitheses; North's version, proceeding by a series of zigzags ('But on the other side . . . Yet . . . But for all that . . .'), creates an effect of moral confusion. Martius is commended for his 'constancie' (the word is Amyot's, translating Plutarch's *apatheian*) that 'was never overcome' by physical hardship or by the temptations of money or pleasure; at the same time he is condemned for being 'so cholericke and impacient, that he would yeeld to no living creature'. Shakespeare may have been struck by similarities to Plutarch's Brutus, who was 'never . . . carried away with pleasure and covetousness' and 'would never yield to any wrong or injustice', but pursued what he believed was right with immovable determination ('what he would, he willeth it vehemently'). Brutus' *apatheia* and his immovable resolution are all part of the characteristic virtue which North labels as 'constancy'. In Martius, on the other hand, Plutarch draws a distinction: his *apatheia* is a virtue, his obstinacy a flaw which vitiates it.

Plutarch would no doubt object that the inconsistency was only apparent and the likeness superficial. Brutus practised true philosophical virtue; Martius by comparison is a barbarian, whose stubbornness proceeds not from rational principle but from pride, anger, and self-will. He resembles not so much Marcus Brutus as Lucius Brutus, whose 'sower stearne nature, not softned by reason' was governed by 'choller and malice'. Caius Martius and Lucius Brutus (near-contemporaries) are products of a primitive society which values courage above all else: 'Now in those days, valiantnes was honoured in ROME above all other vertues: which they call *virtus*, by the name of vertue it selfe, as including in that generall name, all other speciall vertues besides' (p. 236; 1. 4).[16] Such a society can inculcate the *virtus* of brute courage and endurance, but not the Aristotelian balance and moderation ('to like better the meane state, than the higher') which for Plutarch is the essence of virtue. Lacking this, Martius carries his form of

[16] Cf. *Cor.* 2. 2. 83–5. This is, as Russell notes (103), one of the very few passages in which Plutarch acknowledges that moral standards differ in different cultures, that 'our virtues | Lie in th'interpretation of the time' (*Cor.* 4. 7. 49–50).

constancy to excess, and practises it where it is inappropriate, in the forum as well as on the battlefield.[17]

Shakespeare, on the other hand, sees Brutus and Coriolanus (vastly different as they are) as sharing the ideal of being always the same, immovable and 'like themselves'. And the Romes of *Julius Caesar* and *Coriolanus* are sufficiently similar to suggest that this is a peculiarly Roman concept of virtue. No doubt, Coriolanus is extreme; yet Plutarch himself praises him, just before the passage quoted, for showing that even with faulty education a man may be able to 'excell in vertue above the common sorte' (p. 235; I. 2)—a phrase Shakespeare's hero echoes in his double-edged promise to 'exceed the common' (*Cor.* 4. 1. 33). Is there not something in Roman morality, even that of Brutus, which tends towards extreme aspirations?

When Martius comes into conflict with the people, Plutarch condemns his obstinacy as much as their inconstancy—a judgement emphasized by two juxtaposed side-notes in North: '*See the fickle mindes of common people*' and '*The fruites of selfe will and obstinacie*' (p. 243). Plutarch reiterates his criticism of Martius as 'a man too full of passion and choller, and too much given to over selfe will and opinion,' and quotes Plato on 'solitarinesse': 'in the end, all men that are wilfully given to a selfe opinion and obstinate minde, and who will never yeeld to others reason, but to their owne: remaine without companie, and forsaken of all men.' He does at this point acknowledge that Martius' wilfulness is not merely a fault he cannot help but a quality deliberately cultivated: Martius is 'a stoute man of nature, that never yeelded in any respect, as one thinking that to overcome alwaies, and to have the upper hand in all matters, was a token of magnanimitie . . .'. In fact, however (Plutarch insists), it is a token of 'base and faint courage, which spitteth out anger from the most weake and passioned part of the heart, much like the matter of an imposthume'. Governed by his turbulent passions, Martius lacks 'the gravitie

[17] North blurs Plutarch's point that Martius' vices are simply his virtues viewed from a different angle. The passage 'Yet men marvelling . . . was disliked' is translated in Loeb as: 'They did indeed look with admiration upon his insensibility to pleasures, toils, and mercenary gains, to which they gave the names of self-control, fortitude, and justice; but in their intercourse with him as a fellow-citizen they were offended *by it* as ungracious, burdensome, and arrogant' (my emphasis).

[*embrithes*], and affabilitie [*praion*] that is gotten with judgement of learning and reason, which onely is to be looked for in a governour of state' (p. 243; 15. 3–4). Though North obscures the echo, these are precisely the words used in 'Brutus' to describe Brutus' 'gentle [*praeian*] and constant [*embrithê*]' mind. Martius, like Antonius, is for Plutarch an anti-Brutus.

When Martius is banished, North's side-note draws attention to '*Coriolanus constant mind in adversitie*' (p. 246). The text, however, makes it clear that this is a peculiar and perverse kind of constancy.

> *Martius* alone . . . neither in his countenance nor in his gate, did ever shew himselfe abashed, or once let fall his great courage: but . . . did outwardly shew no manner of passion, nor care at all of himselfe. Not that he did patiently beare and temper his good [*sic*] hap,[18] in respect of any reason he had, or by his quiet condition: but because he was so carried away with the vehemencie of anger, and desire of revenge, that he had no sense nor feeling of the hard state he was in, which the common people judge not to be sorow, although in deede it be the very same. For when sorow (as you would say) is set a fire, then it is converted into spite and malice, and driveth away for that time all faintnesse of heart and naturall feare. (pp. 246–7; 21. 1–2)

Though Martius' patience in adversity seems to resemble that of Brutus or Portia, Plutarch insists that this is a parody of true constancy, arising not from reason but from an excess of suppressed emotion.[19] It is this strained and unnatural emotional state which drives Martius in his determination to be revenged upon Rome. His 'obstinate and inflexible rancker' persists until he is confronted with his family; then 'nature so wrought with him' that he 'yeelded to the affection of his bloud, as if he had been violently caried with the furie of a most swift running streame' (p. 254; 34. 2).

Throughout, Plutarch emphasizes the irrational emotional forces which drive Martius. His inflexible stubbornness is derived from pride, irascibility, and self-will, qualities which vitiate his genuine virtues of courage and endurance. In 'The Comparison of Alcibiades

[18] A slip: Amyot has *infortune* (154^r).

[19] A. Luis Pujante, '"No Sense Nor Feeling": A Note on *Coriolanus*, 4. 1', *SQ* 41 (1990), 489–90, draws attention to this passage to explain Coriolanus' oddly insouciant behaviour in 4. 1 as a symptom of 'shock'.

with Martius Coriolanus' Plutarch sums up his tragedy with brutal simplicity:

> And of all his misfortune and ill hap, the austeritie of his nature, and his haughtie obstinate minde, was the only cause: the which of it selfe being hateful to the world, when it is joyned with ambition, it groweth then much more churlish, fierce, and intollerable. (p. 259; 'Comparison of Alcibiades and Coriolanus' 4. 5)

Shakespeare's Aufidius echoes this passage when he suggests that one cause of Coriolanus' tragedy was his inflexibility:

> or whether nature,
> Not to be other than one thing, not moving
> From th' casque to th' cushion, but commanding peace
> Even with the same *austerity* and garb
> As he controll'd the war . . .
>
> (4. 7. 41–5; my emphasis)

In the phrase 'Not to be other than one thing', however, Shakespeare explicitly links Coriolanus' stubbornness with the Stoic virtue of constancy, of being *unus idemque inter diversa*. He thus suggests an analogy which Plutarch would not have accepted. Coriolanus' stubbornness is not merely a fault in a bull-like character untempered by moral training; it is a moral ideal consciously followed in the belief that to be immovable and unyielding is 'a token of magnanimitie'—a belief in which he is supported, up to a point, by his society. If we see in him an absurd and self-destructive rigidity and pride, then that judgement (Shakespeare implies) reflects upon the noble Brutus and upon Roman virtue in general.

Although the Aristotelian triptych which I have described was not planned by Plutarch, it is in keeping with his moral attitudes. Brutus is close to Plutarch's ideal of perfectly tempered, consistent, rational virtue. Antonius and Martius, by contrast, are equally flawed by the dominance of their irrational emotions: Antonius' love of pleasure makes him weak and fickle, a puppet in the hands of others; Martius' pride and anger make him rigid and obstinate, dangerously anti-social in his drive to dominate others.

It may have been his sense of this pattern that drew Shakespeare on from *Julius Caesar* to choose Antony and Coriolanus as heroes.

He reads the 'Lives' (if my reconstruction of his thought is accurate) in the light of the Renaissance idea of constancy, and with an awareness of the problems and paradoxes of the ideal which is foreign to Plutarch's comparatively simple moral judgements. Whereas Plutarch simply admires Brutus and condemns Coriolanus, Shakespeare sees a likeness between them; Coriolanus, in carrying the ideal of constancy to a self-destructive extreme, tests it and exposes its inherent flaws. Antony, similarly, is not just a moral weakling, but a man who deliberately seeks 'variety' of experience instead of the narrowness of Roman constancy. Whereas Plutarch values the mean, Shakespeare is interested in what happens 'when extremities speak' (*Cor.* 3. 2. 42), and in exploring these extremes he explores an extremism which is inherent in the ideal of constancy.[20]

[20] Brockbank (edn. of *Coriolanus*, 28), makes a similar point.

7
'Untired Spirits and Formal Constancy': Julius Caesar

Returning to Shakespeare, the end (in both senses) of this study, it may be appropriate to return to the lines which I quoted at the beginning of the first chapter:

> Let not our looks put on our purposes;
> But bear it as our Roman actors do,
> With untired spirits and formal constancy.
>
> (2. 1. 224–6)

On the surface Brutus is simply urging his fellow conspirators to conceal their true intentions; but the words he uses are heavily loaded. 'Formal constancy' means (as John Dover Wilson noted) 'consistent decorum': playing one's part without slipping out of character.[1] 'Untired spirits' suggests a more Stoic kind of constancy: souls which do not tire but steadfastly withstand adversity. The Ciceronian and Senecan forms of constancy are thus linked. At the same time, both are enclosed within a theatrical metaphor: they are the qualities of 'our Roman actors'. The specifying of *Roman* actors, which may allude to the passage on actors in *De officiis* (1. 114), also seems to imply a logical connection between being Roman and constant and being an actor. At the same time, the perverse attribution of 'constancy' to actors, whose job is to play a number of roles, suggests a potential incongruity between the two halves of the line—between the inner spiritual strength of an 'untired spirit', and the public hypocrisy of assuming a merely 'formal' constancy. This incongruity is underlined by a submerged

[1] *Julius Caesar*, New [Cambridge] Shakespeare (Cambridge, 1949), note ad loc.; he does not explicitly make the connection with Cicero. 'Formal' means 'in outward form or appearance' (*OED* 1c), but with overtones of more pejorative senses: merely in outward appearance (2c), preoccupied with forms (8). Compare the use of 'form' with implications of pretence and deceit in 1. 2. 299 ('*puts on* this tardy form') and 4. 2. 40 ('this sober form . . . hides wrongs').

pun: 'untired'—in the context of 'put on', 'actors', and 'formal'—suggests the wearing of theatrical 'tires' or costumes.[2] Untired spirits, then, are souls which appear naked and undisguised, not assuming a 'formal' appearance. The tensions between the two halves of the line mirror the central tension of the play, not simply between Ciceronian and Senecan constancy, but between the elements in both of inner truth and of external role-playing.[3]

These tensions are central to Shakespeare's first exploration of Roman constancy. Stoic constancy of the Senecan brand has long been recognized as important in *Julius Caesar*.[4] The relevance of Ciceronian decorum has not been noted, in spite of extensive discussion of the play's images of acting and the theatre.[5] Nor—though *Julius Caesar* has long been seen as a 'problem play', deeply concerned with issues of knowledge, judgement and error, rhetoric and persuasion—has the ironic relevance of the Stoic and Neostoic

[2] *OED* 'Tire' v[3] 2b ('To attire, clothe duly'); cf. 'tiring-house', the theatrical term for the backstage area. I have not seen this pun previously noted.

[3] Few critics have looked in detail at these lines. One exception is Jonathan Goldberg, *James I and the Politics of Literature* (Baltimore, 1983), 164, who notes the contradiction between 'resplendent transcendence' and 'the duplicitous form of the actor', but distracts from the central problem by creating unnecessary difficulties over the contrast between genuine and assumed looks.

[4] For earlier discussions of the topic, see above, Ch. 1, n. 9. Robert Ornstein, 'Seneca and the Political Drama of *Julius Caesar*', *JEGP* 57 (1958), 51–6, is not on constancy, but relates to a comment in Seneca's *De beneficiis* (2. 20) on Brutus' political naïvety.

[5] Earlier critics regretted the stiffness of the characters ('more orators than men': Mark Van Doren, *Shakespeare* (London, 1939; New York, 1955), 153). But MacCallum's perception in 1910 (*Shakespeare's Roman Plays*) of a distinction between character and role in Caesar ('he must affect to be what he is not', 231) and Brutus ('a kind of pose', 241) has been taken up by most later critics, many of whom see role-playing as related to the political and ethical nature of Rome. Some of the more important discussions are L. C. Knights, 'Personality and Politics in *Julius Caesar*' (1965; repr. in his *'Hamlet' and Other Shakespearean Essays* (Cambridge, 1979), 82–101); Peter Ure, 'Character and Role from *Richard III* to *Julius Caesar*', in his *Elizabethan and Jacobean Drama*, 22–43; Matthew Proser, *The Heroic Image in Five Shakespearean Tragedies* (Princeton, 1965), 10–50; Stampfer, *Tragic Engagement*, 77–99; John W. Velz, '"If I Were Brutus Now": Role-playing in *Julius Caesar*', *ShakS* 4 (1969), 149–59; Kaufmann and Ronan, '*Julius Caesar*', esp. 20 ('Stoicism is a form of acting'), 37–43; Simmons, *Pagan World*, ch. 3 ('*Julius Caesar*: Our Roman Actors', 65–108); Thomas F. Van Laan, *Role-playing in Shakespeare* (Toronto, 1978), 152–61; Goldberg, *Politics of Literature*, ch. 4 ('The Roman Actor', 164–76); Ralph Berry, 'Communal Identity and the Rituals of *Julius Caesar*', in his *Shakespeare and the Awareness of the Audience* (London, 1985), 75–87; Edward Pechter, '*Julius Caesar* and *Sejanus*: Roman Politics, Inner Selves and the Power of the Theatre', in E. A. J. Honigmann (ed.), *Shakespeare and His Contemporaries* (Manchester, 1986), 60–78.

concept of 'opinion' been perceived.[6] I hope in this chapter to show how Shakespeare constructs Roman constancy as a blend of Senecan *constantia sapientis* and Ciceronian decorum, and how both rest upon and are vitiated by the domination of Rome by opinion. The public temper of Rome is hostile to self-knowledge, in both the individual and the universal sense; in this society decorum becomes a determined playing of inauthentic roles, while aspirations to the heroic stature of the Senecan *sapiens* founder in the gap between claim and reality.

Before I develop this reading, however, a fundamental objection must be faced. Some recent critics have denied the relevance of Stoicism to *Julius Caesar*, on the grounds that, as Plutarch makes clear on the first page of his Life, the historical Brutus was not a Stoic:

> Now touching the GRAECIAN Philosophers, there was no sect nor Philosopher of them, but he heard and liked it: but above all the rest, he loved *Platoes* sect best, and did not much geve him selfe to the new or meane Academie as they call it, but altogether to the old Academie (p. 1054, 2. 1–2)

—that is, the school of Antiochus of Ascalon, which eclectically fused Platonic, Stoic, and sceptical ideas. The debate about Brutus' philosophical position has focused in particular on his reference, in his confused explanation of his attitude to suicide, to 'that philosophy | By which I did blame Cato for the death | Which he did give himself' (5. 1. 100–2). J. C. Maxwell pointed out in 1970 that, though commentators generally explained the 'philosophy' as Stoicism, the Stoics (Cato's school) in fact notoriously approved of suicide, whereas Plato condemned it.[7] Subsequent critics have

[6] R. A. Foakes, 'An Approach to *Julius Caesar*', *SQ* 5 (1954), 259–70, was perhaps the first to note the thematic importance of knowledge and error: 'All is the result of a self-deception, an obsession with names and an ignorance of reality' (270). The epistemological theme has been developed by Ernest Schanzer, *The Problem Plays of Shakespeare* (London, 1963); Mildred E. Hartsock, 'The Complexity of *Julius Caesar*', *PMLA* 81 (1966), 56–62; René E. Fortin, '*Julius Caesar*: An Experiment in Point of View', *SQ* 19 (1968), 341–7; D. J. Palmer, 'Tragic Error in *Julius Caesar*', *SQ* 21 (1970), 399–409 (which Stoically derives error from passion); Wilders, *Lost Garden*, ch. 5 ('Knowledge and Judgement', 79–101). Chang ('Renaissance Historiography') and Rice ('Judgment') relate the theme to Renaissance scepticism, and Vawter, 'After Their Fashion', to Stoic views on fate and divination (an emphasis rather different from mine).

[7] 'Brutus's Philosophy', *N&Q* 215 (1970), 128.

argued inconclusively over the passage and its implications.[8] The most forceful challenge to Stoic readings of the play is that of Gilles Monsarrat, who argues that 'it is unreasonable to father on Shakespeare a philosophic misconception from which his main sources must have preserved him': Shakespeare's Brutus 'is never a Stoic and not always stoical'. More broadly, complaining that '"Stoicism" is almost like a disease in many critical discussions of *Julius Caesar*', Monsarrat suggests that critics like Anson and Brower 'mistake "Romanity" for "Stoicism"'.[9]

For my purposes—concerned as I am with 'constancy' rather than with Stoic philosophy in general—this controversy seems something of a blind alley. I am not concerned (as for instance Vawter is) to argue that Shakespeare had a scholarly knowledge of Hellenistic philosophy, or a precise understanding of the subtle distinctions between the thought of the Stoics and of the Old Academy—which was, in fact, primarily Stoic in its ethical doctrines.[10] In 5.1 he may indeed have himself been confused about the nature of Brutus' 'philosophy' (the source passage in North is, as already noted, deeply ambiguous)—though if so he turns the confusion to dramatic account. But in any case, I do not think Shakespeare's primary concern in this passage is to distinguish between Cato's Stoicism and Brutus' Platonism; he is much more concerned with the problematic relationship between constancy and suicide. Being 'constant'—a Platonic as well as a Stoic virtue—can be held to require either a Senecan suicide, or (in Plato's famous image) a steadfast sticking to one's post.[11] Either a Stoic or a Platonist could reasonably take up either position, and Brutus' wavering between the two serves not so much to pin a philosophical label on him as to illuminate the ambiguity of constancy as a principle.

[8] Mark Sacharoff, 'Suicide and Brutus' Philosophy in *Julius Caesar*', *JHI* 33 (1972), 115–22, lays out the problems but comes to no convincing conclusion; R. F. Fleissner, 'That Philosophy in *Julius Caesar* Again', *Archiv* 222 (1985), 344–5, unconvincingly suggests that 'that philosophy' is Cato's not Brutus'; Wymer, *Suicide and Despair*, 152, argues that, in the light of Neostoic disapproval of suicide, Shakespeare could still have considered Brutus a Stoic; Martindale and Martindale argue that 'Shakespeare deliberately blurs the issue' (*Shakespeare and the Uses of Antiquity*, 168), though they see this as a weakness in the play.

[9] Monsarrat, *Light from the Porch*, 139–44 (141, 143, 144). In a long footnote (141–2 n.) Monsarrat effectively dismantles Vawter's claim that the historical Brutus was a Stoic.

[10] Long, *Hellenistic Philosophy*, 224.

[11] *Phaedo* 61c; see also Wymer, *Suicide and Despair*, 10–11.

More generally, however, it seems undeniable that to represent the 'Romanity' of Brutus, and to a lesser extent of other characters, Shakespeare draws upon the Stoic traditions descending from Seneca and Cicero, and attributes to them attitudes and actions which his audience would clearly have identified as 'stoical'. The objections of Maxwell and Monsarrat to loose assertions about 'Stoicism' are valid; but to deny, on that ground, the illumination which Stoic traditions can throw on the play seems excessively purist.

'A thing unfirm': the world of Julius Caesar

Shakespeare is of course not in any sense original in associating Rome with constancy. The equation of Roman and Stoic virtue had been a commonplace ever since Cicero. Many of the traditional Roman virtues, as defined by the Romans and by later tradition, can be seen as radiating from the central virtue of constancy: fortitude, justice, temperance, *fides*, *gravitas*, all involve steadiness and steadfastness, a refusal to be shifted from one's duty. Rome itself, the Eternal City, is an archetype of stability and permanence, with its straight roads and marble columns and arches, enduring even in ruins—though those ruins also imply the limits of worldly constancy. Rome's solidity, rationality and order are embodied in the 'Roman' simplicity and clarity of *Julius Caesar*'s structure and language.

These Roman qualities are set, however, against a background of mutability, uncertainty, and mystery. It is most potently embodied in the storm, in which Rome is invaded by supernatural disorder: wild beasts roam the streets, the dead walk, and normality is transformed to 'monstrous quality' (1. 3. 68). 'Are you not moved,' Casca demands of Cicero, 'when all the sway of earth | Shakes like a thing unfirm?' (3–4). The subliminal pun suggests that Rome's 'sway', its civilized political order, rests on shaky foundations.[12]

The storm is all the more terrifying because, though it seems meaningful, its meaning is obscure. Characters suggest incompatible explanations: it is a sign of civil war in heaven or divine

[12] The pun is noted by Dover Wilson and Arthur Humphreys (Oxford Shakespeare edn., Oxford, 1984).

anger with mankind (Casca, 1. 3. 11–13), of the unnaturalness of Caesar's tyranny (Cassius, 1. 3. 68–77), of Caesar's impending death (Calphurnia, 2. 2. 30–1) or some other catastrophe (Caesar, 2. 2. 28–9), or simply a natural phenomenon. Cicero, who takes the last view (1. 3. 30), sums up:

> Indeed it is a strange-disposèd time;
> But men may construe things after their fashion,
> Clean from the purpose of the things themselves.
>
> (1. 3. 33–5)

In a play centrally concerned with the problems of knowledge, judgement, and factual and moral error, Cicero's may be taken as a choric comment applicable to much more than the storm.[13]

The disorder and uncertainty of the storm scenes colour the imaginative world of *Julius Caesar* to a surprising degree. All the major characters are complex and changeable, moved by feelings they do not fully understand; the play has a strong undercurrent of powerful, repressed emotions, reflected in imagery of fire, blood, and violence.[14] Similarly, the macrocosm of Rome rests on the dangerously volatile and emotional plebeians. Rome itself is in a process of change from an old to a new order. The characters attempt to control this process, but we know in hindsight that their predictions are wrong and their actions tragically misguided; they move and act in darkness, unsure of anything. Looking into the future near the end of the play, Brutus and Cassius see only that 'the affairs of men rest still incertain' (5. 1. 95), and Brutus utters a heartfelt prayer:

> O that a man might know
> The end of this day's business ere it come!
> But it sufficeth that the day will end,
> And then the end is known.
>
> (5. 1. 123–6)

[13] See Jane Bligh, 'Cicero's Choric Comment in *Julius Caesar*', *English Studies in Canada*, 8 (1982), 391–408, who surveys earlier comments to the same effect.

[14] On imagery, see G. Wilson Knight, *The Imperial Theme* (London, 1931; 3rd edn., 1951), 32–62 ('The Torch of Life') and Charney, *Shakespeare's Roman Plays*, ch. 3. Knight's 'The Eroticism of *Julius Caesar*' (63–95), though eccentric, brings out the elements of irrationality and disorder which conflict with Roman order in the play, and recent criticism has increasingly focused on these: e.g. Spevack's introduction ('What truth ... exists in the play is connected with the "irrational"', 26); Mark Rose, 'Conjuring Caesar: Ceremony, History, and Authority in 1599', *ELR* 19 (1989), 291–304 ('The world of this play is fundamentally mysterious', 298).

His response to the uncertainty of life is a Stoic fatalism: since it is impossible to predict or control the future, one must be prepared to accept with courage and calmness 'the worst that may befall' (96).

The world of *Julius Caesar* is indeed one which naturally leads to Stoicism. Though in theory Stoic ethics rests on a dogmatic theory of knowledge, in practice the close association between Stoicism and scepticism suggests that it can equally be a response to ignorance. The most dramatic example of this is Montaigne's Pyrrho, the sceptic who resorted to an arbitrary and inflexible consistency in a world where no rational certainty was possible. Shakespeare's Romans, in rather the same way, try to create their own constancy within a mutable world. They do this partly through the permanence and stability of Roman institutions, and partly through aspiring as individuals to the virtue of constancy: to be unmoved, unchanged, always the same, rationally consistent and predictable, in a changing world. The ideal of Shakespeare's Romans is to be, in Casca's words, 'not moved, when all the sway of earth | Shakes like a thing unfirm'.[15]

'True fixed and resting quality': Senecan constancy

To be unmoved is the virtue of the Stoic *sapiens*, and this Senecan ideal is most splendidly evoked by Caesar just before his murder:

> I could be well moved if I were as you.
> If I could pray to move, prayers would move me.
> But I am constant as the Northern Star,
> Of whose true fixed and resting quality
> There is no fellow in the firmament.
>
> (3. 1. 58–62)[16]

In declaring that he will not be 'moved', Caesar is making at least three claims: that he will not change his mind, is unmoved

[15] This causal relationship is not always recognized: e.g. Vawter cites Casca's words as showing that constancy is impossible, but does not add that they also show why it is so desirable ('Division', 184).

[16] There is no hint for this speech in Plutarch. The possible influence of earlier theatrical versions of Caesar as a bombastic Senecan tyrant-figure was explored by Harry Morgan Ayres, 'Shakespeare's *Julius Caesar* in the Light of Some Other Versions', *PMLA* 25 (1910), 183–227, and Joan Rees, '*Julius Caesar*: An Earlier Play and an Interpretation', *SQ* 4 (1955), 135–41.

by emotion, and cannot be shaken by external pressures. The most obvious sense is the assertion of immovable will. Caesar refuses to change his decision about Cimber's banishment, and so 'turn preordinance and first decree' into childish capriciousness (38–9). Brutus later takes a very similar stand in refusing (with '*wonderfull constancy*', as North commented) to pardon Lucius Pella (4. 2. 55 ff.). In either case, since the play withholds the facts about Cimber and Pella, we may commend their firmness of principle or condemn their obstinacy. It is clear that both Brutus and Caesar find a positive virtue in not changing their minds, refusing to be 'moved' in the sense (often used in the play) of 'urged' or 'persuaded'. Brutus is typical in expressing to Cassius his reluctance to '[b]e any further moved' (1. 2. 167–8). The plebs, by contrast, are 'moved' (3. 2. 264) only too easily, and literally, by Antony's rhetoric.[17]

'Move' also, in these instances, implies the arousal of emotion. Caesar is denying that he 'bears such rebel blood' (40) as to be moved by emotive appeals. Brutus acknowledges that Caesar shares his own Stoic ideal of rationality: 'I have not known when his affections swayed | More than his reason' (2. 1. 20–1). It does not occur to him that to deny all 'affections' (emotions or friendships) may be as tyrannical as to be governed by them.[18] Having himself acted on these principles in sacrificing his personal affection for Caesar to the public good, he is contemptuous of Cassius' appeals to love or anger:

> Go show your slaves how choleric you are,
> And make your bondmen tremble. Must I budge? . . .
>   By the gods,
> You shall digest the venom of your spleen,
> Though it do split you.
>
> (4. 2. 99–100, 102–4)

[17] 'Move[d]' is also used in this sense at 1. 1. 61; 1. 3. 120; 3. 1. 236; 3. 2. 224. The sense of 'persuaded' is clearest in 1. 3; elsewhere it has clear emotional overtones. Kaufmann and Ronan, '*Julius Caesar*', 24, note the centrality of the word 'move', without distinguishing its senses; Michael E. Mooney, '"Passion, I See, Is Catching": The Rhetoric of *Julius Caesar*', *JEGP* 90 (1991), 31–50, comments on its use in contexts of persuasion.

[18] Levitsky, 'Elements', 242, is clearly wrong to assume that Brutus is criticizing rather than praising Caesar, but the misreading does suggest the potential moral ambiguity of his praise. On Brutus and reason, see Vawter, 'Division', 182, though his comments are extreme.

The man who refuses to be moved by his own passions will not 'budge' in the face of Cassius'.[19] He insists that emotions must be suppressed, even if the effect of that suppression is as painful and self-destructive as Portia's burning coals.

Brutus' Stoic view of emotion is most clearly seen in his advice to the conspirators on the frame of mind in which they must kill Caesar:

> And, gentle friends,
> Let's kill him boldly, but not wrathfully . . .
> And let our hearts, as subtle masters do,
> Stir up their servants to an act of rage,
> And after seem to chide 'em.
>
> (2. 1. 171–2, 175–7)

Brutus sums up the Senecan view that the wise man will do what is right 'boldly' but dispassionately. But the simplicity of this doctrine runs into confusion as Brutus, uneasily aware that you cannot kill a man in a spirit of calm reasonableness, ascribes the necessary emotion to the body rather than the heart or soul. The disjunction seems not only implausible but repellently hypocritical: Brutus' simile puts him in the position of one who orders a crime and then disclaims responsibility for it.[20]

The play thus, in a very traditional way, calls into question Stoic *apatheia*. As Antony tells the plebeians, 'You are not wood, you are not stones, but men' (3. 2. 143); Stoic-stockish impassivity is neither humanly attainable nor desirable. In fact, as I have suggested, Shakespeare's Romans are not passionless. The plebs are governed by emotion; so is Antony, though he is also capable of manipulating both his own feelings and theirs to political ends; and the mob violence which results powerfully demonstrates the dangers of unrestrained passions. Restrained passions, however, can be equally dangerous. Those patricians who, unlike Antony, hold to the Roman code of rationality are in fact more strongly influenced by feelings than they are prepared to acknowledge. Immovable Caesar vacillates between the demands of fear, ambition, and dread of ridicule; shrewd Cassius sacrifices his tactical judgement to his reluctance to oppose the grieving Brutus; Brutus himself seems unaware how far his decision to kill Caesar is

[19] *OED* and editors define 'budge' as 'flinch', but the idea of movement is clearly implied.

[20] See Kaufmann and Ronan, '*Julius Caesar*', 40.

motivated by personal and family pride. The play has an almost Freudian sense of how emotion can work all the more powerfully because it is repressed.

The effect of Stoic constancy, then, is not to eradicate emotion but to repress it. When the word 'constancy' is explicitly used, it is most often in the context of concealment. Brutus' exhortation to 'formal constancy' comes as he advises the conspirators to conceal their true thoughts and feelings; when he urges Cassius to 'be constant' (3. 1. 22) it is because Cassius' panic threatens to reveal the plot. Portia makes 'strong proof of [her] constancy' by giving herself 'a voluntary wound' and concealing her pain (2. 1. 298–9)—proving herself more constant than Brutus, who has been unable to hide his perturbation from her. Later, fearful of letting slip a betraying word under the strain of waiting for news, she prays,

> O constancy, be strong upon my side;
> Set a huge mountain 'tween my heart and tongue.
>
> (2. 4. 6–7)

Constancy is here conceived not as freedom from suffering but as repression of it; its function is to stop up the passage between feeling and expression. The power of the image is increased by the ambiguity of 'upon my side', which suggests an oppressive weight pressing upon the chest and heart.[21] Constancy in *Julius Caesar* is not so much a superhuman imperviousness to pain as an ability to pretend to be impervious—like Seneca's gladiator who, though wounded, 'maketh shew that it is nothing' (*Const.* 16. 2).

The third sense of being 'unmoved' is the Stoic claim of indifference to external evils. Cassius sums up this doctrine when he tells Brutus, rather glibly, 'Of your philosophy you make no use, | If you give place to accidental evils' (4. 2. 199–200). The essence of Stoic philosophy is to enable us to endure 'accidental evils' steadfastly, without 'giving place' to them, in the knowledge that such things are indifferent. Brutus uses the Stoic term when he claims to look on honour and death 'indifferently' (1. 2. 89),[22]

[21] Shakespeare elsewhere uses 'sides' (of the body) in the context of repressing powerful emotions: e.g. *TN* 2. 4. 92; *Lear* (F text) 2. 2. 370.

[22] Brutus' phrasing is suggestively ambiguous. The following lines make it clear that he means 'I am indifferent to death if it comes accompanied by honour'; but the more literal reading, that honour (fame, popular approval) is as 'indifferent' as death, is clearly also a plausible Stoic position.

and Cassius picks it up when he tells Casca, 'I am armed, | And dangers are to me indifferent' (1. 3. 114).

The most obvious 'accidental evil', as in these passages, is death. Both Caesar and Brutus declare it indifferent. Caesar insists that it is not death ('a necessary end') but the fear of death that is an evil: 'Cowards die many times before their deaths' (2. 2. 32, 36). Brutus explains the Senecan technique of meditation on its inevitability: 'With meditating that she must die once, | I have the patience to endure it now' (4. 2. 244–6).[23] We are made aware, however, that Brutus' Stoic indifference to Portia's death is assumed, and a note of strained overstatement in Caesar's lines makes us suspect that he, too, does not find the fear of death as incomprehensible as he claims (2. 2. 34–7). Brutus' true feelings about death are perhaps revealed in the dialogue over Caesar's body:

> BRUTUS. Fates, we will know your pleasures.
> That we shall die, we know; 'tis but the time
> And drawing days out that men stand upon.
> CASCA. Why, he that cuts off twenty years of life
> Cuts off so many years of fearing death.
> BRUTUS. Grant that, and then is death a benefit.
> So are we Caesar's friends, that have abridged
> His time of fearing death.
>
> (3. 1. 99–106)

Caught in Casca's 'sophistical trap', Brutus skids from the claim that death is indifferent to the claim that it is positively desirable.[24] Senecan Stoicism, as we have seen, is always tempted towards a death-wish; Shakespeare's Romans too are tempted to see death as a positive relief from the strain of 'so many years of fearing death' and denying their fear.

Immovable will, passionlessness, indifference to pain and death: all of these aspects of Stoic constancy add up to a claim to rise above humanity, to 'escape man', in Montaigne's phrase. This aspiration is reflected especially in an exaltation of mind and spirit over body, seen in Brutus' reluctance to sleep (4. 2. 281–2) and Portia's voluntary wound; its ultimate act is suicide, the destruction

[23] Benjamin Boyce, 'The Stoic *Consolatio* and Shakespeare', *PMLA* 64 (1949), 771–80, deals with Shakespeare's often ironic use of such Stoic responses to death.

[24] The phrase is Harley Granville-Barker's, *Prefaces to Shakespeare* (London, 1963; first pub. 1930), ii. 227.

of the body to preserve the mind. Set against it is the physical weakness of the characters: epilepsy, fever, deafness, short-sightedness, ague, insomnia, fainting, illnesses real and pretended. Episodes such as Caesar's epileptic fit at the moment of being offered the crown, and the fatal myopia of the 'great observer' Cassius (1. 2. 203), suggest nature reminding the Romans (again in Montaigne's words) of the 'mortalitie . . . and insipiditie' of the human condition, by forcing them to acknowledge flaws 'inexpugnable unto our reason, and to the Stoicke virtue' (2. 2).[25]

The most extreme statement of this aspiration to divinity is, again, Caesar's Northern Star speech. As John Anson first pointed out, Caesar here echoes Lipsius' claim to 'that great title, the neerest that man can have to God, *To be immooveable*'.[26] He represents himself as the pole star (3. 1. 60), the one unmoving point in a mutable world, and as Mount Olympus (74), an image of immovable bulk but also one which combines the connotations of Seneca's two images of constancy: the rock and the god. Caesar is thus more than human, while the rest of mankind, who are 'flesh and blood, and apprehensive' (67), possess only the lower attributes of humanity, in Lipsius' words 'the filth of the bodie and contagion of the senses'.[27] Indeed, as Anson noted, he betrays that he does not see himself as 'flesh and blood' when he declares that his blood cannot be 'thawed' or 'melt[ed]' (41–2); like the icy Angelo (another character who, as his name suggests, aspires to rise above humanity), Caesar 'scarce confesses | That his blood flows' (*MfM* 1. 3. 51–2). Ice-cold and stone-hard, Caesar represents himself as the monstrous Stoic-stock of the anti-Stoic tradition. The hollowness of the claim, already implied by his vacillations in the previous scene, is made brutally clear when 'Olympus' and 'the Northern Star' are reduced to a 'bleeding piece of earth' (257) on the Senate floor.

The constancy of Brutus, Caesar's mirror-image,[28] is subjected

[25] On the motif of sickness see Knight, *Imperial Theme*, 40–2 ('Nearly everyone in the play is ill'); Foakes, 'Approach', 198–9.

[26] Anson, 'Politics of the Hardened Heart', 14–18. This paragraph is strongly indebted to Anson, though I diverge from his subsequent argument.

[27] Vawter ('Division', 177) and most editors, like the *OED*, take 'apprehensive' to mean 'intelligent' (*OED*'s sense 4); I prefer, with Humphreys, to take it as meaning primarily 'capable of perception' (*OED* 2). It seems incongruous in this context for Caesar to praise human beings in general for being intelligent.

[28] Critics who have noted the parallelism of Caesar and Brutus include Norman Rabkin, 'Structure, Convention and Meaning in *Julius Caesar*', *JEGP* 63 (1964), 240–54, and Simmons, *Pagan World*, 87.

to a less brutal critique. Though less prone than Caesar to claim godlike status, Brutus too seeks to rise above humanity by achieving an impossible degree of consistency, rationality, and imperturbability, 'armed so strong in honesty' that external threats pass by him 'as the idle wind' (4. 2. 124–5). It is an admirable ideal, yet its effect in practice is often to make him rigid, cruel, and (most of all) dishonest—since, although he cannot in fact be absolutely constant, he must pretend to himself and others that he is so.

Brutus (despite the claims of some anti-Stoic critics) is clearly neither evil nor mad; for that matter, even Caesar's invocation of the Northern Star is splendid as well as bombastic. The play's treatment of Senecan constancy is not unsympathetic; but it is shown to be a flawed ideal, not humanly attainable, and therefore liable to involve its adherents in continual pretence and self-deception. In Montaigne's formula, it is 'a profitable desire; but likewise absurd'.

Roman opinion

Shakespeare's treatment of Stoic constancy is essentially traditional. What is more original in the play is his sense of the relationship between constancy and Rome: the paradox that such a heroically individualistic, heaven-aspiring ideal should arise out of a society whose values are public-spirited and earthbound, and the deeper irony that, in fact, an ideal which rests on pretence is thoroughly appropriate to a society governed by appearances and 'opinion'.

In *Julius Caesar* virtue is defined as Romanness. The characters are obsessively conscious of their national identity: the words 'Rome' and 'Roman' occur seventy-three times, not merely as labels but often with a moral significance.[29] Cassius tells the conspirators to 'show yourselves true Romans' (2. 1. 222)—that is, courageous and loyal. Brutus urges Messala, 'as you are a Roman [i.e. honest], tell me true,' and Messala replies, 'Then like a Roman [i.e. bravely] bear the truth I tell' (4. 2. 241–2). To 'be a Roman' in this sense, to live up to the virtues the word implies, is the highest possible praise: Brutus' epitaph for Cassius is 'last of

[29] Foakes, 'Approach', 267–9; Berry, 'Communal Identity', in *Awareness*. Word counts here and elsewhere are taken from Marvin Spevack (ed.), *A Complete and Systematic Concordance to the Works of Shakespeare*, 6 vols. (Hildesheim, 1968–70).

all the Romans' (5. 3. 98). To fail to live up to them, for instance by breaking a promise, is to be no true Roman but guilty of 'bastardy' (2. 1. 135–9). Genuine as the Roman virtues are, there is something faintly absurd in this elevation of a place-name into a moral norm. Its self-referentiality also raises moral problems: if virtue is identified as Roman, and Romanness as virtue, by what standards can Rome itself be judged?

Similar problems are raised by another of the play's keywords, 'honour'. What is 'Roman' and hence praiseworthy is defined by the opinions of other Romans, by honour and reputation. But what is honour? Brutus identifies it with 'the general good':

> If it be aught toward the general good,
> Set honour in one eye and death i'th' other,
> And I will look on both indifferently;
> For let the gods so speed me as I love
> The name of honour more than I fear death.
> CASSIUS. I know that virtue to be in you, Brutus,
> As well as I do know your outward favour.
> Well, honour is the subject of my story.
>
> (1. 2. 87–94)

But the honour that is the subject of Cassius' story is (as his image betrays) an 'outward' matter of public recognition; he harps on the contrast between the 'honours that are heaped on Caesar' (135) and the 'dishonourable graves' (139) to which others like himself are relegated. By his deliberate confusion of personal honourableness with public honours, he shows how Brutus' 'honourable metal may be wrought | From that it is disposed' (309–10).[30] Later, in the Forum, Antony hammers the word 'honourable' itself into another shape, so that the crowd revile Brutus' honour as villainy. Brutus, who begged them to 'Believe me for mine honour' (3. 2. 14), can have no easy answer, for how can 'honour' be defined except as that which others regard as honourable?[31]

Such questions, as we have seen, were being urgently debated in

[30] This passage is well discussed by Simmons, *Pagan World*, 95–8.

[31] On 'honour' I am indebted to Norman Council, *When Honour's at the Stake: Ideas of Honour in Shakespeare's Plays* (London, 1973), ch. 3 (60–74). Gary Miles illuminatingly discusses the actual importance of honour in Roman culture, though he oddly concludes that Shakespeare failed to understand, or at least to communicate, 'why his Roman subjects identified public performance and personal worth as completely as they did' ('How Roman', 282).

the late sixteenth century by Neostoics and sceptics like Montaigne. In their terms, the Rome of *Julius Caesar* may be defined as a society governed by 'opinion'. It erects its own standards into moral absolutes, and is dominated by the fallible and fickle judgements of public opinion. The problematic quality of *Julius Caesar*, and its preoccupation with questions of truth and judgement, are thus thematically related to its Roman setting. Not that such problems are exclusively Roman; but the Romans are peculiarly prone to them because their pagan and secular world lacks absolute values. Relying purely on human reason, they fail to recognize how far they are in fact guided by opinion; as Montaigne remarked in the 'Apologie', the two can be hard to distinguish in their 'inconstant vanitie and vaine inconstancy'.

The 'public temper of Rome' (in Eliot's phrase) means that truth is constituted by judgements arrived at through a process of public observation, discussion, and persuasion. Characters continually observe and attempt to 'construe' one another's behaviour and character, as Cassius observes and construes Brutus (1. 2. 34, 47), Caesar and Antony observe Cassius, and everyone observes Caesar.[32] They also continually attempt to persuade one another. The Rome of *Julius Caesar* echoes with rhetoric; not only in the great public scenes but in private encounters and even in soliloquy, characters use language to persuade others (or themselves) to a desired opinion.[33]

In such a society there is a constant temptation to confuse what seems true (or can be made to seem true) with what is true. 'Fashion it thus' (2. 1. 30), Brutus tells himself, construing Caesar's actions after his own fashion. The conspirators want Brutus in their plot because, as Casca puts it,

> he sits high in all the people's hearts,
> And that which would appear offence in us

[32] Leggatt has some shrewd comments on the ways in which 'appearances matter' in the play (*Shakespeare's Political Drama*, 141–3).

[33] On rhetoric, see Gayle Greene, '"The Power of Speech | To Stir Men's Blood": The Language of Tragedy in Shakespeare's *Julius Caesar*', *RenD* 11 (1980), 67–93; John W. Velz, '*Orator* and *Imperator* in *Julius Caesar*: Style and the Process of Roman History', *ShakS* 15 (1982), 55–75; Anne Barton, '*Julius Caesar* and *Coriolanus*: Shakespeare's Roman World of Words', in Philip H. Highfield Jr. (ed.), *Shakespeare's Craft* (Carbondale, Ill., 1982), 24–47 (who argues that rhetoric in this play is 'unequivocally poisonous', 40); and Mooney, 'Rhetoric'.

His countenance, like richest alchemy,
Will change to virtue and to worthiness.

(1. 3. 157–60)

Metellus similarly argues that Cicero's 'silver hairs | Will purchase us a good opinion' (2. 1. 143–4). Their assumption that what matters is how the conspiracy is seen by others is unconsciously echoed by Brutus a little later, when he urges the conspirators to kill Caesar without anger:

This shall make
Our purpose necessary, and not envious;
Which so appearing to the common eyes,
We shall be called purgers, not murderers.

(177–80)

Of course, the fact that the murder *appears* necessary does not *make* it so—any more than the fact that the murderers 'seem to chide' their rage means that they are in fact passionless.[34] Brutus has temporarily lost sight of the distinction he later passionately regrets: 'That every like is not the same, O Caesar, | The heart of Brutus ernes to think upon' (2. 2. 128–9). The Romans of *Julius Caesar* are fatally prone to overlook the difference between 'like' and 'the same'.

The most critical way in which opinion displaces knowledge in the play is the failure of self-knowledge. Shakespeare's Romans are more concerned with the way in which others perceive them than with their own self-awareness—a flaw which, I have suggested, is inherent in both Senecan and Ciceronian Stoicism. The issue is most clearly defined in a passage of Socratic dialogue between Brutus and Cassius:

CASSIUS. . . . Tell me, good Brutus, can you see your face?
BRUTUS. No, Cassius, for the eye sees not itself
But by reflection, by some other things.
CASSIUS. 'Tis just;
And it is very much lamented, Brutus,
That you have no such mirrors as will turn
Your hidden worthiness into your eye,
That you might see your shadow. I have heard
Where many of the best respect in Rome—

[34] See Kaufmann and Ronan, '*Julius Caesar*', 40.

Except immortal Caesar—speaking of Brutus,
And groaning underneath this age's yoke,
Have wished that noble Brutus had his eyes.

(1. 2. 53–64)

Cassius proposes, and Brutus accepts, that it is impossible to see yourself except as reflected in the eyes of others. Self-knowledge can be gained only through the opinions held of you by others, whose opinions in turn are validated by the 'respect' in which *they* are held . . . The sense of endless regression is underlined by Cassius' imagery, which echoes the discussions of honour by Cicero (in *Tusculans* 3) and later writers such as Du Vair. For Cicero, true honour is the accurate reflection of virtue, but false honour, popular reputation, is a mere shadow. Cassius' word 'shadow', which hovers between the two meanings, suggests that the distinction is itself a somewhat shadowy one.[35]

Brutus, in a flash of insight, objects

Into what dangers would you lead me, Cassius,
That you would have me seek into myself
For that which is not in me?

(65–7)

Cassius brushes aside the question; his task is to induce Brutus to abandon his own sense of his 'self', and accept instead the image of Brutus the tyrannicide reflected in Cassius' glass. In the orchard scene we see this process completed, as Brutus is drawn to accept 'the great opinion | That Rome holds of his name' (1. 2. 318–19), as embodied in the cryptic and forged letter which he has to 'piece . . . out' by the light of 'exhalations whizzing in the air' (2. 1. 51, 44). It is a wonderfully suggestive image of the corruption of self-knowledge by 'opinion'. From now on Brutus will, as Cassius wishes, have and be governed by 'that opinion of [him]self | Which every noble Roman bears of [him]' (92–3).

This failure in self-knowledge of the play's most introspective character is symptomatic of a world in which people see their actions most clearly as reflected in the eyes of others. It is not

[35] William O. Scott, 'The Speculative Eye: Problematic Self-Knowledge in *Julius Caesar*', *ShS* 40 (1988), 77–89, discusses this passage, though with the effect of darkening rather than illuminating it. Like other commentators Scott compares *Tro.* 3. 3. 90–118, where the same idea is treated with more overt irony.

surprising that one of the recurring images is that of the theatre, where characters' performances are judged by an audience: Casca sees Caesar's refusal of the crown as a performance clapped and hissed by the people (1. 2. 258–61), and Cassius and Brutus, standing over Caesar's body, speculate how future audiences will respond when the 'lofty scene' is 'acted over' (3. 1. 112–19). The most striking of these images, Brutus' charge to the conspirators to emulate the 'formal constancy' of 'Roman actors', suggests how constancy in this world becomes defined as a form of performance. But the link between constancy and Roman acting, of course, had already been made by Cicero.

'A Roman's part': Ciceronian decorum

The peculiar quality of Roman constancy in *Julius Caesar*, I have suggested, derives from the mingling of its Senecan and Ciceronian definitions. While Senecan Stoic constancy involves an element of pretence, it is Cicero who explicitly recommended his readers to model their behaviour on 'Roman actors'. Shakespeare's Romans, however, take from Cicero's image not its ostensible point—the need to choose appropriate roles—but rather its implications of externality and performance.

For Cicero, every human being has three *personae* or roles which must be played consistently—the role of a human being, the role of oneself as an individual, and the social role—but the first two must take precedence over the last. In *Julius Caesar*—from the opening lines in which Flavius and Murellus berate the plebeians for violating decorum by appearing on the street 'without the sign | Of [their] profession' (1. 1. 4–5)—the social role is primary.[36] Shakespeare's Romans are less concerned with '*play[ing] the man well and duely*' (in Montaigne's phrase), or with knowing

[36] Barbara L. Parker, '"A Thing Unfirm": Plato's *Republic* and Shakespeare's *Julius Caesar*', *SQ* 44 (1993), 30–43 (36), links this episode with a passage in Plato's *Republic* (4. 434) where carpenter and cobbler typify the masses who must not be allowed to meddle in government. If she is right, the play opens with an allusion to Plato's view that a just community depends on each citizen consistently playing a single role, and hence a gesture towards the Platonic assumptions at the root of the whole constancy tradition. (This is not to accept Parker's wider interpretation of Shakespeare's politics as Platonic.)

themselves, than with being consistently Roman, playing 'a Roman's part' (5. 3. 88).

Even individual identity becomes a social role. Names such as 'Brutus' and 'Caesar' become the labels of a *persona*, a publicly defined role which the bearer of the name must play.[37] We see this most clearly in the device which John W. Velz has usefully labelled 'illeism', by which characters refer to themselves (or their listeners) in the third person.[38] Illeism is used most often by Caesar—'Caesar is turned to hear' (1. 2. 19), 'Caesar shall forth' (2. 2. 10), 'Shall Caesar send a lie?' (2. 2. 65)—but also by Brutus, Cassius, Antony, Casca, Portia, and others. Its effect is to suggest the speaker looking at himself or herself from the outside. When Caesar says, 'Caesar should be a beast without a heart | If he should stay at home today for fear' (2. 2. 42–3), he means that this is what others would say of him. When Brutus says that 'poor Brutus, with himself at war, | Forgets the shows of love to other men' (1. 2. 48–9), he is concerned with how his friends will 'construe' his neglect of them.

In such cases the name stands for an ideal self which the speaker must consistently live up to. Caesar must be valiant, Brutus wise, Portia constant, in order to be themselves. 'Shall Caesar send a lie?' implies that Caesar, being Caesar, cannot stoop to such an act. Portia tells Brutus that he is acting out of character ('I should not know you Brutus'), and, when he tries to use illness as an excuse, responds unanswerably, 'Brutus is wise, and were he not in health | He would embrace the means to come by it' (2. 1. 254, 257–8). Brutus, being Brutus, cannot act as unwisely as he claims to be doing.

The relationship between person and name is defined most sharply by Caesar. Advised by Antony not to fear Cassius, he retorts,

> I fear him not.
> Yet if my name were liable to fear,

[37] Foakes, 'Approach', 264–7; Madeleine Doran, 'What Should Be in that "Caesar"?: Proper Names in *Julius Caesar*', in *Shakespeare's Dramatic Language* (Madison, 1976), 120–53; Berry, *Awareness*, 79 (the name as 'a kind of externalized self').

[38] Velz, 'Ancient World', 10. Velz also discusses the device in 'If I Were Brutus Now', but his political interpretation (someone must 'be Caesar') is different from mine.

I do not know the man I should avoid
So soon as that spare Cassius.

(1. 2. 199–202)

He goes on to analyse shrewdly why Cassius is dangerous, yet ends by insisting, 'I rather tell thee what is to be feared | Than what I fear, for always I am Caesar' (212–13). 'Caesar' by definition cannot fear. In asserting 'always I am Caesar', Caesar is making the Stoic claim to be *unus idemque inter diversa*, always the same. This is not exactly a claim to be 'true to himself' (in a sense he is being false to himself, since his earnest denials betray that he does indeed fear Cassius), but rather to be true to his role. 'Caesar' is a publicly assumed role, which Caesar the man must play with decorum and 'formal constancy'. The range of actions possible to him is circumscribed by his role; to allow others to say 'Lo, Caesar is afraid' (2. 2. 101) would be a violation of decorum.

To see one's actions in this way from the outside can be a means of avoiding personal responsibility. When Caesar announces what 'Caesar' thinks, he is not expressing his personal feelings but issuing a press statement about a public figure. His shifts in 2. 2 between third person ('Caesar shall forth') and first person ('I will stay at home') suggest his wavering between the vulnerable human being and the immutable public Caesar. Similarly Brutus, while debating with himself over the murder, speaks of himself as 'I'; having made the decision, he slips self-protectively into the third person:

O Rome, I make thee promise,
If the redress will follow, thou receivest
Thy full petition at the hand of Brutus.

(2. 1. 56–8)

Representing himself as Rome sees him, as a public figure, he avoids the personal implications of the direct statement 'I shall kill Caesar.'

In some ways the Romans of *Julius Caesar* are acting out Cicero's concept of decorum. They see themselves as actors, conceive of virtue as the consistent playing of a part, and are intensely concerned with *aequabilitas*, believing that 'ther is nothing more seemely than an evennesse in all mans lyfe, and everye of his doinges'. They neglect, however, the rest of Cicero's sentence: '... which you can not keepe, if you counterfette an others nature, and lette passe your owne' (1. 111). Lacking self-knowledge, they try instead to act artificial parts imposed on them by their society, the expectations of others, and their own moral aspirations. Casca, an extreme and semi-comic example, seems a man without a self, who changes his *personae* (obsequious courtier, laid-back cynic, superstitious omen-monger, Stoic patriot) as rapidly as he changes his opinions.[39] Others show a clearer tension between natural self and role: Caesar shows fitful glimpses of human warmth and weakness behind the mask of being 'always ... Caesar'; 'gentle Portia' (2. 1. 277) is crushed by her attempts to live up to the role of Brutus' wife and Cato's daughter.

The tension is clearest in Brutus, the gentle philosopher who turns himself into a political assassin, despite his sense that he is being made to 'seek within [him]self | For that which is not in [him]'. He is drawn away from his true self by temptations which Cicero warns against: family tradition, the influence of others, the pressure of public opinion, and, most of all, what Cicero singles out as the greatest enemy of true decorum: the desire to take up a noble role without considering whether one is fitted for it—'for neither is it to anye purpose to fight againste nature nor to ensue any thynge that ye can not atteine' (1. 110). The strain of Brutus' fight against his own nature finally leads him to embrace death with relief.

The most successful characters in *Julius Caesar* are those who eschew consistency and treat their roles as masks to be manipulated and discarded. Both Cassius (in the earlier scenes) and the theatre-loving Antony play with the possibility of alternative roles: 'If I were Brutus now, and he were Cassius ...' (1. 2. 314); 'But were I Brutus, | And Brutus Antony ...' (3. 2. 221–2). Refusing (in Montaigne's words) to treat a 'vizard or apparance' as a 'real essence' (3. 10), they avoid the rigidity of a Brutus or a Caesar. Of course, the flexibility of an Antony has its own dangers. *Antony and Cleopatra* will suggest that the future belongs to Octavius,

[39] The inconsistencies of Casca's characterization have often been criticized (e.g. by Granville-Barker, *Prefaces*, ii. 212), but in a play so concerned with constancy they are surely as deliberate as those of Cleopatra. For his changes of opinion, note e.g. 2. 1. 142, 152.

who maintains his role perfectly because, as far as we can see, he has no identity outside it.

'Like Brutus, like himself'

The Roman idea of constancy in *Julius Caesar*, with its blend of Senecan steadfastness, Ciceronian consistency, role-playing, and concern for public opinion, is perhaps most sharply summed up in the traditional phrase: to be 'like oneself'. The phrase is only used in the last act, and it is in these final scenes that the meaning of constancy is most clearly defined, as Brutus faces its final test, death.

The problems involved in being constant are sharply highlighted in Brutus' double response to the death of Portia. At the end of the quarrel in 4. 2, Brutus, who has been rigidly self-contained in the face of Cassius' passion, bursts into surprising rage at the poet's interruption. Cassius teases him with the lapse from his customary 'philosophy', and Brutus responds (with an odd blend of stark grief and Stoic pride), 'No man bears sorrow better. Portia is dead' (4. 2. 201). The revelation, which forces us to re-evaluate what had up to this moment seemed Brutus' inhuman coldness, is the play's most dramatic demonstration of constancy as the repression of pain. It is illuminated, too, when we learn that Portia, who was so proud of her ability to 'bear . . . with patience' (2. 1. 300), died of '[i]mpatience' of Brutus' absence (4. 2. 204), and by a method horribly appropriate to the Stoic suppression of emotion: swallowing fire (206–10).

A little later, the question of Portia's death is raised again. This time Brutus claims ignorance:

> BRUTUS. Now as you are a Roman, tell me true.
> MESSALA. Then like a Roman bear the truth I tell;
> For certain she is dead, and by strange manner.
> BRUTUS. Why, farewell, Portia. We must die, Messala.
> With meditating that she must die once,
> I have the patience to endure it now.
> MESSALA. Even so great men great losses should endure.
> CASSIUS. I have as much of this in art as you,
> But yet my nature could not bear it so.
>
> (241–9)

In this public response Brutus is at once maintaining decorum, the behaviour appropriate to 'a Roman' and to Brutus, and staging a Senecan 'example of constancy' for the benefit of others like Messala. But in the process of maintaining formal constancy he is forced to dissemble his true feelings and tell a flat lie. The ambiguity of Cassius' half-admiring, half-appalled comment hinges on the meaning of 'art'. Its primary, ostensible meaning is 'The learning of the schools' (*OED* 3)—that is, 'I am as well trained as you in Stoic ethical theory, but I couldn't bear to put it into practice like this.'[40] There is, however, a secondary meaning shared only between Cassius and Brutus: 'Studied conduct or action . . . artfulness' (*OED* 13)—'I thought *I* was a good hypocrite, but how can you bear to act at a moment like this?' Many critics, equally appalled, have explained away the duplicate revelation as a confusion produced by rewriting.[41] I see it rather as central to Shakespeare's portrayal of constancy: as a genuinely noble ideal which nevertheless rests on unnatural suppression of feeling and on 'artful' pretence, both directed toward satisfying the opinions of others.

The possibility of suicide for Brutus himself is first raised in his conversation with Cassius in 5. 1. I have already looked at this problematic passage in relation to the ambiguity of North and the question of 'that philosophy'; here I would note how Shakespeare links these ambiguities to questions about decorum. Brutus shifts from a fumbling first-person attempt to explain his position ('I know not how, | But . . .') to a firm third-person declaration that 'Brutus . . . bears too great a mind' to be led in triumph. The illeism suggests that he has slipped from Stoic philosophy to Roman decorum. Philosophy may claim that it is more constant to endure

[40] For the use of 'art' to mean (Stoic) philosophy, compare Thomas Lodge's *The Wounds of Civil War* (ed. J. W. Houppert, Regents edn., London, 1969), where Marius' question, 'What mean have they left me to cure my smart?' is answered by the echo 'Art' (3. 4. 46).

[41] Most earlier 20th-cent. editors saw this passage as an earlier version of the scene intended to have been replaced by 4. 2. 195–210, and often bracketed it (e.g. Dover Wilson, T. S. Dorsch (Arden, London, 1955)). More recent editors tend to accept that both versions were intended to stand (e.g. the complete Oxford; Humphreys, 79–81), though Spevack, in a confusingly inconclusive discussion, seems to incline towards the duplication theory (149–50). Thomas Clayton, ' "Should Brutus Never Taste of Portia's Death but Once?": Text and Performance in *Julius Caesar*', *SEL* 23 (1983), 237–58, surveys the debate and convincingly defends the existing text.

defeat, but as 'Brutus' and a 'noble Roman' he cannot endure such humiliation; to live on in defeat would be for him, as for Cato in Cicero's discussion (1. 112), a violation of decorum. To preserve the integrity of his *persona*, he must die.

The link between death and decorum is heavily stressed in the scenes which lead up to Brutus' death. Titinius dies with the words: 'this is a Roman's part' (5. 3. 88). In 5. 4 this idea of playing a part to the end, and dying in character, is linked with an echoing insistence on names. Young Cato 'proclaim[s his] name about the field' (3) until he is cut down and Lucillius declares that he will 'be honoured, being Cato's son' (11). Lucillius himself meanwhile is more literally playing a part: 'And I am Brutus, Marcus Brutus, I' (7).[42] When his pretence is discovered, he tells Antony,

> I dare assure thee that no enemy
> Shall ever take alive the noble Brutus.
> The gods defend him from so great a shame.
> When you do find him, or alive or dead,
> He will be found like Brutus, like himself.
>
> (5. 4. 21–5)

The context, with its motifs of names, honour, and acting, throws a light on the implications of the traditional Stoic formula. Acting 'like himself', Brutus, as much as Lucillius, can be seen as a man playing the role of Brutus.[43]

Senecan constancy and decorum finally mingle in Brutus' death scene. His justification for death is Stoic: it is 'more worthy' to choose death, actively asserting one's freedom, than to wait to be killed (5. 5. 24).[44] Under the Stoicism, though, there is a sense that death is positively welcome. When Brutus declares, 'My bones would rest, | That have but laboured to attain this hour' (41–2), he implies the 'teleological fallacy' (life is merely a preparation for death); but we also hear a note of sad futility (has my labour come only to this?) and of relief that the labour is over. The same note of relief is heard in his last words: 'Caesar, now be still. | I killed

[42] Other editors give the line (unassigned in F) to Brutus himself; the difference does not seriously affect my argument.

[43] Foakes ('Approach', 267) notes the importance of the episode but not the significance of 'like himself'; Brower (*Hero and Saint*, 233) connects the phrase in passing with Brutus' 'noble role' but does not develop the insight.

[44] This Stoic idea is not explicit in Plutarch's account.

not thee with half so good a will' (50–1). At the same time he reveals his continued concern with honour and reputation, assuring his followers that he will 'have glory by this losing day' (36), and reassuring himself that Strato, the instrument of his death, is 'a fellow of a good respect' whose life has 'some smatch of honour in it' (45–6). After his death, Strato and Lucillius sum up:

> MESSALA. . . . Strato, where is thy master?
> STRATO. Free from the bondage you are in, Messala.
> The conquerors can but make a fire of him,
> For Brutus only overcame himself,
> And no man else hath honour by his death.
> LUCILLIUS. So Brutus should be found. I thank thee, Brutus,
> That thou hast proved Lucillius' saying true.
>
> (53–9)

This coda brings together the themes of constancy, decorum, honour, and death. Brutus' suicide has proved his Stoic constancy: asserting his freedom and his invulnerability to external evils, he has set his spirit free and left only his despised body to the conquerors. He has died, in Seneca's term, for the sake of *dignitas*: by dying well he escapes the peril of an evil life, ensures he cannot be forced to change or compromise, and remains himself to the end. Thus he preserves not only Senecan constancy but also decorum. Lucillius recalls for us his earlier prediction; Brutus has been 'found . . . like himself', consistent in character to the end.

Nevertheless, the hints of relief and regret in Brutus' dying words remind us that the role he has been playing, with increasing strain, was not necessarily his true self. He has maintained his role to the end and died in the way Lucillius and others expected. Roman opinion will honour him for dying 'like himself'—but, as he himself said, every like is not the same.[45]

The death of Brutus embodies the complexity of 'constancy' in *Julius Caesar*. He simultaneously fulfils the demands of Stoic ethics, remaining 'constant as the Northern Star' in the face of defeat and death, and of Roman decorum, maintaining 'formal

[45] Wymer, *Suicide and Despair*, ch. 7, esp. 150–4, discusses Brutus' suicide in terms very close to my own, noting the sense of 'tragic . . . self-defeat' (135), the tension between inwardness and public persona, and the un-Roman sense of 'dejection [and] weariness' (154).

constancy' and playing his part consistently to the end; in both ways he has been 'always the same' in life, and will remain so in fame after his death. Both ideals, however, involve the strain of pretending to be what he is not, and concealing and suppressing his human weakness. It is not surprising that Brutus welcomes death. Only in death can he end the strain of pretence, and achieve in fact the condition he aspires to: absolute changelessness and immovability, a complete freedom of the mind from the body's weakness, and a complete identification between himself and his public role. Ultimately, to play 'a Roman's part' *is* to die.

8
'I Play the Man I Am': Coriolanus

In the opening scene of *Coriolanus*, the hero is called upon to fight against the Volscians: 'It is your former promise.' 'Sir, it is,' he responds, 'And I am constant' (I. I. 238–9). He means 'I will keep my word'; but, like Brutus' lines on 'formal constancy', the phrase has wider reverberations. In a paradox characteristic of this intensely paradoxical play, the passionate traitor Coriolanus is Shakespeare's most self-consciously 'constant' character, and the play (whose characters could never have heard of Stoicism) is Shakespeare's most searching treatment of the ideal of constancy. Where the earlier play demonstrated how Senecan and Ciceronian elements are interwoven in the construction of Roman constancy, *Coriolanus* sets them against each other, and shows how the internal self-contradictions of the ideal, when it is pushed to its limits, come close to destroying Rome.

'Not to be other than one thing'

It is not surprising that *Coriolanus* is not usually read as a play about Stoic constancy. The Rome of *Coriolanus* is very different from that of *Julius Caesar*, and its hero is no Brutus but a fierce, passionate, violent warrior who seems to have (in Bradley's words) 'not a drop of stoic blood in his veins'.[1] The most recent discussion, by Charles and Michelle Martindale, while acknowledging that the play 'deals centrally with notions of constancy and change', sees the hero as disastrously un-Stoic, and 'his constancy, if it may be so called' as in fact what Lipsius calls 'obstinacy or frowardness'.[2]

[1] A. C. Bradley, '*Coriolanus*', *PBA* (1911–12), 466.

[2] Martindale and Martindale, *Shakespeare and the Uses of Antiquity*, 179–81 (quoting Lipsius, p. 79); I shall argue that this view, while obviously true on one level, misses the play's deeper interrogation of constancy. Earlier discussions of constancy in *Coriolanus* include those of Kaufmann and Ronan, '*Julius Caesar*', 50; Matthew N. Proser, '*Coriolanus*: The Constant Warrior and the State', *College English* 24 (1963), 507–12, rev. and enl. in *Heroic Image*, 135–70 (who argues

This is effectively the view embodied in Plutarch's 'Life', where the kind of 'constancie' (*apatheia*) Martius shows in his endurance of pain and indifference to pleasure is hopelessly vitiated by irrational obstinacy and anger. Yet Plutarch also grants that these virtues and faults are linked in Martius' moral code: he is a man who 'never yeelded', believing that 'to overcome alwaies . . . was a token of magnanimitie'. I believe that Shakespeare, drawing on this hint, sees Coriolanus' strengths and weaknesses as related to an ideal of constancy.

This ideal is for Shakespeare the essence of Roman virtue, and the differences between its manifestations in Coriolanus and in Brutus are partly a matter of historical development. In the Rome of *Coriolanus*, centuries earlier than that of *Julius Caesar*, 'constancy' takes the form of a simple heroic code, made up of the warrior virtues which the Romans called *virtus* and *fides*: courage to stand fast in battle, honour which tells the truth and keeps its word. Over time this simple code will evolve into the more philosophical ethics of a Brutus; but the value Rome places on steadfastness and consistency remains the same.

The constancy of Coriolanus partakes of both these basic qualities. His steadfastness is embodied in the repeated image of him standing firm in battle while others flee. He contemptuously calls his cowardly followers 'these movers' (1. 6. 4),[3] despises those who 'budge' in the face of the enemy (1. 7. 44), and challenges Aufidius: 'Let the first budger die the other's slave' (1. 9. 5). He is not only steadfast himself but inspires steadfastness in other men; as Cominius reports, he 'stopped the fliers' (2. 2. 103). Cominius' eulogy presents him as a colossus in battle, who transcends bodily weakness by the power of his untired spirit ('his doubled spirit | Requickened what in flesh was fatigate'

over-simply that 'his constancy lies in this: he is always the potential killer' (*Heroic Image*, 154)); Kranz, '"Too Great a Mind"', 150–6 (who relates his pursuit of Stoic 'integrity of mind' to his insistence on Rome's political integrity). Many critics, of course, have written perceptively on Coriolanus' inflexibility without explicit reference to Stoicism or constancy: e.g. William Rosen, *Shakespeare and the Craft of Tragedy* (Cambridge, Mass., 1960), 161–207 ('a kind of predetermined, unalterable being', 205); A. P. Rossiter, '*Coriolanus*', in *Angel with Horns* (London, 1961), 235–52, who notes the 'depressing paradox' that his attempt to be unyielding makes him as 'unstable and trustless' (252) as the plebs he despises.

[3] 'Movers' may imply 'removers' (of loot), but I think the idea of lack of steadfastness is dominant; cf. Brockbank's note ad loc. in the Arden edn. (For the sake of simplicity I refer to the hero as 'Coriolanus' throughout.)

(116–17)), and whose almost inhuman insensibility to wounds and pain recalls Seneca's invulnerable *sapiens* or his iron-skinned Hercules. These warrior qualities are present in Plutarch's Martius, but Shakespeare surrounds him with the aura of the Senecan Stoic hero, and suggests that his heroism arises from Volumnia's stoical 'precepts that would make invincible | The heart that conned them' (4. 1. 10–11). His prayer for his son—

> that thou mayst prove
> To shame unvulnerable, and stick i'th' wars
> Like a great sea-mark standing every flaw
> And saving those that eye thee!
>
> (5. 3. 72–5)

—expresses the ideal of constancy in its noblest form: the immovability of the Stoic hero, like that of a lighthouse, serves as an 'example of constancy' which guides others to safety.

The other aspect of Coriolanus' constancy, his consistency, is partly a Roman insistence on *fides*, being constant to one's former promises. The most damning insult he can throw at Aufidius is 'I do hate thee | Worse than a promise-breaker' (1. 9. 1–2). More fundamentally, it is a determination to remain consistently true to the same beliefs and values. Coriolanus' contempt for 'the mutable rank-scented meinie' (3. 1. 70) is largely based on their fickleness and unreliability:

> He that trusts to you,
> Where he should find you lions finds you hares,
> Where foxes, geese. You are no surer, no,
> Than is the coal of fire upon the ice,
> Or hailstone in the sun. . . .
> Hang ye! Trust ye?
> With every minute you do change a mind,
> And call him noble that was now your hate,
> Him vile that was your garland.
>
> (1. 1. 168–72, 179–82)

In attacking them as the embodiment of inconstant opinion, he defines himself as consistent in standing by his fixed beliefs. He is no more willing to compromise his views than to run away from an enemy in battle. In the political conflicts of Act 3 he insists upon the consistency of his position ('This was my speech, and I will speak't again', 3. 1. 65), refusing to modify it in the interests of tact or timing, or to accept the excuse that he overstated it through 'choler': 'Were I as patient as the midnight sleep, | By Jove, 'twould be my mind' (88–9). Behind the insistence on intellectual consistency is an ideal of reliability. Coriolanus is proud that everyone knows what to expect from him, and that he is seen to be always the same.

Aufidius, in his strange, convoluted analysis of Coriolanus, suggests that constancy (consistency), as much as pride or lack of judgement, may be the key to his tragedy. It is his 'nature' to be the same under all circumstances,

> Not to be other than one thing, not moving
> From th' casque to th' cushion, but commanding peace
> Even with the same austerity and garb
> As he controlled the war.
>
> (4. 7. 41–5)

In the Senecan formula, Coriolanus is *unus idemque inter diversa*. As Aufidius suggests, this is both a virtue and a flaw. His steadfastness makes him a great warrior, and his integrity gives him heroic standing in a world of intriguers and compromisers. But his rigid refusal to adapt to different circumstances, his determination to behave in the forum exactly as he does on the battlefield, is disastrous, and his predictability makes him vulnerable to both manipulation and ridicule. His repeated knee-jerk response to the charge of 'traitor', exploited by both the tribunes and Aufidius, makes him seem mechanically predictable. The constant tragic hero at times seems uncomfortably like a Jonsonian humour character, 'speaking his speech again' like the pub bore, locked into a comically obsessive pattern of behaviour.[4]

The constancy of Coriolanus, in its blend of steadfastness and consistency, is a typically Roman blend of the two traditions of constancy. Coriolanus has the rocklike and godlike strength and

[4] O. J. Campbell, *Shakespeare's Satire* (Oxford, 1943), 198–217, takes this view to an extreme, seeing the play as a 'tragical satire' in which Shakespeare 'mocks and ridicules' the hero throughout; Rossiter more convincingly suggests ('*Coriolanus*', 245) that Shakespeare keeps him just on the verge of becoming a Jonsonian 'humour'. Katherine Stockholder, 'The Other Coriolanus', *PMLA* 85 (1970), 228–36, also invokes Jonson, and Bergson on the comic effect of automatism, seeing the play as about 'the tragic process by which a man limits himself to his type, and by which "types" tend to become comic'.

the heroic superiority of Seneca's *sapiens* (or of Hercules, his literalized image); but his concern for integrity and self-consistency can also be read in terms of Ciceronian decorum. This ambiguity becomes clearer if we examine the values of the Rome which has created Coriolanus.[5]

Roman virtue and the identity of Coriolanus

Roman virtue in *Coriolanus* is essentially *virtus*: manly courage. Plutarch's observation that in early Rome *virtus* was 'honoured ... above all other vertues' and called 'by the name of vertue itself' is put into Cominius' mouth as a programmatic statement of Roman values:

> It is held
> That valour is the chiefest virtue, and
> Most dignifies the haver.
>
> (2. 2. 83–5)[6]

[5] The argument of the following section is indebted to Simmons's reading (*Pagan World*, ch. 2, 18–64) of Coriolanus as the product and embodiment of Roman values, who must finally be destroyed because of the clash between his absolute and Rome's pragmatic interpretation of those values. Paster similarly sees Rome's tragedy as its necessary sacrifice of 'its best and most characteristic product' (*Idea of the City*, 90); and Jonathan Dollimore, *Radical Tragedy* (Brighton, 1984), 218–30, from a very different perspective to Simmons's, draws a similar distinction between Coriolanus' 'essentialist' view of virtue and the Roman view of it as a social construct. Earlier critics who have seen Coriolanus as embodying Roman values (often as part of a severe critique of those values) include R. F. Hill, '*Coriolanus*: Violentest Contrareity', *Essays and Studies*, NS 17 (1964), 12–23; W. I. Carr, '"Gracious Silence": A Selective Reading of *Coriolanus*', *English Studies*, 46 (1965), 221–34; Clifford Davidson, '*Coriolanus*: A Study in Political Dislocation', *ShakS* 4 (1968), 263–74; Stockholder, 'The Other Coriolanus'; Anthony Miller, '*Coriolanus*: The Tragedy of *Virtus*', *Sydney Studies in English*, 9 (1983–4), 37–60. On the play's treatment of *virtus* and heroism, Brower's ch. 9 in *Hero and Saint* ('Achilles in the Forum') brings out the clash between heroic and civic values, but not the irony that Coriolanus' Homeric virtues *are* the official civic values of Rome. John W. Velz, 'Cracking Strong Curbs Asunder: Roman Destiny and the Roman Hero in *Coriolanus*', *ELR* 13 (1983), 58–69, and Anne Barton, 'Livy, Machiavelli, and Shakespeare's *Coriolanus*', *ShS* 38 (1985), 115–29, see Coriolanus as a heroic anachronism in a changing Rome. Two other studies of classical ideals in the play, Waith, *Herculean Hero*, ch. 5, and R. Poisson, 'Coriolanus as Aristotle's Magnanimous Man', in W. F. McNeir and T. N. Greenfield (eds.), *Pacific Coast Studies in Shakespeare* (Portland, 1966), 210–24, too uncritically identify the hero's values with the play's.

[6] On Cominius' speech see Brower, *Hero and Saint*, 355–7; Simmons, *Pagan World*, 18–20; Davidson, 'Political Dislocation', 271 ('Coriolanus represents not virtue but *virtus*').

Coriolanus, calling for volunteers on the field, sums up the elements of *virtus*: love of blood and war, love of country, desire for a 'brave death' and posthumous glory (1. 7. 67–72). Volumnia's account in 1. 3 of the principles on which she brought up her son makes clear the dominance of warlike courage and desire for glory over all other values. As many critics have noted, the placing of such sentiments in a woman's mouth provides an ironic perspective on Rome's masculine values and the unnaturalness of a world in which a mother cheerfully sends her son to death (18–21), a bleeding wound is lovelier than a mother's breast (42–5), and an angry little boy tearing a butterfly to pieces is 'a noble child' (69).[7]

'Noble' is itself a key word in the Roman vocabulary; it and its cognates occur eighty-five times in the play, and are insistently associated with the hero, from his first acclamation as 'noble Martius!' (1. 1. 161) to the promise in the final line that he will have 'a noble memory' (5. 6. 154).[8] The code of *virtus* is an aristocratic one, proper to the patrician class, 'the honoured number | Who lack not virtue' (3. 1. 76–7). It is directed towards individual heroic achievement—to do great deeds, achieve honour and glory, 'exceed the common' (4. 1. 33).

This is not, in other words, intrinsically a public-spirited ideal. The Roman warrior-noble and the Stoic *sapiens* are paradoxically alike in their heroic individualism: both fight, stand fast, and endure wounds (literally or figuratively) for the sake of individual self-assertion and self-perfection. Cicero shrewdly defined this problem in his discussion in *De officiis* 1 of *magnitudo animi*, 'greatnesse of corage', a concept which includes both warlike courage and the stoical principles which underpin it. Such a virtue is of immense 'profite' to a community, but can also be dangerously anti-social in its encouragement of 'wilfulnesse' and 'overseking of

[7] The ironic treatment of Roman values in this passage has often been noted: e.g. L. C. Knights, 'Shakespeare and Political Wisdom: A Note on the Personalism of *Julius Caesar* and *Coriolanus*', *Sewanee Review*, 41 (1953), 43–55; Carr, '"Gracious Silence"', 225–7; Stockholder, 'Other Coriolanus', 235–36; Miola, *Shakespeare's Rome*, 171–2. Wilson Knight, 'The Royal Occupation: An Essay on *Coriolanus*' (*Imperial Theme*, 154–98), stresses the unnatural, metallic imagery which characterizes both the play's Rome and Coriolanus in particular.

[8] Michael Goldman, 'Characterizing Coriolanus', *ShS* 34 (1981), 73–84, notes (82) that 'noble' occurs more often in *Coriolanus* than in any other Shakespeare play.

rule'.[9] Rome faces this danger when its exemplar of virtue is Coriolanus, the solitary arrogant superman who is characteristically 'himself alone | To answer all the city' (1. 5. 22–3).

On the other hand, the very fact that Roman virtue is defined as 'nobility' means that it is tied to social values. To be 'noble' is to live up to the values of the Roman noble class. Like being 'Roman' in *Julius Caesar*, this is a social construct; who is 'noble' is defined by the judgements of other nobles. These judgements are expressed in the form of 'honour'—the mainspring of Roman virtue, as Volumnia makes very clear with her insistent repetition, in the opening lines of 1. 3, of 'honour', 'renown', 'fame', 'good report'. Rome's men do great deeds on behalf of Rome, and Rome rewards them with honour (praise) and honours (titles, triumphs, consulships). Through this process of conferring and receiving honour, the individualistic pursuit of 'nobility' or *magnitudo animi* is tied to the service of the Roman state.[10]

This dependence upon honour means that Rome's morality, again, rests upon opinion. In *Coriolanus* as in *Julius Caesar*, a good Roman acts for the sake of others' opinions, and to be virtuous means to be seen and said to be virtuous. Virtue does not truly exist unless it is publicly recognized; so, when Coriolanus refuses honours, Cominius jokingly threatens to put him in manacles '[l]ike one that means his proper harm' (1. 10. 56), for to refuse to have his deeds honoured and validated by public opinion is tantamount to denying his own existence, and so a form of suicide. Coriolanus, however, instead of being rewarded with honours, 'pays himself with being proud' (1. 1. 31–2). His honour is not affected by the opinions of others; like the *sapiens* he steadfastly pursues his own ideal of virtue. That is, at least, how he sees himself. His tragic disillusionment comes from his discovery that his virtue is in fact defined by the opinions of others—which means,

[9] Miola's discussion of Cicero in the play (*Shakespeare's Rome*, 181–92), focusing on *De oratore*, does not discuss this passage, but ends by quoting *De officiis* 3 and drawing a similar contrast between Cicero's social and Coriolanus' potentially anti-social morality. Rebhorn's analysis of aristocratic 'emulation' in *Julius Caesar* ('Crisis of the Aristocracy') is also relevant to the earlier Rome of *Coriolanus*.

[10] On the much-discussed question of 'honour' I am most indebted to Simmons and to D. J. Gordon's classic 'Name and Fame: Shakespeare's *Coriolanus*', in G. I. Duthie (ed.), *Papers Mainly Shakespearian* (Edinburgh, 1964), 40–57. Other useful discussions are by Norman Rabkin, *Shakespeare and the Common Understanding* (New York, 1967), 119–44 (esp. 130–33), and Platt, *Rome and Romans*, 86–116.

in the final analysis, by those embodiments of mere opinion, the plebeians. The Roman concept of virtue, which for him has been absolute truth, is for Rome a matter of opinion, a convenient assumption: 'It is *held* | That valour is the chiefest virtue . . .'. Roman virtue is a social construct, and so, he comes to recognize, is he.

Coriolanus is the creation of Rome and the embodiment of Roman virtue. This, as J. L. Simmons has pointed out, is Shakespeare's crucial departure from Plutarch's conception: 'Shakespeare, with grim irony, urges Coriolanus not as a victim of neglect but as the epitome of Roman cultivation.'[11] Cominius presents Coriolanus as the unique embodiment of Roman *virtus*. 'If it be' that valour is the chiefest virtue, then 'The man I speak of cannot in the world | Be singly counterpoised' (2. 2. 85–7). *If* Rome's conception of virtue is correct, then Coriolanus is the perfect man.

The extent to which Coriolanus is the product of his society is made very clear in Volumnia's account of his upbringing (1. 3. 1–25); in none of Shakespeare's other tragedies are we given such an explicit account of how the hero's character was formed. We hear the 'precepts' with which she used to 'load' her son, and of the moral pressures she placed on him to conform to her ideal. Coriolanus, it seems, could hardly have become other than the man he is. Volumnia truly tells him, 'Thou art my warrior. | I holp to frame thee' (5. 3. 62–3). This is not merely maternal influence; Volumnia also represents patrician Rome, as she implies when she says, 'I am in this | Your wife, your son, these senators, the nobles' (3. 2. 64–5). Through Volumnia, Rome constructs Coriolanus.[12] *Coriolanus* is the most deterministic of Shakespeare's tragedies in its stress on the inescapable moulding influence of environment and upbringing—as *Antony and Cleopatra*, with its sense of the fluidity of human character, is the least so. There is a tragic irony in Coriolanus' desire to 'stand | As if a man were author of himself' (5. 3. 35–6): more than most men he is the creation of others, and bound by the self which his society has created for him.[13]

[11] Simmons, *Pagan World*, 20.

[12] This is of course an over-simplified view of the mother–son relationship, but its psychological complexity has been exhaustively explored by other critics. I agree with Lisa Lowe, '"Say I Play the Man I Am": Gender and Politics in *Coriolanus*', *Kenyon Review*, NS 8 (1986), 86–95 (an otherwise rather strained reading) that the relationship must be read in political as well as psychological terms (90).

[13] This irony is noted by e.g. Bradley, '*Coriolanus*', 466; Carr, '"Gracious Silence"', 230.

This social determinism is symbolized by the fact that the hero's very name is given to him by Rome. Seizing upon an episode in Plutarch, Shakespeare extends his use in *Julius Caesar* of names as symbols of the public self; the name by which the hero is known, 'Coriolanus', is not his birth-name, but is given to him as one of his war honours. He, who refuses other honours as degrading and irrelevant, accepts this one, and so lets not merely his actions but his very identity be defined by the opinions of others. When he is banished from Rome he loses this name and identity, becoming 'a kind of nothing, titleless' (5. 1. 13).

We clearly have a double vision of Coriolanus and his relationship with Rome. On the one hand, he towers above humanity as a Herculean and godlike figure, the embodiment of heroic *magnitudo animi*; on the other hand, he is tied to his society as Rome's soldier-servant, moulded by his upbringing and given his rank, honours, name, and identity by Rome. The contradiction is reflected in two different interpretations of Coriolanus' constancy, as a Senecan Stoic heroism aspiring to divinity, or as the decorous Ciceronian playing of a social role. It gradually becomes clear, to us and to Coriolanus, that while he sees himself in the former light, Rome sees him in the latter; and the conflict becomes focused on the question of whether he is being himself or playing a role.[14]

Rome sees Coriolanus as playing a role: that of the heroic Roman warrior. An image in Cominius' eulogy—'When he might act the woman in the scene, | He proved best man i'th' field' (2. 2. 96–7)—hints that the battlefield is another kind of 'scene' on which

[14] Almost all critical discussions of Coriolanus touch on role-playing, but most too simply contrast his 'nature' with his role. Exceptions include Carr, who argues that 'People are continually acting parts . . . Coriolanus, on the other hand, fits his so completely that it has become his nature' ('"Gracious Silence"', 224); Philip Edwards, 'Person and Office in Shakespeare's Plays', *PBA* 56 (1970), 93–109 ('Coriolanus' "nature" . . . is . . . a second nature', 97); and Michael Taylor, 'Playing the Man He Is: Role-playing in Shakespeare's *Coriolanus*', *Ariel* 15 (1984), 19–28, who argues that Coriolanus' 'authentic self is irrepressibly social' (but sees his submission too simply as a return to his true Roman role). Constance C. Relihan, 'Appropriation of the "Thing of Blood": Absence of Self and the Struggle for Ownership in *Coriolanus*', *Iowa State Journal of Research*, 62 (1988), 407–20, argues too sweepingly that Coriolanus 'has no private self' (417). Zvi Jagendorf, '*Coriolanus*: Body Politic and Private Parts', *SQ* 41 (1990), 455–69, ingeniously links Coriolanus' aversion to playing a 'part' to his obsession with wholeness and unity: 'To admit that the self-authored man is "a part" is an absurdity. He must be a whole . . .' (468). The play on words suggests very neatly how the communal quality of theatre can undermine the acting of constancy.

Coriolanus has chosen to play his part. The patricians find his consistent playing of this part admirable but somewhat excessive. Volumnia asks him,

> as thou hast said
> My praises made thee first a soldier, so,
> To have my praise for this, perform a part
> Thou hast not done before.
>
> (3. 2. 107–10)

A soldier is one part, a politician is another, and Coriolanus must be prepared to change roles. Coriolanus cannot see it in this way: for him soldiership is not a 'part' but his nature and his very identity. With his ideal of being always the same, acting is for him a contemptible hypocrisy. Yet he is forced to perform 'a part | That I shall blush in acting' (2. 2. 145–6) when he is thrust in front of the people to beg first their votes, then their forgiveness. Standing like an actor in a ridiculous costume, displaying his scars like stage props, to be applauded or hissed by an audience he despises, he suffers not merely humiliation but a traumatic insight into the nature of his role and the meaning of his life:

> *For your voices* I have fought,
> Watched *for your voices*, *for your voices* bear
> Of wounds two dozen odd; battles thrice six
> I have seen and heard of *for your voices*, have
> Done many things, some less, some more.
>
> (2. 3. 126–30; my emphasis)

His career, in the eyes of Rome, has been a performance to win applause from others, his heroic pursuit of constancy merely the decorous acting of a part. But for Coriolanus the deeds and ideals were real. He may have been acting, but the part he was performing is his true self.

He tries to express this insight in a crucial passage during his argument with Volumnia:

> Why did you wish me milder? Would you have me
> False to my nature? Rather say I play
> The man I am.
>
> (3. 2. 13–15)

The final phrase brilliantly sums up the paradox of Ciceronian decorum: an ideal which depends upon self-knowledge and truth to oneself, but also upon a striving for self-consistency which entails consciously acting the part of oneself. Coriolanus is fumbling to express the paradox of his own situation, a paradox he can only suggest by simultaneously admitting and denying that he is an actor. His self ('The man I am') is the creation of Rome, which has moulded him. In the pragmatic eyes of Rome, it is a part in which he has been cast. For Coriolanus, however, the role has become his 'nature'. He cannot, as Volumnia casually suggests, change roles temporarily; the role is himself, and he has no identity separate from it, no 'self' different from the persona perceived by Rome. Where the role-players of *Julius Caesar* suffered a painful discrepancy between public role and private self, in Coriolanus the two are identical. Nevertheless, 'I play | The man I am' does not mean simply and tautologically 'I am myself.' Volumnia's impatient response, 'You might have been enough the man you are | With striving less to be so' (18–19), misses the point. Coriolanus is being himself, but also (as he now realizes) consciously 'striving' to 'play' himself, to remain true to his ideal of self-consistency. He must not lapse even for a moment into playing a different part,

> Lest I surcease to honour mine own truth,
> And by my body's action teach my mind
> A most inherent baseness.
>
> (121–3)

Thus, paradoxically, the man who despises acting comes to define his own moral code in terms of theatrical decorum. He has found an appropriate part, identified himself totally with it, and plays it with such unalterable consistency that he cannot step outside it.

Cicero, however, advises that the ideals of appropriateness and consistency must be moderated by a sense of what is socially necessary and possible. We should play the part which is appropriate for us, but if circumstances force us to play one which is not appropriate, to violate decorum, then 'all care . . . must bee employed: that, if we do them not comlye, yet wyth as lyttle uncomlynesse as may be' (*Off.* 1. 114). Decorum as a social virtue depends on such adaptability. Coriolanus, identifying himself entirely with his part, turns (in Montaigne's words) a 'vizard and apparance' into his 'real essence' (3. 10). In doing so, he endows decorum with the heroic absoluteness of Senecan *constantia sapientis*, and provides a model for those scholars who see in *De officiis* the root of the 'bastard Stoicism' of the individualistic hero-villains of Elizabethan drama. 'I play | The man I am' can become a formula for the pursuit of absolute selfhood. That this is a perversion of Cicero's doctrine, however, the ending of the play will remind us.

Coriolanus predictably fails in his indecorous performances before the plebeians; but the consequences are not what he feared. Rather than betraying his 'own truth' and lapsing into 'baseness', he becomes fully aware for the first time that what he is upholding *is* his own truth, not Rome's; that, although Rome has constructed him out of its official ideals of *virtus* and constancy, only he truly believes in these values as moral absolutes. Banished, he retorts, 'I banish you' (3. 3. 127), and leaves Rome to pursue his ideal of constancy in 'a world elsewhere' (139).[15]

The image of the hero banishing his city focuses the ironies of the relationship between Coriolanus and Rome. Shakespeare takes Cicero's analysis of the dangers of *magnitudo animi* as a social ideal, and pursues its implications. Heroic constancy is central to Rome's official morality, of which Coriolanus is the perfect embodiment. But he practises Roman virtue too constantly, plays his role too consistently, is, finally, 'too noble' (3. 1. 255), and the society which created him is forced to cast him out.

Keeping a constant temper: Coriolanus outside Rome

In the last two acts Coriolanus, Rome's creation and champion, becomes its enemy and would-be destroyer. Such a treasonous reversal of allegiance seems on the face of it to be a complete abandonment of constancy (fidelity) and hence of constancy (consistency). Yet in another sense Coriolanus becomes not less but more constant. His promise to his friends that they will hear 'never of me aught | But what is like me formerly' (4. 1. 53–4) is paradoxically true, even though when they next hear of him he is

[15] Martindale and Martindale, *Shakespeare and the Uses of Antiquity*, 179–80, relate this passage to Seneca's and Lipsius' strictures on travel as a way of escaping one's own inner disorder; but Coriolanus travels, not in order to change his state of mind, but in order to remain the same.

leading an army against them. Exiled from Rome, he pushes the Roman ideal of constancy to its logical and destructive extreme.[16]

Justifying his treason on his first appearance in Antium, Coriolanus describes a world of moral chaos:

> O world, thy slippery turns! Friends now fast sworn,
> Whose double bosoms seem to wear one heart . . .
> shall within this hour,
> On a dissension of a doit, break out
> To bitterest enmity. So fellest foes,
> Whose passions and whose plots have broke their sleep
> To take the one the other, by some chance,
> Some trick not worth an egg, shall grow dear friends
> And interjoin their issues. So with me.
> My birthplace hate I, and my love's upon
> This enemy town.
>
> (4. 4. 12–13, 16–24)

Nothing in the Roman plays shows more clearly why Rome values constancy. It is as a bulwark against this vision of a world of meaningless chance and irrational change that Rome sets up its codes of constancy—codes which impose rational predictability on the vagaries of human behaviour, oppose an immovable steadfastness to the changeableness of fortune, and set up firmly agreed Roman opinions to make up for the inaccessibility of absolute truth. Coriolanus has discovered the artificiality of the codes, but outside them he can see nothing constant at all. Rather than endure this vision of the absurdity of life, he retreats into constancy, becoming not changeable but even more rigidly true to the inflexible nature that Rome has forged in him.

Coriolanus' position may be compared to the sceptical constancy of Pyrrho in Montaigne's 'Of Vertue': a determination, in an absurd world where absolute truth is unknowable, to follow consistently one's 'own truth'. Ultimately, I have suggested, all Roman constancy is in this sense 'sceptical', since the norms to which Romans are called on to be constant (being 'Roman', being 'noble', being 'Caesar') are arbitrarily defined by Roman opinion rather than, as in Stoic theory, by the clear truths of reason and nature. The

[16] Waith defends Coriolanus against critics who see irony here: 'he is not inconstant. Shakespeare makes it clear that his first allegiance is always to his personal honour' (*Herculean Hero*, 131). But this in itself, of course, contributes to the play's critique of constancy and honour.

scepticism, the latent desperation, and the potential absurdity of such constancy are made very clear in Coriolanus, as he pursues his straight course through the world's 'slippery turns' with the implacable determination of Pyrrho walking into the ditch.

His resolution continues to be represented, in these scenes, in images of immovability. As in *Julius Caesar*, Shakespeare plays with the various senses of being 'moved'. Menenius tells Coriolanus that he was 'moved to come to thee . . . being assured none but myself could move thee' (5. 2. 73–5); repulsed, he bitterly reports to Sicinius that it is as easy to move Coriolanus as to displace 'yon coign o'th' Capitol, yon corner-stone . . . with your little finger' (5. 4. 1–5).[17] Aufidius comments on the rejection of Menenius, 'You keep a constant temper' (5. 2. 94). The Volscian guards also pay tribute to his constancy with a Senecan image: 'He's the rock, the oak, not to be wind-shaken' (110). As much as Stoic heroes like Caesar or Brutus, Coriolanus scorns emotional appeals and will not allow his affections to sway more than his reason.

This is, of course, a strange and perverse kind of constancy. Plutarch, as we have seen, insisted that there was no likeness between Martius' obstinacy, driven by wounded pride and rage, and the rational virtue of a Brutus. Shakespeare, by his repeated echoes of Stoic motifs and images, suggests that the distinction is not so clear. Coriolanus is stubborn, rigid, and harsh; so, very often, is the Stoic hero. He is motivated by pride; that is a traditional accusation against the Stoics, to some extent supported by *Julius Caesar*. And if he is driven by passion rather than reason, that too is not necessarily unlike the Stoic. Montaigne in 'Of Drunkennesse' suggested that heroic constancy (steadfastness), though traditionally associated with reason and self-control, is in fact a kind of heroic madness attainable only in brief moments of overmastering emotion. This is the kind of constancy we find in Seneca's Hercules and in many later 'Herculean heroes', figures who have many of the attributes of the Stoic hero without his theoretical passionlessness. It is in this Stoic tradition that I would locate Coriolanus.

Coriolanus most strikingly resembles the Stoic hero in his aspiration to be like a god. Earlier in the play the tribune Brutus

[17] The irony of Menenius' simile is increased if one associates it with Seneca's contrast between the Capitol, which can be conquered, and the unconquerable constancy of the *sapiens* (*Const.* 6. 8). Miola acutely notes 'a touch of the "northern star" complex' in these passages (*Shakespeare's Rome*, 200).

accused him of speaking of the people 'as if you were a god | To punish, not a man of their infirmity' (3. 1. 85–6). Now, outside Rome, he increasingly strives (in his mother's words) to 'imitate the graces of the gods' (5. 3. 151), to rise above humanity, cut himself off from human ties and human weaknesses, and 'stand | As if a man were author of himself | And knew no other kin' (35–7). Menenius, echoing Seneca's aphorism that 'a good man onely differeth from God but in time', comments that 'He wants nothing of a god but eternity and a heaven to throne in' (5. 4. 23–5).

But Menenius' description also has less godlike overtones:

> This Martius is grown from man to dragon. He has wings, he's more than a creeping thing. . . . [H]e no more remembers his mother now than an eight-year old horse. The tartness of his face sours ripe grapes. When he walks, he moves like an engine, and the ground shrinks before his treading. He is able to pierce a corslet with his eye, talks like a knell, and his 'hmh!' is a battery. He sits in his state as a thing made for Alexander. (12–22)

He is not only a god but also an animal, a machine, a statue; in Seneca's image, he is a rock, too hard and insensible to feel pain or tenderness. In rejecting his own humanity he has become both more and less than human. This is the paradox implicit in much debate about the Stoic ideal, most memorably stated by Montaigne: when men attempt to 'escape man', 'insteade of transforming themselves into Angels, they transchange themselves into beastes'.[18] Coriolanus' constancy in these final acts is magnificent if regarded like a natural force; in human terms, it is appalling.

This double view of the hero as god and as beast or thing has been present throughout the play.[19] When Sicinius wonders at

[18] Platt (*Rome and Romans*, 105, 118–19) also quotes Montaigne on the 'savage infirmity' of despising one's own being.

[19] On this dual imagery, see Charney, *Shakespeare's Roman Plays*; Derek Traversi, *Shakespeare: The Roman Plays* (London, 1963), 233–4, 265; Christopher Givan, 'Shakespeare's *Coriolanus*: The Premature Epitaph and the Butterfly', *ShakS* 12 (1979), 143–58 ('to deify is to reify', 155). F. N. Lees, '*Coriolanus*, Aristotle and Bacon', *RES* NS 1 (1950), 114–25, convincingly related this dualism to Aristotle's dictum in the *Politics* that the man who cannot live in society is either a beast or a god. But the images of Coriolanus as a 'thing' of stone or metal are better explained by reference to the Senecan images of god and rock, and the traditional dichotomy which sees the Stoic as superhuman or subhuman or both (like Erasmus' godlike statue or Montaigne's angel/beast). Moreover, to suggest that Shakespeare is drawing not only on Aristotle but also on the Stoic tradition is to acknowledge that Coriolanus' inability to live in society is the result, not only of his flawed nature (as Aristotle or Plutarch would suggest), but also of the moral ideal he pursues.

Coriolanus' transformation, Menenius responds, 'There is differency between a grub and a butterfly; yet your butterfly was a grub' (5. 4. 11–12). Both superhumanity and subhumanity were already latent in the Roman Coriolanus, as we have seen in Cominius' description of him as a heroically implacable war machine. In developing both to the near-destruction of his humanity he is, the play suggests, merely taking to its logical conclusion the inhumanity of the Roman warrior code which has shaped him. Cominius says that Coriolanus is the Volscians' 'god' and

> leads them like a thing
> Made by some other deity than nature,
> That shapes man better . . .
>
> (4. 6. 94–6)

The 'other deity' which has made Coriolanus is, I would suggest, Rome—which attempts to reshape men and make them better than nature created them, at the cost of making them in some ways worse.[20]

The controlling irony of these final scenes is that Coriolanus sets out to destroy Rome in the name of the values that Rome has taught him and the nature that Rome has shaped in him. The irony is encapsulated in the motif of the hero's name. Coriolanus, Cominius says, is 'a kind of nothing, titleless, | Till he had forged himself a name o'th' fire | Of burning Rome' (5. 1. 12–14). Kenneth Burke brilliantly pointed out that, if he became 'Coriolanus' by sacking Corioles, the name he would forge in the fire of Rome would have to be 'Romanus'.[21] He will become the perfect Roman by destroying Rome. The Roman ideal of constancy logically leads the hero who pursues it to a point where he becomes no longer human, and, in order to remain consistent with the ideals his society has taught him but has failed to live up to, has to destroy it.

Constancy, decorum, and nature: the submission

Coriolanus' constancy in these final acts has been represented as a distorted form of Senecan Stoic heroism; his submission, in 5. 3, is worked out in terms of the principles of Ciceronian decorum.

[20] Richard S. Ide, *Possessed with Greatness: The Heroic Tragedies of Chapman and Shakespeare* (London, 1980), 183, makes the same association.

[21] '*Coriolanus*—and the Delights of Faction', *Hudson Rev.* 19 (1966), 185–202 (197).

From the beginning of the encounter with his family Coriolanus finds his feelings in conflict with his resolution to be constant. He declares:

> But out, affection!
> All bond and privilege of nature break;
> Let it be virtuous to be obstinate.
> . . . I'll never
> Be such a gosling to obey instinct, but stand
> As if a man were author of himself
> And knew no other kin.
>
> (24–6, 34–6)

In the name of his quasi-Stoic principle that it is 'virtuous to be obstinate', he is determined to deny the natural bonds which tie him to imperfect humanity and to act as if he were 'author of himself', like a god, self-created and self-determining. Yet the hypothetical terms he uses ('As if', 'Let it be') betray a sense that his basic assumptions are false: obstinacy is not normally a virtue, and a man is not really author of himself.[22] Even as he declares his immovable strength, he admits his weakness:

> I melt, and am not
> Of stronger earth than others. My mother bows,
> As if Olympus to a molehill should
> In supplication nod; and my young boy
> Hath an aspect of intercession which
> Great nature cries 'Deny not'.
>
> (29–33)

The natural bonds of 'affection' towards mother, child, wife, and country are too strong to be dismissed by an act of will. Menenius unwittingly defined why Coriolanus cannot be like a god: he lacks 'eternity and a heaven to throne in'. Being mortal and on earth, he must finally recognize the natural ties which bind him to the rest of humanity, and 'melt' from rock to common clay.

During this struggle between constancy and nature, Coriolanus sees himself once again as an actor:

[22] This device of setting up an ethical hypothesis is a recurring one in the play: compare Cominius on Roman *virtus* ('It is held . . . If it be . . .'), and, for a minor example, the Volscian guard's 'though it were as virtuous to lie as to live chastely' (5. 2. 28–9).

> Like a dull actor now
> I have forgot my part, and I am out
> Even to a full disgrace.
>
> (40–2)

It is a crucial moment of insight. Coriolanus, who despised acting as hypocrisy and inconstancy, has already been forced to define his ideal in terms of consistent acting: 'I play | The man I am.' Now he recognizes that his godlike Senecan constancy is itself a role—a role, moreover, which is not true to his deepest nature and which, as he finds himself forgetting his lines and lapsing out of character, he cannot maintain with consistency or decorum. The whole situation, in fact, violates decorum: as Volumnia kneels 'unproperly' (54) to her own son, proper roles are reversed in a way which he feels as an apocalyptic disintegration of the natural order of things (58–62). It is an 'unnatural scene' (185). Can it be right to maintain a constancy which leads to such indecorum?

Coriolanus is facing the contradiction Cicero recognized in *De officiis*:

> For in such wise we muste worke, as againste all nature [*universam naturam*] wee never strive: which thing avoided, let us folow our owne proper nature [*propriam naturam*]. (*Off.* 1. 110)

You must consistently follow your own nature only so far as it is not in conflict with nature in the universal sense. Coriolanus has attempted to be true to his own nature (albeit a 'nature' which is to a large extent a social construct). He has attained an awe-inspiring degree of consistency and steadfastness, rising above humanity and renouncing all human ties. But such a state is itself inconsistent with universal nature: that 'Great nature' which cries out that he must not deny the pleas of his own child. In such a conflict, universal nature is, in Cicero's words, 'muche the surer, and the steadfaster'. Coriolanus' individual self-assertion, and the social values of Rome, must give way to it.

This is the principle of *homologia*, harmony and consistency with nature, which underlies the Stoic ideal of constancy in both its Senecan and Ciceronian forms—though it tends to become overlaid in the former by an unnatural ideal of moral perfection, and in the latter by public role-playing. It is also the principle which underlies Montaigne's late 'philosophy of nature'. Fundamental to

Montaigne's moral vision is the ideal of knowledge of and consistency with both our own nature and universal nature—a consistency not to be found in a pursuit of rigid self-consistency or of an impossible Stoic constancy. That Shakespeare shares this ideal, and sees the failure of Rome in its failure to share it, is, I think, implied in *Julius Caesar*. It is more explicit in *Coriolanus*, where the hero's pursuit of absolute constancy is brought directly into conflict with *universa natura*. The tragedy of Coriolanus is that, while he attempts to 'play | The man I am', he does not know how to '*play the man well and duely*'. Unlike Brutus and Caesar, however, Coriolanus is granted at least a moment of insight into his own failure, and at the climax of the play submits to universal nature.[23]

The insight is only temporary: his character is too rigidly formed for permanent change. On his return to the Volscians he is the same man as ever, still boasting (despite his double betrayal) of the consistency of his actions (5. 6. 71–3). Like Shakespeare's other Roman heroes, Coriolanus dies 'like himself'; his death is entirely consistent with his life in its mingling of violence, nobility, and suicidal obstinacy. Dying like Brutus with a concern for his *dignitas*, his last thought is a desperate desire that his posthumous reputation be consistent with the truth about himself as he sees it. He repudiates Aufidius' definition of him as 'traitor' and 'boy', and insists instead upon the heroic image that future 'annals' will record:

> If you have writ your annals true, 'tis there
> That, like an eagle in a dove-cote, I
> Fluttered your Volscians in Corioles.
> Alone I did it. 'Boy'!
>
> (114–17)

[23] Many critics (e.g. Campbell, Rabkin, Traversi, Waith) read the submission scene much more bleakly or ironically, seeing Coriolanus as giving way to his social conditioning or his mother's domination. While acknowledging the ironies, I prefer the more positive readings of Bradley ('the conquest of passion by simple human feelings': '*Coriolanus*', 468), or R. B. Parker, '*Coriolanus* and "th'Interpretation of the Time"', in J. C. Gray (ed.), *Mirror Up to Shakespeare: Essays in Honour of G. B. Hibbard* (Toronto, 1984), 261–76 ('affirmation of the familial link on which a healthy society has to be built', 275). Hermann Heuer, 'From Plutarch to Shakespeare: A Study of *Coriolanus*', *ShS* 10 (1957), 50–9, is a good discussion of 'nature' in this scene.

Aufidius' final words promise him what he wanted: 'a noble memory' (154). It is a truly Roman death. Nevertheless, for a moment Coriolanus had an insight into a kind of virtue less limited than the ideal of constancy.

Coriolanus is Shakespeare's definitive critique of the contradictions of 'constancy', and its potentially destructive consequences for an individual or a society which hold it as the supreme virtue. *Antony and Cleopatra*, probably written a little earlier, takes the argument in a different direction. What would it be like to base a life on the positive value of inconstancy?

9

'Infinite Variety': Antony and Cleopatra

Antony and Cleopatra and *Coriolanus* represent the opposing wings of the 'triptych' which Shakespeare borrowed from Plutarch. To put it in its starkest terms, Coriolanus falls because he is too constant, Antony because he is not constant enough—and in love with a woman who is inconstancy incarnate.[1] So much is implicit in Plutarch. But where Plutarch saw his subjects as merely driven to disaster by moral flaws and irrational compulsions, Shakespeare sees each as pursuing—blindly, confusedly, and self-destructively—a genuine moral ideal. Coriolanus' ideal is that of constancy, '[n]ot to be other than one thing': an ideal taught him by Volumnia and Rome, and bearing a strong likeness to the Stoic codes of *Julius Caesar*. Antony's ideal is un-Roman and un-Stoic, and is best defined in the words of Montaigne: in a mutable world, he chooses to embrace 'the benefit of inconstancy' (3. 4, p. 57).

'Let Rome in Tiber melt': mutability and Roman constancy

More perhaps than any other of Shakespeare's plays, *Antony and Cleopatra* is dominated by a sense of mutability.[2] Almost every critic has commented on this quality of the play: its 'Heracleitian' universe of 'flux, conflict, and paradox' (Stephen A. Shapiro); the sense of 'something deliquescent in the reality behind the play' (John F. Danby); the fact that its characters '[b]oth within and

[1] Other critics have seen a similar relationship between the plays: Bullough defines it in terms of irascible and concupiscible passion (*Narrative and Dramatic Sources*, 454–5); Howard Erskine-Hill, *The Augustan Idea in English Literature* (London, 1983), ch. 6 (134–63), sees them as a 'diptych' representing opposed types of heroic 'intemperance', with Octavius (and Menenius) as 'approximate mean' (155).

[2] The obvious exception is *Troilus and Cressida*. But whereas *Troilus* almost equates mutability with 'decay', *Antony* stresses uncertainty and unpredictability, and its mutations can be positive as well as destructive.

without . . . inhabit a medium in perpetual movement' (Emrys Jones).[3] It is a quality which separates *Antony and Cleopatra* from the other two Roman plays, which are set primarily in the city of Rome and dominated by a sense of Rome's physical, political, and moral solidity and stability. Occasional, corner-of-the-eye glimpses of a chaotic and incomprehensible world outside the city walls—the storm in *Julius Caesar*, Coriolanus' panicky vision of the world's 'slippery turns'—remind us both of the artificiality of that order and of why its construction was necessary; but Rome's solidity remains central. In *Antony and Cleopatra*, that solidity has melted away.

The change is partly historical. Eternal Rome itself is changing, from republic to empire. A flawed but functioning commonwealth which structured the lives of its citizens has now become an arena for competing warlords. The play's political world is under the domination of fortune (a word which occurs forty-six times): a world of confusion, intrigue, rumour, treachery, abrupt rises and falls, whose symbols are the waxing and waning moon to which Pompey, with unconscious irony, compares his 'crescent' power (2. 1. 10), and the 'varying tide' which Octavius uses as an image of popular favour:

> This common body,
> Like to a vagabond flag upon the stream,
> Goes to, and back, lackeying the varying tide,
> To rot itself with motion.
>
> (1. 4. 44–7)

Its paradigm is the scene on Pompey's galley: the world rulers drunk and dancing on a floating ship, unaware that at any moment the ship may be cut adrift and their throats casually slit.[4] The political world of *Antony and Cleopatra* is that envisaged by the Stoics: a 'confusion' (in Montaigne's words) in which every

[3] Stephen A. Shapiro, 'The Varying Shore of the World: Ambivalence in *Antony and Cleopatra*', *MLQ* 27 (1966), 18–32 (25); John F. Danby, 'The Shakespearean Dialectic: An Aspect of *Antony and Cleopatra*', in *Scrutiny*, 16 (1949), 196–213 (198); Emrys Jones, introd. to New Penguin edn. (Harmondsworth, 1977), 12. The best discussion of mutability and ambiguity in the play is the first chapter of Janet Adelman, *The Common Liar: An Essay on 'Antony and Cleopatra'* (New Haven, 1973); this is still the best book-length study of any of the Roman plays, and I am indebted both to Adelman's text and her wide-ranging notes.

[4] This scene is well discussed by Jones, 21–2.

man 'doth hourely see himselfe upon the point of his fortunes overthrow and downefall' (3. 2), and nothing is to be relied upon except the constancy of the individual human soul.[5]

The human soul, however, is no more stable. There is perpetual motion, as Jones points out, within as well as without the characters. Cleopatra's capriciousness goes without saying; Antony too shifts unpredictably between extremes of sensuality and austerity, love and jealousy, courage and self-pity. Cleopatra's line 'Let him for ever go—let him not, Charmian' (2. 5. 116) captures the fluidity of their emotions and their relationship. Even the most rational characters suffer unpredictable changes of mood: Enobarbus pragmatically betrays Antony and then dies of grief, Octavius weeps for the death of Antony whom he has driven to death. This paradox of mourning for one's enemies, which Montaigne cited to illustrate 'the volubilitie and supplenesse of our minde' (1. 37), recurs in the play as an example of how (in Antony's words), 'The present pleasure, | By revolution low'ring, does become | The opposite of itself' (1. 2. 118–20). Human emotions too 'revolve' like fortune's wheel.

Truth itself seems to be in a state of flux. We hear a babble of reports and contradictory 'choric' comments; see events and characters alter as we view them from different perspectives; watch the characters themselves (even the lovers) fail to understand one another; find our expectations mocked, and our desire to understand thwarted when the play withholds crucial information from us.[6] The fascination of the Roman plays with problems of knowledge is here omnipresent; *Antony and Cleopatra* seems

[5] On 'fortune', see Michael Lloyd, 'Antony and the Game of Chance', *JEGP* 61 (1962), 548–54; Marilyn L. Williamson, 'Fortune in *Antony and Cleopatra*', *JEGP* 67 (1968), 423–9; and Frederick Kiefer, *Fortune and Elizabethan Tragedy* ([San Marino, Calif.], 1983), 319–29. David Kaula, 'The Time Sense of *Antony and Cleopatra*', *SQ* 15 (1964), 211–23, is a subtle treatment of the play's various attitudes to time and change. Charles A. Hallett, 'Change, Fortune, and Time: Aspects of the Sublunar World in *Antony and Cleopatra*', *JEGP* 75 (1976), 75–89, clearly enunciates the Platonic-Stoic assumptions which (in my view) the play questions: 'What we must grasp . . . is what his audience would have grasped immediately: change is destructive. One must rise above it. The natural—Edenic—state of man is the state of rest' (86).

[6] See, for example, Adelman's discussion of the problems of Cleopatra's 'betrayal' of Antony in the final battle (*Common Liar*, 15–16 and n. 9), and Ronald R. MacDonald, 'Playing Till Doomsday: Interpreting *Antony and Cleopatra*', *ELR* 15 (1985), 78–99, on the play's subversion of the convention of the reliable messenger (85–9).

to demand that we pass judgements while undermining our ability to do so.[7]

The poetry itself is pervaded by images of mutability: flowing water, tides, mud, quicksands, wind and rain, the moon, transformation, melting, and decay. In the very first speech dotage 'o'erflows', glowing eyes 'bend' and 'turn', a heart becomes a bellows and a fan, 'the triple pillar of the world' is 'transformed | Into a strumpet's fool' (1. 1. 1–13). We are in a Daliesque or Ovidian world in which things undergo perpetual, grotesque transformations, climaxing in Antony's comparison of himself to the shapes which form and dissolve in clouds (4. 15. 1–14).[8]

Shakespeare's sense of universal mutability in *Antony and Cleopatra* no doubt owes something to Ovid's *Metamorphoses*, and something to Christian commonplaces about the instability of worldly things. More specifically, it echoes the preoccupations of Stoicism and Neostoicism: Seneca's descriptions of a world under the domination of fortune, Lipsius' vision of 'the alterations of all humaine affares: and the swelling and swaging of them as of the sea' (p. 111). Most of all, I believe, it is indebted to Montaigne. His vision in the 'Apologie' of universal flux, in which nothing is certain because 'both the judgeing and the judged . . . [are] in continuall alteration and motion'; his stress on the inconsistency of human character, in which 'all is but changing, motion, and inconstancy' (2. 1) and it is impossible to wrest our actions into any semblance of consistency; his assertion that '[t]he world runnes all on wheeles. All things therein moove without intermission; yea the earth, the rockes of *Caucasus*, and the Pyramides of Ægypt,' so that even his own self goes 'unquietly and staggering, with a naturall drunkenesse' (3. 12)—these seem the best commentaries on the world of *Antony and Cleopatra*. Shakespeare may be echoing this last passage when, in the galley scene, Menas wishes that the whole world be drunk '[t]hat it might go on wheels' (2.

[7] On problems of truth and judgement, see Schanzer, *Problem Plays*, ch. 3, and Benjamin T. Spencer, '*Antony* and the Paradoxical Metaphor', *SQ* 9 (1958), 373–8. Michael Neill, in the excellent introduction to his recent Oxford edition (Oxford, 1994), notes that 'Philo's opening words, "Nay but" set the keynote for . . . a play always arguing with itself, in which . . . no point of view . . . is allowed to go unquestioned or unqualified' (100–1); the comment irresistibly recalls Montaigne's motto that 'To any reason an equal reason may be opposed'.

[8] On the play's imagery, see Charney, *Shakespeare's Roman Plays*, ch. 4, and Wilson Knight, *Imperial Theme*, 199–262, esp. 232–40 on images of melting and dissolution.

7. 89). The colloquial phrase can imply either effortless gliding or wild careering; its ambiguity suggests, both in Florio and in Shakespeare, the mixture of exhilaration and vertigo such a world can induce.[9]

The Stoic response to such a world is summed up by Lipsius: 'Imprint CONSTANCIE in thy mind amid this casuall and inconstant variablenesse of all things' (p. 111). Such constancy is Rome's traditional virtue, and is still associated with it in *Antony and Cleopatra*. The imagery enforces a contrast between Roman stability and Egypt's abandonment to flux: Egypt is associated with water, the tides, the overflowing fertility of the Nile; Rome with dry land and with symbols of restraint, control, and geometrical rigidity—the arch, the set-square, the unslipping knot. When Antony declares, 'Let Rome in Tiber melt, and the wide arch | Of the ranged empire fall' (1. 1. 35–6), he is symbolically renouncing Rome's ordered stability for Egyptian fluidity and change. Yet the contrast is more symbolic than real. Rome's republican order has already 'melted' into civil war; the distinctions between Rome and Egypt begin to blur and dissolve as Antony takes to Egyptian life, Pompey hopefully tries to put on an 'Alexandrian feast' (2. 7. 91), and Dolabella is converted to the 'religion' of Cleopatra's love (5. 2. 195), while Cleopatra dies 'after the high Roman fashion' (4. 16. 89). Cleopatra's phrase is one of very few where the word 'Roman' has the moral connotations it had in *Julius Caesar*; in *Antony* 'Rome' is a place-name, not a moral norm, and Romans are guided mainly by political expediency.[10]

Roman constancy is represented most obviously by Octavius

[9] See the note ad loc. in M. R. Ridley's Arden edn. (London, 1954), and (on the double meaning) *OED*, 'Wheel' sb. 15b. Though the phrase is commonplace, its association in both contexts with drunkenness (and with pyramids: cf. 2. 7. 18) suggests Shakespeare may have had the Montaigne passage in his mind. Neill (introduction, 80–5) also invokes Montaigne's influence on the play's treatment of 'the discontinuous and histrionic nature of identity' (82), citing several of the same passages as I do.

[10] The decay of the Roman ideal in *Antony* is well discussed by Cantor (*Shakespeare's Rome)* in his introduction (esp. 23–30; on the blurring of Rome and Egypt, 26) and ch. 4 (127–154). See also Robert Ornstein, 'The Ethic of the Imagination: Love and Art in *Antony and Cleopatra*', in J. R. Brown and B. Harris (eds.), *Later Shakespeare* (London, 1966), 31–46 (35–8); Dipak Nandy, 'The Realism of *Antony and Cleopatra*', in Arnold Kettle (ed.), *Shakespeare in a Changing World* (London, 1964), 172–94 (a Marxist reading). Michael Lloyd, 'The Roman Tongue', *SQ* 10 (1959), 461–8, and his 'Game of Chance', focus respectively on Rome's dependence on opinion and on fortune.

Caesar.[11] Consistent, temperate, rational, unemotional, Octavius defines his values on his first appearance by eloquently condemning Antony's sensual excesses (1. 4. 4–10, 16–33) and praising his former steadfast endurance of hardship (56–71). These are traditional Roman judgements: Coriolanus would have endorsed Octavius' praise of *virtus*, Brutus his insistence on the superiority of spirit to body.

Nevertheless, Octavius is an inadequate representative of the Roman Stoic ideal. If he never surrenders to passion, he seems to have no passions to overcome; if he is steadfast, he never has any serious adversity to test him; he does not defy fortune but is carried along by it to success, becoming in Cleopatra's phrase 'Fortune's knave, | A minister of her will' (5. 2. 3–4). A telling example of his debasement of Stoic ideas is the advice of his emissary Thidias to Cleopatra: 'Wisdom and fortune combating together, | If that the former dare but what it can, | No chance may shake it' (3. 13. 79–81). The doctrine that the wise man cares only for what is in his power meant, for the Stoics, that nothing matters except virtue; in Thidias' mouth it becomes a cynical tip to accept the inevitable and join the winning side. Octavius' aim is success, and his values pragmatic. He is willing for the sake of argument to 'grant it is not | Amiss' (1. 4. 16–17) for Antony to indulge his vices, if only they were not politically damaging. Virtue is for him a matter of appearances. Preoccupied with public opinion (despite his contempt for the people), he is anxious to '[l]et the world see | His nobleness well acted' (5. 2. 43–4). His rebuke to his sister for not allowing him to organize a public welcome for her—she has 'prevented | The ostentation of our love; which, left unshown, | Is often left unloved' (3. 6. 51–3)—is almost a *reductio ad absurdum* of the Roman assumption that appearance and reality are identical.[12]

[11] My view of Octavius is influenced by Cantor, *Shakespeare's Rome*, 29–30, and Adelman, *Common Liar*, 25, who notes his concern for self-justification; see also J. Leeds Barroll's subtle and devastating analysis in 'The Character of Octavius', *ShakS* 6 (1972), 231–88. Pompey is seen by Martindale and Martindale as a figure of Stoic constancy (*Shakespeare and the Uses of Antiquity*, 181–3), but this is surely to ignore the irony with which the play treats his reliance on fortune, his wishful thinking (e.g. 2. 1. 18–20), and his purely formal notion of honour (which amounts to an insistence on 'deniability' in the crimes his subordinates commit on his behalf).

[12] Commentators disagree (e.g. Case versus Ridley in the Arden edn.) whether Octavius means that unshown love is unfelt or is thought to be unfelt; the point, I think, is his confusion of the two ideas.

In a sense Octavius is the ultimate development of Roman constancy. But he represents a diminished form of the ideal, lacking any trace of the flawed greatness of the other Roman heroes: Brutus' pursuit of perfection, Caesar's Olympian pride, Coriolanus' imitation of the graces of the gods. In Octavius the merely 'formal' strain in Roman virtue has completely displaced its heroic aspirations. Antony, on the other hand, continues to aspire to godlike greatness—but not through constancy.

'Whom everything becomes': the ideal of inconstancy

In Plutarch's Life, Antonius' fatal flaw is inconstancy: unable to remain consistently true to his better, Roman self, he is led astray by emotion, sensuality, and Cleopatra. Many critics, whether or not they accept Plutarch's moral priorities, would accept the basic assumption. Antony is fatally divided between two worlds, Rome and Egypt, and the opposed sets of values they represent—variously defined as politics and love, reason and feeling, order and freedom, the World and the Flesh, public and private life.[13] It is not (on this view) so much that Antony rejects Rome for Egypt, as that he is unable to make a clear choice between them. Instead he wavers back and forth, swayed now by Cleopatra, now by Octavius, acted upon by others rather than acting, making critical decisions by whim or default, until he is at last cornered and forced to a messy and ignoble death.

There is an element of truth in this view, but it is inadequate. Antony is not simply unable to choose between the two worlds between which he moves; he positively refuses to choose between them. He is not satisfied to be bound to either Rome or Egypt, but wants to combine both: to be both soldier and lover, have both honour and pleasure, be great both in public and in private life.[14]

[13] The tendency to allegorize Rome and Egypt is cogently criticized by Adelman, *Common Liar*, 193–4, and Wilders, *Lost Garden*, 118–19.

[14] Critics who see Antony's tragedy in his lack of single-mindedness include Laurence Edward Bowling, 'Antony's Internal Disunity', *SEL* 4 (1964), 239–46; J. Leeds Barroll, 'Shakespeare and the Art of Character: A Study of Anthony', *ShakS* 5 (1971), 159–235 ('the tragic shapelessness of Anthony's identity', 221); Martindale and Martindale, *Shakespeare and the Uses of Antiquity*, 184 ('Antony's problem, like Hamlet's . . . is that he cannot make up his mind'). My own view is influenced by Julian Markels, *The Pillar of the World: 'Antony and Cleopatra' in Shakespeare's Development* (Columbus, Oh., 1968), who sees Antony as positively choosing not to choose between Rome and Egypt, and A. Caputi, 'Shakespeare's *Antony*

Antony is not given to philosophical statements, and it is perhaps overstating the case to speak of his 'ideal' or his 'philosophy'. But the principle behind his actions seems very close to that which Montaigne voices in 'Of Three Commerces or Societies':

> Our chiefest sufficiency is, to apply our selves to divers fashions. It is a being, but not a life, to bee tied and bound by necessity to one onely course. The goodliest mindes are those that have most variety and pliablenesse in them. (3. 3, p. 99)

Antony refuses to be 'bound . . . to one onely course'. Rejecting the Stoic ideal '[n]ot to be other than one thing', to be *unus idemque inter diversa*, he wants to be many things, and respond in 'divers fashions' to diverse situations. He is willing to surrender to the variousness and mutability of his world, and to change in response to it; to adopt different modes of behaviour in Rome or in Egypt, to seek a variety of transient pleasures ('There's not a minute of our lives should stretch | Without some pleasure now' (1. 1. 48–9)), to be responsive to the different 'qualities of people' (1. 1. 56), to indulge in games of self-transformation such as exchanging clothes with Cleopatra (2. 5. 22–3). Enobarbus seems to speak for him when he says, 'Every time | Serves for the matter that is then born in't' (2. 2. 9–10). Antony echoes this when he advises Octavius, at the feast on Pompey's galley, to 'Be a child o'th' time' (2. 7. 96): respond appropriately to the changing demands of each situation. This is just what Coriolanus would or could not do; and Octavius too rejects the principle with his retort, 'Possess it, I'll make answer' (97): don't respond to situations, control them.[15]

Cleopatra is the very embodiment of the mutability which Antony embraces.[16] As 'our terrene moon' (3. 13. 156) and 'serpent of old

and Cleopatra: Tragedy without Terror', *SQ* 16 (1965), 183–91, who stresses his choice of the 'inclusiveness' (190) embodied in Cleopatra; both Markels and Caputi, however, tend to exaggerate his success and play down the painfulness of his end.

[15] This interpretation of Octavius' reply, though debatable, is accepted by Ridley, Dover Wilson (New Shakespeare, Cambridge, 1950), Jones, and Everett (Signet edn., New York, 1964).

[16] Useful older discussions of Cleopatra's inconsistency include MacCallum, *Shakespeare's Roman Plays*, 418–21, who quotes suggestively from La Rochefoucauld ('La constance en amour est une inconstance perpétuelle . . .' (420 n.)) and Granville-Barker, *Prefaces*, iii, 81–96 ('She is true enough to the self of the moment' (91)). Recent feminist critics find more positive value in it. Clare Kinney, 'The Queen's Two Bodies and the Divided Emperor: Some Problems of Identity in *Antony and Cleopatra*', in A. M. Hazelkorn and B. S. Travitsky (eds.), *The Renaissance Englishwoman in Print* (Amhurst, Mass., 1990), 177–86, stresses her identification

Nile' (1. 5. 25), she is identified with the the play's chief symbols of flux. 'Variety and pliablenesse' are her leading qualities: 'Age cannot wither her, nor custom stale | Her infinite variety' (2. 2. 241–2). Enobarbus is no doubt thinking primarily of her range of sexual arts, but Cleopatra's 'variety' goes deeper than that; her fascination for Antony, and for us, lies in her unpredictability, her darting momentary interest in anything, her mercurial changes of mood in which genuine feelings mingle with play-acting ('If you find him sad, | Say I am dancing; if in mirth, report | That I am sudden sick' (1. 3. 3–5)) so as to keep even Antony perpetually off balance. He sums up this quality in her with a mixture of exasperation and admiration:

Fie, wrangling queen,
Whom everything becomes—to chide, to laugh,
To weep; how every passion fully strives
To make itself, in thee, fair and admired!

(1. 1. 50–3)

Whatever Cleopatra does, she does with absolute commitment, and it 'becomes' her, is beautiful and appropriate in her.

Cleopatra returns the compliment a few scenes later, when questioning Alexas about Antony's departure:

CLEOPATRA. What, was he sad or merry?
ALEXAS. Like to the time o'th' year between the extremes
Of hot and cold, he was nor sad nor merry.
CLEOPATRA. O well divided disposition! Note him,
Note him, good Charmian, 'tis the man; but note him.
He was not sad, for he would shine on those
That make their looks by his; he was not merry,
Which seemed to tell them his remembrance lay
In Egypt with his joy; but between both.
O heavenly mingle! Be'st thou sad or merry,
The violence of either thee becomes;
So does it no man else.

(1. 5. 49–60)

with Egypt in its 'multiplicity' (182), as opposed to Rome's competitive individualism; Jyotsna Singh, 'Renaissance Antitheatricality, Antifeminism, and Shakespeare's *Antony and Cleopatra*', *RenD* NS 20 (1989), 99–121, and Mary Ann Bushman, 'Representing Cleopatra', in Dorothea Kehler and Susan Baker (eds.), *In Another Country* (Metuchen, NJ, 1991), see her conscious role-playing as a strategy for subverting or evading male and Roman concepts of essential, consistent identity.

She seems at first to be praising Antony for a kind of Roman temperance, a refusal to over-indulge any emotion. The last lines, however, give the idea an unexpected twist. Commentators fret over the illogicality of 'The violence of either thee becomes,' the Arden editor suggesting that Cleopatra must mean '*Even if* he had run to either extreme it would still have become him.' Her meaning is, I think, more paradoxical. She evokes the ideal of temperance only to subvert it. Antony's 'heavenly mingle' is not a grey area between opposite extremes of emotion, but a mingling of two emotions both so strong that they cancel one another out. This phrase sums up the ideal that Cleopatra and Antony live by: not to choose a single consistent course, or find a happy mean between opposites, but to combine 'the violence of either', to fuse conflicting extremes and experience all aspects of life to their fullest. Like Montaigne's, it is an ideal of 'variety' as opposed to Stoic constancy—but more extreme, paradoxical, and 'violent' than the moderate adaptability Montaigne recommended.

In rejecting constancy, Antony is in a sense also rejecting decorum. For Cicero, decorum depends upon consistency: 'stedfastnes . . . becommeth moste of all' (1. 120). You must choose a single appropriate role and play it consistently throughout life. Cicero acknowledges that young people may sometimes find the choice of role difficult, but not that it may be a lifelong problem; the middle-aged Antony's refusal to choose would clearly appear to him both immature and indecorous.

In another sense, however, Antony and Cleopatra are not defying but redefining decorum. It is significant that, of only three uses by Shakespeare of the word, two occur in *Antony and Cleopatra*, and both are spoken by Egyptians: Iras' prayer to Isis to 'keep decorum' and cuckold Alexas (1. 2. 67), and Cleopatra's assertion that 'majesty, to keep decorum, must | No less beg than a kingdom' (5. 2. 17–18).[17] The first use is facetious, the second grandiloquent but edged with irony (since the very idea of a queen begging is grossly indecorous). Nevertheless, Cleopatra and her court invoke the principle of decorum more explicitly than any other characters in Shakespeare. Yet Cleopatra's actions frequently outrage conventional ideas of decorum: hopping forty paces through the public

[17] The third is *MfM* 1. 3. 30–1 ('The baby beats the nurse, and quite athwart | Goes all decorum').

street, or physically assaulting a messenger, would not normally be thought 'fitting' for a queen; and if 'stedfastnes . . . becommeth moste of all,' Cleopatra is the least decorous of human beings. Clearly, as Janet Adelman has pointed out, there is something odd and un-Roman about 'Egyptian decorum'.[18]

Moreover, the words 'become' and 'becoming', which Grimalde used to translate Cicero's *decet* and *decorum*, occur with unusual regularity in the play, often in this sense.[19] Cleopatra tells Antony that 'my becomings kill me when they do not | Eye well to you' (1. 3. 97–8); Octavius responds to Lepidus' defence of Antony's faults with the grudging hypothesis, 'Say this becomes him' (1. 4. 21); Lepidus tells Enobarbus that it 'shall become [him] well' to entreat Antony to moderation (2. 2. 2); Enobarbus, speaking of Cleopatra's 'infinite variety', declares that 'vilest things | Become themselves in her' (2. 2. 244–5); Octavius orders Thidias (cryptically) to '[o]bserve how Antony becomes his flaw' (3. 12. 34). The question of what 'becoming' means, and how one decides what 'becomes' a person, is subtly but insistently raised.

The most striking uses of the word are the two passages quoted earlier, in which Antony declares that 'everything becomes' Cleopatra, and Cleopatra says that the violence of either mirth or sadness 'becomes' Antony. Whatever Cleopatra does, she is observing decorum, because everything is appropriate or 'comely' for her; whatever extremes of emotion Antony flies to, they are decorous for him (if for no one else). Decorum for Antony and Cleopatra does not, as it does for Cicero or for Roman tradition, involve self-consistency. They are themselves so diverse and universal in their potentialities that nothing they do can be inconsistent with

[18] Adelman's brief discussion (*Common Liar*, 141–5) is very suggestive, though she defines 'Egyptian decorum' in terms of 'excess' rather than variety, and does not put it in a Ciceronian or Stoic context. Less useful is McAlindon's treatment in *Shakespeare and Decorum* (ch. 6), which judges the lovers by the conventional standard, seeing them as initially condemned and mocked for indecorum but redeemed by their decorous deaths. Other critics invoke decorum more in an aesthetic than an ethical sense: e.g. Phyllis Rackin, 'Shakespeare's Boy Cleopatra, the Decorum of Nature, and the Golden World of Poetry', *PMLA* 87 (1972), 201–12; Ide, *Possessed with Greatness*, ch. 5 (102–31); J. Leeds Barroll, *Shakespearean Tragedy: Genre, Tradition, and Change in 'Antony and Cleopatra'* (Washington, 1984), 168–75.

[19] Spevack (*Concordance)* lists seventeen occurences, compared with four in *Julius Caesar* and nine in *Coriolanus*.

themselves. Hence, nothing can be indecorous: even 'vilest things' become them.

Shakespeare also exploits the double meaning of the word 'become', linking the ideas of decorum and change. As Adelman notes, when Cleopatra speaks of 'my becomings', the word seems to embrace 'both the things that are becoming to her and the things she becomes'.[20] Enobarbus' 'vilest things become themselves' suggests not only that they become (befit) Cleopatra but also that they become truly themselves, achieving their own perfection and being transformed from vileness into something rich and strange. In this non-Platonic world, decorum is not a matter of *being* but of *becoming*, continually changing to adapt to the world's changes.

Antony and Cleopatra redefine decorum by emptying it of its Ciceronian and Roman associations with constancy. For a complex individual in a perpetually changing world, decorum cannot be defined as being always the same: it must involve the ability to become a variety of different things, to explore one's full potential, to 'be a child o'th' time'. This development illustrates the chameleon quality of the concept of decorum itself. Rome's code of public-spirited formal role-playing, Coriolanus' pursuit of truth to his rigidly defined self, and Antony and Cleopatra's pursuit of 'infinite variety' can all be justified by selective reference to *De officiis* 1.

The idea of being oneself, or 'like oneself', similarly becomes divorced from constancy. When Lucillius in *Julius Caesar* said that his general would be found 'like Brutus, like himself', his meaning was clear: Brutus, being Brutus, would necessarily kill himself. When Enobarbus, in answer to Lepidus' plea to entreat Antony to gentle speech, says, 'I shall entreat him | To answer like himself' (2. 2. 3–4), the meaning is less clear, for Antony is much less predictable. Enobarbus wants him to take a firm stand; Lepidus wants him to be yielding; in the event, he moves through a variety of stances (generosity, pride, flippancy, dignified apology) towards a politic compromise. Which of these is 'like himself'? What does it mean for Antony to be 'like himself'?

[20] Adelman, *Common Liar*, 145; McAlindon, *Shakespeare and Decorum*, 186, and Michael Goldman, *Acting and Action in Shakespearean Tragedy* (Princeton, 1985), 124–6, also note the double meaning of 'becoming'. Adelman invokes the Platonic distinction, without taking the further step of contrasting this 'becoming' with Platonic-Stoic consistency.

This question is insistently raised in the first scene. The burden of Philo's opening speech is that Antony is no longer himself: the great general is 'transformed | Into a strumpet's fool' (1. 1. 12–13). Antony speaks, on the contrary, as one who has found his true self ('Here is my space', 36); but Cleopatra accuses him of falsehood, and concludes—with teasing, sibylline ambiguity—'Antony | Will be himself' (45). No doubt, but what does that mean? Antony's answer, 'But stirred by Cleopatra' (45), implies that he will only be truly himself when under her influence. Once the lovers have gone, however, Philo and Demetrius restate their very different judgement:

> Sir, sometimes when he is not Antony
> He comes too short of that great property
> Which still should go with Antony.
>
> (59–61)

Antony is not being Antony, and is failing to play the part of himself with decorum.[21] Their criticism begs the question: what *is* Antony?

For Shakespeare's other Roman heroes the aim of being 'like oneself' is straightforward: their single and consistent 'selves' are defined by their social roles and the opinions of others. When Julius Caesar claims to be 'always . . . Caesar', everyone knows what that means. Antony, however, is not socially defined: the political vacuum that is Rome has no official role for him, nor is he concerned about the opinions of his peers (he has none, except Octavius) or of the people. He must construct his own identity. Yet he refuses to do this by tying himself to a single consistent and predictable self, like Julius Caesar's. Antony can only be defined as being like Antony; his model is the crocodile which, as he helpfully tells Lepidus, is 'shaped . . . like itself' (2. 7. 41). What it means to be 'like Antony' is something he must himself decide from moment to moment.

Unlike the decorum pursued by Brutus, Caesar, and Coriolanus, or the Roman codes of being 'Roman' or 'noble', this ideal of being Antony does not depend upon the opinions of others; it demands self-knowledge. It is like those other codes, however, in

[21] 'Property', I think, here includes the sense of propriety, fitness, decorum (*OED* 7). See also Neill's discussion of 'The Properties of the Self' (introduction, 112–23).

its self-defining circularity. Whereas the Romans of *Julius Caesar*, defining virtue as 'being Roman', could look to the stable society around them to define what that meant, Antony can only define what is proper for him in terms of his own continually changing self. It is not surprising that, in the mutable world of *Antony and Cleopatra*, he is in danger of losing himself.

The dissolution of Antony

I have argued that it is inadequate to see Antony's inconstancy merely as weakness. But there is no denying that his Montaignian ideal of variety, however attractive in theory, in practice appears as vacillation. In the first scene Antony grandly rejects Rome for Egypt; in the second '[a] Roman thought hath struck him' (I. 2. 77) and he resolves to break his 'Egyptian fetters' (I. 2. 110). In the third he finds a heroic compromise, declaring that he goes to Rome as Cleopatra's 'soldier-servant' (I. 3. 70); and this is maintained in I. 5 in his message from 'the firm Roman to great Egypt' (42–3), Alexas' picture of him soberly mounting his spirited horse (47–9), and Cleopatra's praise of his 'heavenly mingle' (58). Momentarily we glimpse an Antony who has successfully blended the 'violence' of Roman soldiership and Egyptian love. Once he reaches Rome, however, the precarious equilibrium collapses, as Antony apologizes to Octavius for his 'poisoned hours' (2. 2. 95) and patches up a political marriage—shortly to be broken. Antony's 'well-divided disposition' is most often disastrously divided against itself. Unlike the immovable Julius Caesar or Coriolanus, he is in ceaseless movement back and forth, like the 'vagabond flag' of Octavius' image, which '[g]oes to, and back, lackeying the varying tide, | To rot itself with motion' (I. 5. 45–7).

Antony's lack of 'singleness of aim' makes him vulnerable to the single-minded Octavius.[22] While Octavius, possessor rather than child of the time, moves towards his goal of power, Antony abandons himself to the power of fortune. We see this most clearly in his decision to fight at sea, which is shown not only as a tactical

[22] The phrase is A. C. Bradley's, 'Shakespeare's *Antony and Cleopatra*' in his *Oxford Lectures on Poetry* (London, 1920), 279–305 (288).

blunder but also as a symbolic choice of Egyptian flux over Roman stability—

> Let th'Egyptians
> And the Phoenicians go a-ducking; we
> Have used to conquer standing on the earth
> And standing foot to foot.
>
> (3. 7. 63–6)

—and of 'chance and hazard' over 'firm security' (47–8). In a way he is following a principle, but the principle is foolish, and his feeble afterthought that 'if we fail, | We then can do't at land' (52–3) exposes the weakness of a moral position based on trying to have it both ways.

In the later acts we are increasingly invited to judge Antony from a Stoic perspective, as a man whose surrender to fortune leaves him without the inner strength to withstand adversity. Buffeted by external crises and his own emotions, he swings wildly between heroism and self-pity, overconfidence and despair, infatuation and jealousy, and weakly attempts to evade his problems by Montaignian 'diversions': 'Let's to supper, come, | And drown consideration' (4. 2. 44–5). Enobarbus keeps up a cool quasi-Stoic commentary, dismissing Antony's courage, for instance, in Senecan style as merely the displacement of one irrational emotion by another: 'To be furious | Is to be frighted out of fear' (3. 13. 197–8). Antony's case, he concludes (in a double-edged comment that can cut both at Antony and at Stoicism), goes against the Stoic claim that the rational mind is unaffected by external adversity:

> I see men's judgments are
> A parcel of their fortunes, and things outward
> Do draw the inward quality after them
> To suffer all alike.
>
> (3. 13. 30–3)

In Stoic terms, Antony, lacking inner constancy, depends for his stability on external things which may fail him at any time: honour and love. His honour, the military authority and respect he commands, begin to melt away in defeat, and he discovers the truth of his glib assertion to Octavia: 'If I lose mine honour, | I lose myself' (3. 4. 22–3). The love of Cleopatra is equally under the control of fortune: how is it possible to rely on the incarnation of mutability? Shakespeare carefully leaves us as well as Antony in the dark as to whether she ever in fact betrays him, but there is ample room for suspicion that her 'inconstancy' may embrace infidelity as well as inconsistency.

When he discovers Cleopatra allowing Thidias to kiss her hand, Antony is thrown into a paroxysm of rage and panic, as his sense of both Cleopatra's identity and his own seem to disintegrate. Complaining, as his servants hesitate to obey him, that '[a]uthority melts from me' (3. 13. 90), he desperately asserts, 'I am | Antony yet' (92–3). But he is no longer sure who Cleopatra is: 'what's her name | Since she was Cleopatra?' (98–9). 'Not know me yet?' (160) Cleopatra asks him; but Antony is preoccupied with his own identity, and pathetically chides Octavius for 'harping on what I am, | Not what he knew I was' (144–5). Finally, as Cleopatra swears her fidelity, Antony recovers his love and courage in a burst of bravado, and Cleopatra rejoices: 'since my lord | Is Antony again, I will be Cleopatra' (188–9). The names 'Antony' and 'Cleopatra' echo through the scene, as 'Brutus' and 'Caesar' did in *Julius Caesar*, and as in the earlier play the names seem to stand for ideal selves which the characters must live up to. But where in *Julius Caesar* the roles implied by the names were clearly defined, in *Antony and Cleopatra* they are shifting, ambiguous, and continually changing. Antony cannot define from moment to moment what Cleopatra is, nor, as he tries to depend upon her, what he himself is.

Finally, defeated and betrayed, the hero who tried to explore a variety of selves finds his very existence melting away like the evanescent shapes in the clouds:

> That which is now a horse even with a thought
> The rack distains, and makes it indistinct
> As water is in water. . . .
> My good knave Eros, now thy captain is
> Even such a body. Here I am Antony,
> Yet cannot hold this visible shape, my knave.
>
> (4. 15. 9–14)

His response is to embrace, at last, Stoic constancy. 'Nay, weep not, gentle Eros. There is left us | Ourselves to end ourselves' (21–2). By the familiar Stoic paradox, he will assert his selfhood by killing himself, and preserve his *dignitas* by placing himself beyond change. His dying exchange with Cleopatra echoes the words of Strato and Lucillius over Brutus' body:

> ANTONY. . . . Not Caesar's valour
> Hath o'erthrown Antony, but Antony's
> Hath triumphed on itself.
> CLEOPATRA. So it should be,
> That none but Antony should conquer Antony.
> But woe 'tis so!
>
> (4. 16. 14–18)

Like other Roman heroes, Antony dies 'like himself', insisting that his death is worthy of and consistent with his self, and, by pronouncing his own third-person epitaph, attempting to define what posterity will say of him.[23] By doing so he defines what being 'like Antony' means. At last, in death, he acquires a fixed and constant identity. It is largely that of the Roman soldier, 'a Roman by a Roman | Valiantly vanquished' (4. 16. 59–60); as Stephen Shapiro puts it, Antony 'is clasped by death in the posture of a noble Roman and held rigid'.[24] But it is also that of Cleopatra's lover, dying on the last of many thousand kisses. His suicide is that of a Stoic 'conqueror of myself', but also that of a joyful 'bridegroom' (4. 15. 62, 100). In his last moments Antony reaches again the precarious equilibrium he occasionally touched, and fixes his identity at that point of rest.

The satisfactoriness of this resolution is qualified, however, by the mess and muddle which surrounds it. If his suicide is a performance, it is reduced almost to farce by the accidents which beset it: the unscripted and inconvenient suicide of a minor character, the bungled business of the stabbing, the awkward staging of the death scene which requires Antony to be hauled up to Cleopatra on ropes, the cross-purposes of the lovers' final dialogue. Antony's Stoic death seems like a tragicomic attempt to attain stability in a world whose chaotic mutability undercuts any such attempt.[25]

[23] Miola, *Shakespeare's Rome*, 147–51, compares Antony's suicide with those of Brutus and Cassius; his conclusion that they are similar 'only in externals' seems overstated.

[24] Shapiro, 'Varying Shore', 28.

[25] James C. Bulman, *The Heroic Idiom of Shakespearean Tragedy* (Newark, 1985), has an excellent analysis of how these scenes both evoke and undercut heroic expectations (192–9).

Marble-constancy and the fleeting moon

It is Cleopatra, in the final act, who succeeds where Antony failed in staging a death with true Stoic constancy and decorum—and, at the same time, achieving a paradoxical reconciliation of the values of constancy and inconstancy.

As soon as Antony is dead Cleopatra declares her intention to die, and 'do it after the high Roman fashion' (4. 16. 89). Ironically it is Cleopatra, rather than any Roman, who voices the most explicit and eloquent statement of Stoic principles in all the Roman plays:

> My desolation does begin to make
> A better life. 'Tis paltry to be Caesar.
> Not being Fortune, he's but Fortune's knave,
> A minister of her will. And it is great
> To do that thing that ends all other deeds,
> Which shackles accidents and bolts up change,
> Which sleeps and never palates more the dung,
> The beggar's nurse, and Caesar's.
>
> (5. 2. 1–8)

Cleopatra, in her willingness to die, is more truly free and 'great' than Octavius, whose commitment to worldly success makes him merely 'Fortune's knave'. Suicide will take her out of the power of fortune and mutability into a constant state in which she can never change or be affected by the world's changes. Cleopatra, who previously embodied the play's mutable world, now seems to reject mutability and choose instead to be (in the play's first and only use of the word) 'constant' as marble:

> My resolution's placed, and I have nothing
> Of woman in me. Now from head to foot
> I am marble-constant. Now the fleeting moon
> No planet is of mine.
>
> (234–7)

It is easy by such selective quotations to make Cleopatra seem purely Stoic, an Egyptian Portia.[26] In fact our total impression is

[26] McAlindon, for instance, sees a 'final change . . . from levity to gravity, from weakness into unchanging nobility . . . from becoming into being' (*Shakespeare and Decorum*, 210).

more complex. Despite her assertions of 'resolution', she keeps her options open, and seems finally to decide on death only when she learns of the plan to lead her in triumph. Even then she is not petrified into the single-minded marble-constancy which which Brutus faces death. She remains various and mercurial, under the influence of 'the fleeting moon', to the very end. As she prepares for death, sentiments of Roman nobility and Stoic resolution are mingled with almost every other possible mood—pride, tenderness, vanity, jealousy, humour and mockery, 'immortal longings', love both ideal and sensual. Her final thoughts dart unpredictably back and forth, from admiration to jealousy of Iras, to a fascinated sympathy with the asp, to a flash of malicious mockery of Octavius, to the tender fantasy of 'the baby at my breast' (304), to the final thought of Antony mingled with what seems like a sensuous enjoyment of the sensation of dying: 'As sweet as balm, as soft as air, as gentle' (306). She remains to the end a knot of contradictions, summed up in the audaciously indecorous clash of registers in Charmian's epitaph: 'A lass unparalleled' (310).

Such a death is in many ways thoroughly un-Stoic. Yet its motives and manner are very close to those of the traditional Stoic suicide as defined by Seneca and practised by Cato or Brutus. Cleopatra dies 'like herself', for the sake of *dignitas*, to preserve and fix her identity unchangingly; she stages her own death as a public demonstration of what she is and will remain. Octavius, by leading her in triumph, wants to define her as Rome sees her, transfixing her forever '[i]'th' posture of a whore' (217). Instead, she puts on her own performance, with appropriate setting, costumes, and properties, in Shakespeare's most magnificent presentation of the Senecan 'posture of dying'. Dying with perfect decorum in a way 'fitting for a princess | Descended of so many royal kings' (321–2), she defines forever the image that posterity will have of her.

The difference between Cleopatra's death and the other Stoic suicides of the plays lies in her concept of decorum. To die 'like herself' is not for her so simple as for a Brutus or a Coriolanus. Although she claims to renounce the fleeting moon in favour of marble-constancy, Cleopatra in her death unites the two. She does not reject her un-Roman, un-Stoic qualities—emotionalism, sensuality, frivolity, capriciousness, changeableness—but combines them with a new Stoic dignity and resolution. In death she attains constancy, and will remain 'always like herself' forever; but that self is not single and simple, *unus idemque*, but multiple and various, embracing all her contradictory qualities. Thus she achieves a paradoxical fusion of 'the violence of either' of the play's two conflicting forces, constancy and mutability: she becomes constant in inconstancy, or (in Spenser's phrase) 'eterne in mutabilitie'.[27]

Cleopatra's triumphant evasion of the choice between constancy and mutability makes the ending of *Antony and Cleopatra* more liberating than those of the other two Roman plays. Nevertheless, it is an extraordinary achievement, scarcely to be imitated, and one possible only in death. Moreover, it does not provide so neat a closure as the structure of my book, perhaps rather wishfully, has suggested; if the accepted dating of the Roman plays is correct, their final image of constancy is not Cleopatra's ambiguous triumph but Coriolanus' futile death. Turning back from the romance-like ending of *Antony and Cleopatra* to the confines of Rome's walls and opinions, the inextricable contradictions of Ciceronian decorum and Senecan constancy, and the helpless frustration of Coriolanus' pursuit of the principle that 'were man | But constant, he were perfect', Shakespeare suggests that the problems he has raised cannot really be resolved—not, at least, in the purely secular world his Romans inhabit.

[27] *Faerie Queene*, 3. 6. 47; compare Bate on the vision of Ovid's *Metamorphoses* 15: 'change itself becomes constancy, instability a fixed principle' (*Shakespeare and Ovid*, 6–7). Martindale and Martindale independently formulate Cleopatra's achievement in very similar terms—'a paradoxical and moving combination of fleeting moon and marble-constancy' (*Shakespeare and the Uses of Antiquity*, 189)—though without fully spelling out the implications of the paradox. Earlier critics who have influenced my reading of the play's ending include Ide, *Possessed with Greatness*, 127–8 (on Cleopatra's fusion of art and nature); Ornstein, 'Ethic of the Imagination'; Rackin, 'Shakespeare's Boy Cleopatra'; Anne Barton, *'Nature's Piece 'Gainst Fancy': The Divided Catastrophe in 'Antony and Cleopatra'* (London, 1973); Adelman, *Common Liar*, ch. 3; Duncan S. Harris, 'Again for Cydnus: The Dramaturgical Resolution in *Antony and Cleopatra*', *SEL* 17 (1977), 219–31.

Bibliography

PRIMARY SOURCES

AUGUSTINE, *Concerning the City of God against the Pagans*, tr. Henry Bettenson, introd. David Knowles (Harmondsworth, 1972).

CALVIN, JEAN, *Calvin's Commentary on Seneca's 'De Clementia'*, ed. and tr. Ford Lewis Battles and André Malan Hugo (Leiden, 1969).

—— *Institutes of the Christian Religion*, ed. John T. McNeill, tr. Ford Lewis Battles, Library of Christian Classics (2 vols., London, 1961).

CHAUCER, GEOFFREY, *The Riverside Chaucer*, gen. ed. Larry D. Benson (Oxford, 1988).

CICERO, *Academica*, in *De Natura Deorum; Academica*, ed. and tr. H. Rackham, Loeb Classical Library (London, 1933).

—— *De finibus bonorum et malorum*, ed. and tr. H. Rackham, Loeb Classical Library (2nd edn., London, 1931).

—— *De officiis*, ed. and tr. Walter Miller, Loeb Classical Library (London, 1913).

—— *Marcus Tullius Ciceroes thre bookes of duties to Marcus his sonne*, tr. Nicholas Grimalde (2nd edn., with parallel Latin text, London, 1558).

—— *Cicero on Moral Obligation: A New Translation of Cicero's 'De Officiis'*, tr. John Higginbotham (London, 1967).

—— *On Duties*, tr. Miriam T. Griffin and E. M. Atkins, Cambridge Texts in the History of Political Thought (Cambridge, 1991).

—— *De oratore*, ed. and tr. E. W. Sutton and H. Rackam, Loeb Classical Library (2nd edn., London, 1948).

—— *Letters to Atticus*, ed. and tr. E. O. Winstedt, Loeb Classical Library, iii (London, 1918).

—— *Tusculan Disputations*, ed. and tr. J. E. King, Loeb Classical Library (2nd edn., London, 1945).

—— *Those fyve questions, which Marke Tullye Cicero disputed in his Manor of Tusculanum*, tr. John Dolman (London, 1561).

CORNWALLIS, SIR WILLIAM, *Essayes of Sir William Cornwallis, the Younger*, ed. Don Cameron Allen (Baltimore, 1946).

DU VAIR, GUILLAUME, *The Moral Philosophie of the Stoicks*, tr. Thomas James [1598], ed. Rudolf Kirk (New Brunswick, NJ, 1951).

—— *The True Way to Vertue and Happiness. Intreating specially of Constancie in publike Calamities, and private Afflictions* [*De la constance*], tr. [Andrew Court] (1623). [Repr. with new title-page of *A Buckler against adversitie: or a treatise of constancie* (London, 1622).]

ELYOT, SIR THOMAS, *The Boke Named The Governour*, introd. Foster Watson, Everyman's Library (London, 1907).

—— *Of the Knowledge which Maketh a Wise Man*, ed. Edwin Johnston Howard (Oxford, Oh., 1946).

ERASMUS, DESIDERIUS, *The Handbook of the Militant Christian* [*Enchiridion militis Christiani*], in *The Essential Erasmus*, ed. and tr. John P. Dolan (New York, 1964), 24–93.

—— *The Praise of Folie*, tr. Sir Thomas Chaloner [1549], ed. Clarence H. Miller, Early English Text Society OS 257 (London, 1965).

HALL, JOSEPH, *Heaven on Earth, and Characters of Vertues and Vices*, ed. Rudolf Kirk (New Brunswick, NJ, 1948).

JONSON, BEN, *Works*, ed. C. H. Herford and Percy and Evelyn Simpson (11 vols., Oxford, 1925–52).

LIPSIUS, JUSTUS, *Two Bookes of Constancie* [*De constantia*], tr. Sir John Stradling [1595], ed. Rudolf Kirk (New Brunswick, NJ, 1939).

LODGE, THOMAS, *The Wounds of Civil War*, ed. J. W. Houppert, Regents series (London, 1969).

MARSTON, JOHN, *The Poems of John Marston*, ed. Arnold Davenport (Liverpool, 1961).

MASSINGER, PHILIP, *The Roman Actor*, in *The Plays and Poems of Philip Massinger*, ed. Philip Edwards and Colin Gibson, iii (Oxford, 1976).

MIDDLETON, THOMAS, and ROWLEY, WILLIAM, *The Changeling*, ed. N. W. Bawcutt, Revels Plays (2nd edn., London, 1961).

MONTAIGNE, MICHEL DE, *Les Essais de Michel de Montaigne: Édition conformé au texte de l'exemplaire de Bordeaux*, ed. Pierre Villey, 2nd edn. rev. V.-L. Saulnier *et al.* (Paris, 1965).

—— *Essays*, tr. John Florio [1603], introd. L. C. Harmer, Everyman's Library (3 vols., London, 1910).

—— *The Complete Essays*, tr. M. A. Screech (Harmondsworth, 1993).

PLATO, *Phaedo*, in *The Last Days of Socrates*, tr. Hugh Tredennick, Penguin Classics (Harmondsworth, 1954).

PLUTARCH, *Lives*, ed. and tr. Bernadotte Perrin, Loeb Classical Library, vols. iv (London, 1916), vi (1918), xi (1920).

—— *Les Vies des hommes illustres, Grecs & Romains, comparees l'une avec l'autre par Plutarque de Chaeronee*, tr. Jacques Amyot (2nd edn., Paris, 1565).

—— *The Lives of the Noble Grecians and Romanes, Compared Together by that Grave Learned Philosopher and Historiographer, Plutarke of Chareronea*, tr. [Sir] Thomas North (2nd edn., London, 1595).

—— *Shakespeare's Plutarch: The Lives of Julius Caesar, Brutus, Marcus Antonius, and Coriolanus in the Translation of Sir Thomas North*, ed. T. J. B. Spencer (Harmondsworth, 1964).

SENECA, *The Workes of Lucius Annaeus Seneca, Newly Inlarged and Corrected*, tr. Thomas Lodge (2nd edn., London, 1620).

—— *Ad Lucilium epistulae morales*, ed. and tr. Richard M. Gummere, Loeb Classical Library, vols. i (London, 1917), ii (1920), iii (1925).

—— *Moral Essays*, ed. and tr. John W. Basore, Loeb Classical Library, vols. i (London, 1928), ii (1932), iii (1935).

—— *Tragedies*, ed. and tr. Frank Justus Miller, Loeb Classical Library (2 vols., London, 1917).

—— *Seneca His Tenne Tragedies Translated into English*, ed. Thomas Newton [1581], introd. T. S. Eliot (2 vols., London, 1927).

SHAKESPEARE, WILLIAM, *The Complete Works*, ed. Stanley Wells and Gary Taylor (Oxford, 1986).

—— *Antony and Cleopatra*, ed. John Dover Wilson, The New [Cambridge] Shakespeare (Cambridge, 1950).

—— *Antony and Cleopatra*, ed. M. R. Ridley, based on the edn. of R. H. Case, Arden Shakespeare (London, 1954).

—— *Antony and Cleopatra*, ed. Barbara Everett, Signet Classic Shakespeare (New York, 1964).

—— *Antony and Cleopatra*, ed. Emrys Jones, New Penguin Shakespeare (Harmondsworth, 1977).

—— *The Tragedy of Anthony and Cleopatra*, ed. Michael Neill, Oxford Shakespeare (Oxford, 1994).

—— *Coriolanus*, ed. Philip Brockbank, Arden Shakespeare (London, 1976).

—— *Hamlet*, ed. Harold Jenkins, Arden Shakespeare (London, 1982).

—— *Julius Caesar*, ed. John Dover Wilson, The New [Cambridge] Shakespeare (Cambridge, 1949).

—— *Julius Caesar*, ed. T. S. Dorsch, Arden Shakespeare (London, 1955).

—— *Julius Caesar*, ed. Arthur Humphreys, Oxford Shakespeare (Oxford, 1984).

—— *Julius Caesar*, ed. Marvin Spevack, New Cambridge Shakespeare (Cambridge, 1988).

—— *Titus Andronicus*, ed. J. C. Maxwell, Arden Shakespeare (3rd edn., London, 1961).

SPENSER, EDMUND, *The Faerie Queene*, ed. A. C. Hamilton (London, 1977).

TACITUS, *Works*, ed. and tr. John Jackson, Loeb Classical Library, vol. v (London, 1937).

SECONDARY SOURCES

ADDINGTON, MARION H., 'Shakespeare and Cicero', *N&Q* 165 (1933), 116–18.

ADELMAN, JANET, *The Common Liar: An Essay on 'Antony and Cleopatra'* (New Haven, 1973).

ANSON, JOHN, '*Julius Caesar*: The Politics of the Hardened Heart', *ShakS* 2 (1966), 11–33.

ANZAI, TETSUO, *Shakespeare and Montaigne Reconsidered*, Renaissance Monographs 12 (Tokyo, 1986).

ARNOLD, E. VERNON, *Roman Stoicism* (Cambridge, 1911).

AYRES, HARRY MORGAN, 'Shakespeare's *Julius Caesar* in the Light of Some Other Versions', *PMLA* 25 (1910), 183–227.

BAKER, HERSCHEL, *The Dignity of Man: Studies in the Persistence of an Idea* (Cambridge, Mass., 1947).

BALDWIN, T. W., *William Shakspere's Small Latine & Lesse Greeke* (2 vols., Urbana, Ill., 1944).

BARISH, JONAS, *The Antitheatrical Prejudice* (Berkeley, 1981).

BARROLL, J. LEEDS, *Shakespearean Tragedy: Genre, Tradition, and Change in 'Antony and Cleopatra'* (Washington, 1984).

—— 'Shakespeare and the Art of Character: A Study of Anthony', *ShakS* 5 (1971), 159–235.

—— 'The Character of Octavius', *ShakS* 6 (1972), 231–88.

BARTON, ANNE, '*Julius Caesar* and *Coriolanus*: Shakespeare's Roman World of Words', in Philip H. Highfield Jr. (ed.), *Shakespeare's Craft: Eight Lectures* (Carbondale, Ill., 1982), 24–47.

—— *'Nature's Piece 'Gainst Fancy': The Divided Catastrophe in 'Antony and Cleopatra'*, Inaugural Lecture, Bedford College, University of London (London, 1973).

—— 'Livy, Machiavelli, and Shakespeare's *Coriolanus*', *ShS* 38 (1985), 115–29.

BATE, JONATHAN, *Shakespeare and Ovid* (Oxford, 1993).

BECKINGHAM, C. F., 'Seneca's Fatalism and Elizabethan Tragedy', *MLR* 32 (1937), 434–48.

BELSEY, CATHERINE, 'Senecan Vacillation and Elizabethan Deliberation: Influence or Confluence?', *RenD* 6 (1973), 65–88.

BENNETT, ROGER E., 'Sir William Cornwallis's Use of Montaigne', *PMLA* 48 (1933), 1080–9.

BERRY, RALPH, *Shakespeare and the Awareness of the Audience* (London, 1985).

BEVAN, EDWYN, *Stoics and Sceptics* (Oxford, 1913).

BLIGH, JANE, 'Cicero's Choric Comment in *Julius Caesar*', *English Studies in Canada*, 8 (1982), 391–408.

BOWLING, LAURENCE EDWARD, 'Antony's Internal Disunity', *SEL* 4 (1964), 239–46.

BOYCE, BENJAMIN, 'The Stoic *Consolatio* and Shakespeare', *PMLA* 64 (1949), 771–80.

BRADEN, GORDON, *Renaissance Tragedy and the Senecan Tradition: Anger's Privilege* (New Haven, 1985).

BRADLEY, A. C., '*Coriolanus*', *PBA* (1911–12), 457–73.

—— 'Shakespeare's *Antony and Cleopatra*', in his *Oxford Lectures on Poetry* (London, 1920), 279–305.

BROWER, REUBEN A., *Hero and Saint: Shakespeare and the Greco-Roman Heroic Tradition* (Oxford, 1971).

BULLOUGH, GEOFFREY (ed.), *Narrative and Dramatic Sources of Shakespeare*, v (London, 1964).

BULMAN, JAMES C., *The Heroic Idiom of Shakespearean Tragedy* (Newark, 1985).

BURKE, KENNETH, '*Coriolanus*—and the Delights of Faction', *Hudson Review*, 19 (1966), 185–202.

BURKE, PETER, *Montaigne*, Past Masters (Oxford, 1981).

BUSHMAN, MARY ANN, 'Representing Cleopatra', in Dorothea Kehler and Susan Baker (eds.), *In Another Country: Feminist Perspectives on Renaissance Drama* (Metuchen, NJ, 1991), 36–49.

CAMPBELL, O. J., *Shakespeare's Satire* (Oxford, 1943), 198–217.

CANTOR, PAUL A., *Shakespeare's Rome: Republic and Empire* (Ithaca, NY, 1976).

CAPUTI, A., 'Shakespeare's *Antony and Cleopatra*: Tragedy without Terror', *SQ* 16 (1965), 183–91.

CARR, W. I., '"Gracious Silence": A Selective Reading of *Coriolanus*', *English Studies*, 46 (1965), 221–34.

CAVE, TERENCE, 'Problems of Reading in the *Essais*', in I. D. McFarlane and Ian Maclean (eds.), *Montaigne* (Oxford, 1982), 133–66.

CHANG, J. S. M. J., '*Julius Caesar* in the Light of Renaissance Historiography', *JEGP* 69 (1970), 63–71.

CHARNEY, MAURICE, *Shakespeare's Roman Plays: The Function of Imagery in the Drama* (Cambridge, Mass., 1961).

CLAYTON, THOMAS, '"Should Brutus Never Taste of Portia's Death but Once?": Text and Performance in *Julius Caesar*', *SEL* 23 (1983), 237–58.

COUNCIL, NORMAN, *When Honour's at the Stake: Ideas of Honour in Shakespeare's Plays* (London, 1973).

CRAIG, HARDIN, 'The Shackling of Accidents: A Study of Elizabethan Tragedy', *PQ* 19 (1940), 1–19.

—— '*Coriolanus*: Interpretation', in W. F. McNeir and T. N. Greenfield (eds.), *Pacific Coast Studies in Shakespeare* (Portland, Ore., 1966), 199–209.

CROLL, MORRIS W., *Style, Rhetoric, and Rhythm*, ed. J. Max Patrick *et al.* (Princeton, 1966).

CUNLIFFE, JOHN W., *The Influence of Seneca on Elizabethan Tragedy* (London, 1893).

DANBY, JOHN F., 'The Shakespearean Dialectic: An Aspect of *Antony and Cleopatra*', in *Scrutiny*, 16 (1949), 196–213.

DAVIDSON, CLIFFORD, '*Coriolanus*: A Study in Political Dislocation', *ShakS* 4 (1968), 263–74.

DEAN, PAUL, 'Tudor Humanism and the Roman Past: A Background to Shakespeare', *RQ* 41 (1988), 84–111.

DIEHL, HUSTON, *An Index of Icons in English Emblem Books 1500–1700* (Norman, Okla., 1986).

DOLLIMORE, JONATHAN, *Radical Tragedy: Religion, Ideology and Power in the Drama of Shakespeare and His Contemporaries* (Brighton, 1984).

DORAN, MADELEINE, *Endeavors of Art: A Study of Form in Elizabethan Drama* (Madison, 1954).

—— *Shakespeare's Dramatic Language* (Madison, 1976).

DOUGLAS, A. E., 'Cicero the Philosopher', in T. A. Dorey (ed.), *Cicero*, Studies in Greek and Latin Literature and Its Influence (London, 1964), 135–70.

EDWARDS, PHILIP, 'Person and Office in Shakespeare's Plays' *PBA* 56 (1970), 93–109.

ELIOT, T. S., 'Seneca in Elizabethan Translation' and 'Shakespeare and the Stoicism of Seneca', in his *Selected Essays* (3rd edn., London, 1951), 65–105 and 126–46.

ELLRODT, ROBERT, 'Self-consciousness in Montaigne and Shakespeare', *ShS* 28 (1975), 37–50.

ERSKINE-HILL, HOWARD, *The Augustan Idea in English Literature* (London, 1983).

EVANS, GARETH LLOYD, 'Shakespeare, Seneca, and the Kingdom of Violence', in T. A. Dorey and Donald R. Dudley (eds.), *Seneca*, Studies in Latin Literature and Its Influence (London, 1965), 123–59.

FLEISSNER, R. F., 'That Philosophy in *Julius Caesar* Again', *Archiv*, 222 (1985), 344–5.

FOAKES, R. A., 'An Approach to *Julius Caesar*', *SQ* 5 (1954), 259–70.

FORTIN, RENÉ E., '*Julius Caesar*: An Experiment in Point of View', *SQ* 19 (1968), 341–7.

FRAME, DONALD M., *Montaigne: A Biography* (London, 1965).

FRENCH, MARILYN, *Shakespeare's Division of Experience* (New York, 1981).

GALINSKY, G. KARL, *The Herakles Theme: The Adaptations of the Hero in Literature from Homer to the Twentieth Century* (Oxford, 1972).

GILBERT, ALLAN H., 'Seneca and the Criticism of Elizabethan Tragedy', *PQ* 13 (1934), 370–81.

GILL, CHRISTOPHER, 'Panaetius on the Virtue of Being Yourself', in Anthony Bulloch *et al.* (eds.), *Images and Ideologies: Self-definition in the Hellenistic World* (Berkeley, 1993), 330–53.

GIVAN, CHRISTOPHER, 'Shakespeare's *Coriolanus*: The Premature Epitaph and the Butterfly', *ShakS* 12 (1979), 143–58.

GOLDBERG, JONATHAN, *James I and the Politics of Literature* (Baltimore, 1983).

GOLDMAN, MICHAEL, 'Characterizing Coriolanus', *ShS* 34 (1981), 73–84.

—— *Acting and Action in Shakespearean Tragedy* (Princeton, 1985).

GORDON, D. J., 'Name and Fame: Shakespeare's *Coriolanus*', in G. I. Duthie (ed.), *Papers Mainly Shakespearian* (Edinburgh, 1964), 40–57.

GRANVILLE-BARKER, HARLEY, *Prefaces to Shakespeare* (4 vols., London, 1930; illus. edn., introd. and notes by M. St Clare Byrne, 1963).

GREEN, DAVID C., *Plutarch Revisited: A Study of Shakespeare's Last Roman Plays and Their Source* (Salzburg, 1979).

GREEN, JEFFREY MARTIN, 'Montaigne's Critique of Cicero', *JHI* 36 (1975), 595–612.

GREENE, GAYLE, '"The Power of Speech I To Stir Men's Blood": The Language of Tragedy in Shakespeare's *Julius Caesar*', *RenD* 11 (1980), 67–93.

GRIFFIN, MIRIAM T., *Seneca: A Philosopher in Politics* (Oxford, 1976).

GRIMAL, PIERRE, *Sénèque 'De constantia sapientis': Commentaire* (Paris, 1953).

GUTHRIE, W. K. C., *The Gods of the Greeks* (London, 1950).

HALL, JOAN LORD, '"To Play the Man Well and Duely": Role-playing in Montaigne and Jacobean Drama', *Comparative Literary Studies*, 22 (1985), 173–86.

HALLETT, CHARLES A., 'Change, Fortune, and Time: Aspects of the Sublunar World in *Antony and Cleopatra*', *JEGP* 75 (1976), 75–89.

HARMON, ALICE, 'How Great Was Shakespeare's Debt to Montaigne?', *PMLA* 57 (1942), 988–1008.

HARRIS, DUNCAN S., 'Again for Cydnus: The Dramaturgical Resolution in *Antony and Cleopatra*', *SEL* 17 (1977), 219–31.

HARTFORD, G. F., 'T. S. Eliot on the Stoicism of Seneca', *English Studies in Africa*, 33 (1990), 1–14.

HARTSOCK, MILDRED E., 'The Complexity of *Julius Caesar*', *PMLA* 81 (1966), 56–62.

HAYDN, HIRAM, *The Counter-Renaissance* (New York, 1950).

HEUER, HERMANN, 'From Plutarch to Shakespeare: A Study of *Coriolanus*', *ShS* 10 (1957), 50–9.

HICKS, R. D., *Stoic and Epicurean* ([London, 1910]; repr. New York, 1962).

HILL, R. F., '*Coriolanus*: Violentest Contrariety', *Essays and Studies*, NS 17 (1964), 12–23.

HODGEN, MARGARET T., 'Montaigne and Shakespeare Again', *Huntingdon Library Quarterly*, 16 (1952–3), 23–42.

HOOKER, ELIZABETH ROBBINS, 'The Relation of Shakespeare to Montaigne', *PMLA* 17 (1902), 312–66.

HOOPES, ROBERT, *Right Reason in the English Renaissance* (Cambridge, Mass., 1962).

HUNT, H. A. K., *The Humanism of Cicero* (Melbourne, 1954).

HUNTER, G. K., 'A Roman Thought: Renaissance Attitudes to History

Exemplified in Shakespeare and Jonson', in Brian S. Lee (ed.), *An English Miscellany Presented to W. S. Mackie* (Cape Town, 1977), 93–118.

HUNTER, G. K., 'Seneca and the Elizabethans: A Case-study in "Influence"', and 'Seneca and English Tragedy', in *Dramatic Identities and Cultural Tradition* (Liverpool, 1978), 159–73 and 174–213.

IDE, RICHARD S., *Possessed with Greatness: The Heroic Tragedies of Chapman and Shakespeare* (London, 1980).

JAGENDORF, ZVI, '*Coriolanus*: Body Politic and Private Parts', *SQ* 41 (1990), 455–69.

KAUFMANN, R. J., 'The Seneca Perspective and the Shakespearean Poetic', *CompD* 1 (1967), 182–98.

—— and RONAN, CLIFFORD J., 'Shakespeare's *Julius Caesar*: An Apollonian and Comparative Reading', *CompD* 4 (1970), 18–51.

KAULA, DAVID, 'The Time Sense of *Antony and Cleopatra*', *SQ* 15 (1964), 211–23.

KERFERD, G. B., 'Cicero and Stoic Ethics', in John R. C. Martyn (ed.), *Cicero and Virgil: Studies in Honour of Harold Hunt* (Amsterdam, 1972), 60–74.

KIEFER, FREDERICK, 'Seneca's Influence on Elizabethan Tragedy: An Annotated Bibliography', *RORD* 21 (1978), 17–34.

—— *Fortune and Elizabethan Tragedy* ([San Marino, Calif.], 1983).

—— 'Senecan Influence: A Bibliographic Supplement', *RORD* 28 (1985), 129–42.

KINNEY, CLARE, 'The Queen's Two Bodies and the Divided Emperor: Some Problems of Identity in *Antony and Cleopatra*', in Anne M. Hazelkorn and Betty S. Travitsky (eds.), *The Renaissance Englishwoman in Print* (Amhurst, Mass., 1990), 177–86.

KNIGHT, G. WILSON, *The Imperial Theme: Further Interpretations of Shakespeare's Tragedies Including the Roman Plays* (London, 1931; 3rd edn., 1951).

KNIGHTS, L. C., 'Shakespeare and Political Wisdom: A Note on the Personalism of *Julius Caesar* and *Coriolanus*', *Sewanee Review*, 41 (1953), 43–55.

—— 'Personality and Politics in *Julius Caesar*', in *'Hamlet' and Other Shakespearean Essays* (Cambridge, 1979), 82–101.

KRANZ, DAVID L., 'Shakespeare's New Idea of Rome', in P. A. Ramsey (ed.), *Rome and the Renaissance: The City and the Myth* (Binghamton, NY, 1982), 371–80.

—— '"Too Great a Mind": The *Mentis Integritas* of Shakespeare's Roman Heroes', *Classical and Modern Literature* 4 (1984), 143–65.

KRISTELLER, PAUL OSKAR, 'The Moral Thought of Renaissance Humanism', in his *Renaissance Thought II: Papers on Humanism and the Arts* (New York, 1965), 20–68.

LEES, F. N., '*Coriolanus*, Aristotle and Bacon', *RES* NS 1 (1950), 114–25.

LEGGATT, ALEXANDER, *Shakespeare's Political Drama: The History Plays and the Roman Plays* (London, 1988).

LEVI, ANTHONY [A. H. T.], *French Moralists: The Theory of the Passions 1585 to 1649* (Oxford, 1964).

LEVITSKY, RUTH M., '"The Elements Were So Mix'd..."', *PMLA* 88 (1973), 240–5.

LLOYD, MICHAEL, 'The Roman Tongue', *SQ* 10 (1959), 461–8.

—— 'Antony and the Game of Chance', *JEGP* 61 (1962), 548–54.

LOGAN, GEORGE M., 'The Relation of Montaigne to Renaissance Humanism', *JHI* 36 (1975), 613–32.

LONG, A. A., *Hellenistic Philosophy: Stoics, Epicureans, Sceptics* (2nd edn., London, 1986).

—— and SEDLEY, D. N., *The Hellenistic Philosophers* (2 vols., Cambridge, 1987).

LOWE, LISA, '"Say I Play the Man I Am": Gender and Politics in *Coriolanus*', *Kenyon Review*, NS 8 (1986), 86–95.

LUCAS, F. L., *Seneca and Elizabethan Tragedy* (Cambridge, 1922).

MCALINDON, T., *Shakespeare and Decorum* (London, 1973).

MACCALLUM, M. W., *Shakespeare's Roman Plays and Their Background* (London, 1910; repr. New York, 1967, introd. T. J. B. Spencer).

MACDONALD, RONALD R., 'Playing Till Doomsday: Interpreting *Antony and Cleopatra*', *ELR* 15 (1985), 78–99.

MACKENDRICK, PAUL, with SINGH, KAREN LEE, *The Philosophical Books of Cicero* (London, 1989).

MARKELS, JULIAN, *The Pillar of the World: 'Antony and Cleopatra' in Shakespeare's Development* ([Columbus, Oh.], 1968).

MARTINDALE, CHARLES, and MARTINDALE, MICHELLE, *Shakespeare and the Uses of Antiquity: An Introductory Essay* (London, 1990).

MAXWELL, J. C., 'Brutus's Philosophy', *N&Q* 215 (1970), 128.

MAYER, C. A., 'Stoïcisme et purification du concept chez Montaigne', *Studi Francesci*, 70–2 (1980), 487–93.

MILES, GARY B., 'How Roman are Shakespeare's "Romans"?', *SQ* 40 (1989), 257–83.

MILLER, ANTHONY, '*Coriolanus*: The Tragedy of *Virtus*', *Sydney Studies in English*, 9 (1983–4), 37–60.

MIOLA, ROBERT S., *Shakespeare's Rome* (Cambridge, 1983).

—— *Shakespeare and Classical Tragedy: The Influence of Seneca* (Oxford, 1992).

MONSARRAT, GILLES D., *Light from the Porch: Stoicism and English Renaissance Literature* (Paris, 1984).

MOONEY, MICHAEL E., '"Passion, I See, is Catching": The Rhetoric of *Julius Caesar*', *JEGP* 90 (1991), 31–50.

MOTTO, ANNA LYDIA, *Seneca Sourcebook: Guide to the Thought of Lucius Annaeus Seneca in the Extant Prose Works* (Amsterdam, 1970).

NANDY, DIPAK, 'The Realism of *Antony and Cleopatra*', in Arnold Kettle (ed.), *Shakespeare in a Changing World* (London, 1964), 172–94.

ORNSTEIN, ROBERT, 'Seneca and the Political Drama of *Julius Caesar*', *JEGP* 57 (1958), 51–6.

—— *The Moral Vision of Jacobean Tragedy* (Madison, 1960).

—— 'The Ethic of the Imagination: Love and Art in *Antony and Cleopatra*', in J. R. Brown and B. Harris (eds.), *Later Shakespeare*, Stratford-upon-Avon Studies 8 (London, 1966), 31–46.

Oxford Classical Dictionary, ed. N. G. L. Hammond and H. H. Scullard (2nd edn., Oxford, 1970).

PALMER, D. J., 'Tragic Error in *Julius Caesar*', *SQ* 21 (1970), 399–409.

PALMER, RALPH GRAHAM, *Seneca's 'De Remediis Fortuitorum' and the Elizabethans* (Chicago, 1953).

PARKER, BARBARA L., '"A Thing Unfirm": Plato's *Republic* and Shakespeare's *Julius Caesar*', *SQ* 44 (1993), 30–43.

PARKER, R. B., '*Coriolanus* and "th'Interpretation of the Time"', in J. C. Gray (ed.), *Mirror Up to Shakespeare: Essays in Honour of G. B. Hibbard* (Toronto, 1984), 261–76.

PASSMORE, JOHN, *The Perfectibility of Man* (London, 1970).

PASTER, GAIL KERN, *The Idea of the City in the Age of Shakespeare* (Athens, Ga., 1985).

PECHTER, EDWARD, '*Julius Caesar* and *Sejanus*: Roman Politics, Inner Selves and the Power of the Theatre', in E. A. J. Honigmann (ed.), *Shakespeare and His Contemporaries: Essays in Comparison* (Manchester, 1986), 60–78.

PETERSSON, TORSTEN, *Cicero: A Biography* ([London, 1920], repr. New York, 1963).

PHILLIPS, MARGARET MANN, 'Erasmus and the Classics', in T. A. Dorey (ed.), *Erasmus*, Studies in Latin Literature and Its Influence (London, 1970).

PLATT, MICHAEL, *Rome and Romans According to Shakespeare* (London, 1976; 2nd edn., Lanham, Md., 1983).

POISSON, R., 'Coriolanus as Aristotle's Magnanimous Man', in W. F. McNeir and T. N. Greenfield (eds.), *Pacific Coast Studies in Shakespeare* (Portland, Ore., 1966), 210–24.

POPKIN, RICHARD H., *The History of Scepticism from Erasmus to Spinoza* (Berkeley, 1979).

PRATT, NORMAN T., *Seneca's Drama* (Chapel Hill, NC, 1983).

PRICE, HEREWARD T., '"Like Himself"', *RES* 16 (1940), 178–81.

PROSER, MATTHEW, '*Coriolanus*: The Constant Warrior and the State', *College English*, 24 (1963), 507–12.

—— *The Heroic Image in Five Shakespearean Tragedies* (Princeton, 1965).

PROSSER, ELEANOR, 'Shakespeare, Montaigne, and "the Rarer Action"', *ShakS* 1 (1965), 261–4.

PUJANTE, A. LUIS, '"No Sense Nor Feeling": A Note on *Coriolanus*, 4.1', *SQ* 41 (1990), 489–90.

RABKIN, NORMAN, 'Structure, Convention, and Meaning in *Julius Caesar*', *JEGP* 63 (1964), 240–54.

—— *Shakespeare and the Common Understanding* (New York, 1967).

RACKIN, PHYLLIS, 'The Pride of Shakespeare's Brutus', *Library Chronicle (Univ. of Pennsylvania)*, 32 (1966), 18–33.

—— 'Shakespeare's Boy Cleopatra, the Decorum of Nature, and the Golden World of Poetry', *PMLA* 87 (1972), 201–12.

REBHORN, WAYNE A., 'The Crisis of the Aristocracy in *Julius Caesar*', *RQ* 43 (1990), 75–111.

REES, JOAN, '*Julius Caesar*: An Earlier Play and an Interpretation', *SQ* 4 (1955), 135–41.

RELIHAN, CONSTANCE C., 'Appropriation of the "Thing of Blood": Absence of Self and the Struggle for Ownership in *Coriolanus*', *Iowa State Journal of Research*, 62 (1988), 407–20.

RICE, JULIAN C., '*Julius Caesar* and the Judgment of the Senses', *SEL* 13 (1973), 238–55.

RIST, J. M., *Stoic Philosophy* (Cambridge, 1969).

—— 'Zeno and Stoic Consistency', *Phronesis*, 22 (1977), 161–74.

ROBERTSON, JOHN M., *Montaigne and Shakespeare and Other Essays on Cognate Questions* (London, 1897; rev. and enl., 1909).

ROSE, MARK, 'Conjuring Caesar: Ceremony, History, and Authority in 1599', *ELR* 19 (1989), 291–304.

ROSEN, WILLIAM, *Shakespeare and the Craft of Tragedy* (Cambridge, Mass., 1960).

ROSENMEYER, THOMAS G., *Senecan Drama and Stoic Cosmology* (Berkeley, 1989).

ROSS, G. M., 'Seneca's Philosophical Influence', in C. D. N. Costa (ed.), *Seneca*, Greek and Latin Studies (London, 1974), 116–65.

ROSSITER, A. P., '*Coriolanus*', in his *Angel with Horns and Other Shakespeare Lectures*, ed. Graham Storey (London, 1961), 235–52.

RUSSELL, D. A., *Plutarch*, Classical Life and Letters (London, 1972).

SACHAROFF, MARK, 'Suicide and Brutus' Philosophy in *Julius Caesar*', *JHI* 33 (1972), 115–22.

SAMS, HENRY W., 'Anti-Stoicism in Seventeenth- and Early Eighteenth-Century England', *Studies in Philology*, 41 (1944), 65–78.

SANDBACH, F. H., *The Stoics* (London, 1975).

SANDYS, JOHN EDWIN, *A History of Classical Scholarship* (2 vols., Cambridge, 1908).

SAUNDERS, JASON LEWIS, *Justus Lipsius: The Philosophy of Renaissance Stoicism* (New York, 1955).

SAUNDERS, JASON LEWIS (ed.), *Greek and Roman Philosophy after Aristotle*, Readings in the History of Philosophy (New York, 1966).

SAYCE, R. A., *The Essays of Montaigne: A Critical Exploration* (London, 1972).

SCHANZER, ERNEST, *The Problem Plays of Shakespeare* (London, 1963).

SCOTT, WILLIAM O., 'The Speculative Eye: Problematic Self-Knowledge in *Julius Caesar*', *ShS* 40 (1988), 77–89.

SCREECH, M. A., *Montaigne and Melancholy: The Wisdom of the 'Essays'* (London, 1983).

SHAPIRO, STEPHEN A., 'The Varying Shore of the World: Ambivalence in *Antony and Cleopatra*', *MLQ* 27 (1966), 18–32.

SIMMONS, J. L., *Shakespeare's Pagan World: The Roman Tragedies* (Brighton, 1974).

—— 'Shakespeare and the Antique Romans', in P. A. Ramsey (ed.), *Rome and the Renaissance: The City and the Myth* (Binghamton, NY, 1982), 77–92.

SINGH, JYOTSNA, 'Renaissance Antitheatricality, Antifeminism, and Shakespeare's *Antony and Cleopatra*', *RenD* NS 20 (1989), 99–121.

SKINNER, QUENTIN, *The Foundations of Modern Political Thought* (2 vols., Cambridge, 1978).

SONNENSCHEIN, E. A., 'Shakspere and Stoicism', *University Review*, 1 (1905), 23–41.

SPENCER, BENJAMIN T., '*Antony* and the Paradoxical Metaphor', *SQ* 9 (1958), 373–8.

SPENCER, T. J. B., 'Shakespeare and the Elizabethan Romans', *ShS* 10 (1957), 27–38.

SPENS, JANET, 'Chapman's Ethical Thought', *Essays and Studies*, 11 (1925), 145–69.

SPEVACK, MARVIN (ed.), *A Complete and Systematic Concordance to the Works of Shakespeare* (6 vols., Hildesheim, 1968–70).

STAMPFER, JUDAH, *The Tragic Engagement: A Study of Shakespeare's Classical Tragedies* (New York, 1968).

STOCKHOLDER, KATHERINE, 'The Other Coriolanus', *PMLA* 85 (1970), 228–36.

TANNER, R. G., 'Cicero on Conscience and Morality', in John R. C. Martyn (ed.), *Cicero and Virgil: Studies in Honour of Harold Hunt* (Amsterdam, 1972), 87–112.

TAYLOR, GEORGE COFFIN, *Shakspere's Debt to Montaigne* (New York, 1925).

—— 'Montaigne-Shakespeare and the Deadly Parallel', *PQ* 22 (1943), 330–7.

TAYLOR, MICHAEL, 'Playing the Man He Is: Role-playing in Shakespeare's *Coriolanus*', *Ariel* 15 (1984), 19–28.

THOMAS, VIVIAN, *Shakespeare's Roman Worlds* (London, 1989).

TRAVERSI, DEREK, *Shakespeare: The Roman Plays* (London, 1963).

URE, PETER, *Elizabethan and Jacobean Drama: Critical Essays*, ed. J. C. Maxwell (Liverpool, 1974).

VAN DOREN, MARK, *Shakespeare* (London, 1935; New York, 1955).

VAN LAAN, THOMAS F., *Role-playing in Shakespeare* (Toronto, 1978).

VAWTER, MARVIN L., '*Julius Caesar*: Rupture in the Bond', *JEGP* 72 (1973), 311–28.

—— '"Division 'tween Our Souls": Shakespeare's Stoic Brutus', *ShakS* 7 (1974), 173–95.

—— '"After Their Fashion": Cicero and Brutus in *Julius Caesar*', *ShakS* 9 (1976), 205–19.

VELZ, JOHN W., *Shakespeare and the Classical Tradition: A Critical Guide to Commentary* (Minneapolis, 1968).

—— '"If I Were Brutus Now": Role-playing in *Julius Caesar*', *ShakS* 4 (1969), 149–59.

—— 'The Ancient World in Shakespeare: Authenticity or Anachronism? A Retrospect', *ShS* 31 (1978), 1–12.

—— '*Orator* and *Imperator* in *Julius Caesar*: Style and the Process of Roman History', *ShakS* 15 (1982), 55–75.

—— 'Cracking Strong Curbs Asunder: Roman Destiny and the Roman Hero in *Coriolanus*', *ELR* 13 (1983), 58–69.

VERBEKE, GERARD, *The Presence of Stoicism in Medieval Thought* (Washington, 1983).

VILLEY, PIERRE, *Les Sources et l'évolution des Essais de Montaigne* (2 vols., 2nd edn., Paris, 1933).

WAITH, EUGENE, *The Herculean Hero in Marlowe, Chapman, Shakespeare, and Dryden* (London, 1962).

WELLS, CHARLES, *The Wide Arch: Roman Values in Shakespeare* (London, 1993).

WELLS, HENRY W., 'Senecan Influence on Elizabethan Tragedy: A Re-estimation', *Shakespeare Assoc. Bulletin*, 19 (1944), 71–84.

WENLEY, R. M., *Stoicism and Its Influence*, Our Debt to Greece and Rome (n.d. [1925?]).

WILDERS, JOHN, *The Lost Garden: A View of Shakespeare's English and Roman History Plays* (London, 1978).

WILLIAMSON, MARILYN L., 'Fortune in *Antony and Cleopatra*', *JEGP* 67 (1968), 423–9.

WYMER, ROWLAND, *Suicide and Despair in the Jacobean Drama* (Brighton, 1986).

ZANTA, LÉONTINE, *La Renaissance du Stoïcisme au XVIe siècle* (Paris, 1914; repr. Geneva, 1975).

Index

Works are listed under authors' names, except for the three Roman plays (*Antony and Cleopatra*, *Coriolanus*, *Julius Caesar*), which are given separate entries. Characters in the Roman plays are also separately indexed. Bold type indicates major discussions.

Printed in the United States
1248800001B/112